THE
SHERMAN
LETTERS

CORRESPONDENCE BETWEEN

GENERAL AND SENATOR SHERMAN

FROM 1837 TO 1891

EDITED BY

RACHEL SHERMAN THORNDIKE

NEW YORK

1894

Discover more lost history from BIG BYTE BOOKS

Contents

INTRODUCTION

Soon after beginning the work of arranging my father's papers for publication, I found a series of letters which awoke my deepest interest. They covered a period extending from 1837 to 1891, and proved to be the complete correspondence between my father and his brother John during those (more than fifty) years.

These letters, exchanged by two brothers of such eminence, and many of them written during the most stirring events of our country's history, seem to me unique. They form a collection, complete in itself $ they are of great historical value, and the expressions of opinion which they contain are so freely given as to furnish an excellent idea of the relations that existed between my father and his brother.

Realizing all this, I have decided to publish the correspondence by itself; and in so doing, my chief desire has been to let the letters speak for themselves, and to put them in such form that they may be easily understood. I feel sure that they will command a very general interest and be accorded that ready sympathy which was so freely and lovingly expressed at the time of my father's death.

RACHEL SHERMAN THORNDIKE.

BOSTON, July, 1894.

CHAPTER I

IN the year 1836 William Tecumseh Sherman, then a lad of sixteen, entered West Point as a cadet. He was appointed from his native State, Ohio. He travelled east by stage, spent a week at Washington, a few days in Philadelphia, and another week in New York, thus becoming, for his age and time, a much-travelled boy. He is described as being a tall, slim, loose-jointed lad, with red hair, fair, burned skin, and piercing black eyes. He himself says that in New York some of his relations looked upon him as "an untamed animal just caught in the Par West." He must indeed have had a rural look. That his strong individuality and intense interest in life were even then developed none who knew him later can doubt.

His earliest letters are labored and boyish. He had not acquired a vocabulary or the fluency of pen which later developed itself to an almost wonderful degree. He was nervous and quick in all his thoughts and actions. He wrote a running hand, difficult to read, and rendered so by the race his pen had to run with his thoughts. His boyish letters are interesting, therefore, only because they are his, and I have quoted but few of them. He was three years older than his brother John, and in some cases assumed the role of adviser in an amusing way. In giving these letters to the public, I presuppose some knowledge of my father's and uncle's lives, and shall only note the chief events, in order to connect the letters. The first letter was written, as may be seen, eighteen months after my father's entrance at West Point.

West Point, N.Y., Dec. 0, 1837.

Dear Brother: In compliance with your request I sent you a paper shortly after the reception of your letter, which I should have answered much sooner had I not been till within a few days past under the impression that it had been done. This excuse is sufficient, I suppose, for my long delay, especially as a letter from me is not very desirable.

I hope that you still have as favorable opinions as ever with respect to your employment, for in my opinion a man's success in his profession depends upon the impressions he receives at the beginning; for if these are favorable, most undoubtedly he will endeavor to succeed, and success will be the necessary consequence. You have now been engaged at that employment about a year and must be by this time quite an expert engineer. I would not be much astonished if when I came home I would find you superintendent of some public work. I have not received many letters from home lately; in fact, I am almost too busy to write many, and if I do not answer all their letters immediately upon their reception, they follow my example apparently, which is the cause of it, I presume; but after our examination in January I will endeavor to be a little more punctual and expect the same of my correspondents. At present we are very much engaged in preparing for the examination which takes place immediately after Christmas. I think I will still have about the same standing as I have now in Mathematics and French, but in Drawing I think I will be among the first five. Preparation for the Christmas spree is now all the go. I have joined in with about a dozen others and laid the foundation for a very good dinner costing about three dollars apiece. I wish we could get ahold of some of our western turkeys, chickens, and the like, which cannot be obtained here except at an enormous price, and as money is something to us like teeth, we are obliged to go without. Winter seems to be very reluctant about setting in. The weather at present is more like spring than winter. This time last winter, the river was closed, and we had fine skating, but no doubt it will soon set in with a vengeance, giving us our full share of north winds, which it generally deals out very liberally to the inhabitants of the Highlands. It is now about half-past nine, and we are obliged to go to bed at ten. You must, therefore, allow me to come to a conclusion, wishing you at the same time to give my best love to all the family when you next write home. Do not fail to write soon. From

Your affectionate brother,

JOHN SHERMAN, Esqr. W. T. SHERMAN.

The second letter was written when, at the end of his second year, he returned to Ohio on his two months furlough. I have often heard my mother say how his training at West Point had developed him physically; how straight and strong he was, how clear and bright-eyed, and what light-heartedness and pride were in his bearing and tread. He evidently failed that summer to see John, who was at work in another part of the State.

WEST POINT, N.Y., Sept. 15, 1838.

Dear Brother: I did go to the salt works, as I proposed when you were at home, and was there three or four days. While there I made arrangements to go with the Misses Clark to a relative of theirs (Mr. Walker), from thence to Beverly; but unfortunately it rained, and we got several duckings before we got to Mr. W.'s (twelve miles), and when there was told it was thirty miles farther. Consequently I was obliged, much against my wish, to relinquish my design of visiting you. After a few days' stay at the salt works, we returned to Lancaster. When I had been home a few days grandma and Taylor came down from Mansfield on the way to Dayton. Mother, Lamp, and I accompanied them, and had a very fine trip. Lamp and I went to Oxford College to see Phil, from there to Cincinnati, where I stayed a couple of days, then returned to Dayton, where I found them all ready to return home. We travelled together until we got to Columbus, where we found Mr. Ewing. Mother and the rest went on home. Phil and I remained until the next day, and then went home in the carriage. My furlough had nearly expired, and I could only stay home two days more, at the end of which time James, grandma, and I went to Mansfield, where we found them all well except Mr. Parker, who was not very well. We stopped at Mary's and Uncle John's a few minutes on our way up. Prom Mansfield I went with Taylor in his buggy to Sandusky on the lake. We stopped all night at Uncle Daniel's, whom I saw for the first time. He is a very fine old man, but do not think he resembles father (if you recollect him). Prom Sandusky I went to Buffalo by water, then to Niagara Balls, thence to New York City, where I spent two days with our relatives, then to West Point, where I have been a little more than two weeks studying very hard indeed.

Your affectionate brother,

W. T. SHERMAN.

In the next letter, dated October 15th, is a touch of elder-brotherly advice. The one following, of June 9, 1839, begins to show greater fluency and ease of expression. He is evidently worried over rumors from home of John's speculations in salt. Considering John's age and his own, respectively not yet sixteen and nineteen years, the trouble of mind seems premature. The speculation did not turn out successfully, but would have done so had not the river refused to rise at the proper moment. But the risks were so small that they failed seriously to cripple John's prospects in life.

In the next letter, of April 13th, the young cadet expresses his satisfaction at the failure of his brother's speculations, fearing that success might have lured him into greater temptations. The belligerent spirit shown against Great Britain was very shortly outgrown.

WEST POINT, N.Y., Oct. 15, 1838.

Dear Brother:

I suppose that by this time you have become quite an expert engineer, — much better acquainted with "Jacob staffs," chains, compasses, etc., than you used to be with Euclid and Virgil; and I hope to hear from you soon that you have become highly pleased with your occupation. you will go home; and if you are detained there by the weather, which will probably be the case, I would advise you to continue your study of the mathematics or whatever else may be connected with your business. You must write to me soon, and tell me all about your campaign or trip, and what particular office you fill in the company, etc., etc. Excuse the shortness of this.

Your affectionate brother,

W. T. SHERMAN.

MILITARY ACADEMY,

WEST POINT, Jan. 9, 1839.

Dear Brother: I am now writing upon the risk of your not receiving this, for I hear that you are engaged in speculating in salt, and are waiting for the river to rise to take a load down to Cincinnati. Are you doing this on borrowed capital or not? Or does it interfere in the least with your duties as engineer? If it does, I would advise you not to engage in it at any rate, even if you can make a fortune by it; for a reputation for a strict and rigid compliance to one's duties, whatever they may be, is far more valuable than a dozen loads of salt. If, however, you do engage in it, of course I wish you success, a pleasant trip to Cincinnati, and hope you will make a long stay, for Lampson's sake.

I suppose you know that we have two examinations here every year, one in January and the other in Juno. At the latter a number of gentlemen from all parts of the United States attend by invitation of the Secretary of War, and of course we all endeavor to be well prepared in our studies, both for our own good and that the persons (always influential) may carry off a good opinion of the Institution. The course of studies we are engaged in this year has always had the reputation of being the most difficult of the four, and that justly; therefore to be prepared for the coming June examination I expect to be very studious and busy, and if between this time and then I be not very regular in my correspondence, you may know what to attribute it to and excuse it.

Your affectionate brother,

W. T. SHERMAN.

MILITARY ACADEMY,

WEST POINT, N.Y., April 13, 1839.

Dear Brother:

It appears that although you were pleased with Cincinnati as a city, you were not with the visit, taken all in all. Prom this I judge that your speculations did not turn out as well as expected. You must not be astonished if I say that if such be the case I am glad of it, because, had you succeeded, your attention would have been turned from your present business, with your success in which so many are interested. I presume by this time you must be nearly done with the works on the Muskingum. Those dams and locks of which you have spoken will no doubt be some of the finest specimens of workmanship in Ohio, and the more I think of it, the more I regret that I did not go and see them last summer. By the arrangement I suppose steamboats will be able to go up as far as Zanesville. I presume you have heard of these Maine difficulties before now. All is now calm in that quarter, the troops having been withdrawn from the disputed territory by both parties, and as far as our Government is concerned the thing is in a fair way of being amicably adjusted, but doubts are entertained with regard to the course which England will adopt. All anxiously await the return of the steamship *Great Western* which carried out the news, and as the time of her usual return has passed by several days, it is supposed that the time of her departure from England had been delayed in order to receive the news by the ship *Liverpool,* that left New York about eight or ten days after her; and as among the latter were the proceedings of Congress and the President's message, there is every Reason to expect by this vessel some decisive news, and if they are ready for war, I think we will soon be. For my part, there is no nation that I would prefer being at variance with than the British, in this case more especially as our cause is plainly right and just. If anything occurs soon, I will write again or send the paper containing it....

Your affectionate brother,

W. T. SHERMAN.

The following group of letters carry the cadet through his graduation and into his twenty-first year. They are already very consequential and full of ideas of affairs, even discussing State debts and the advantages of farming life. But they show his life at West Point to have been happy and contented. As he says himself in his memoirs, he never rose above the ranks; was never chosen to be an officer; and yet, except for his demerits, his standing was excellent. And he seems always contented with his treatment, though looking forward to freedom from duties after graduation. His grave reasoning on a choice of army corps is most natural, as every young cadet knows, and the reasons that influenced him are still about the same.

MILITARY ACADEMY,

West Point, N.Y., Aug. 31, 1839.

Dear Brother:

The encampment (my last) is now over, and we are once more in barracks and to-morrow will commence our studies, commencing with Civil Engineering. This year's course of study is by far the most important of the four, as well as the most interesting, embracing as it does Engineering both Civil and Military, the construction of fortifications as well as the manner of attacking and defending them, Mineralogy and Geology, Rhetoric, Moral Philosophy, International and Common Law, Artillery and Infantry Tactics, as well as many other minor studies, which the scientific officer requires. When these shall have been completed, and the next nine months shall have passed away, we will receive diplomas and commissions in the army, and I hope a furlough along with them. Of course we look forward with no common pleasure to so fruitful a time as that; indeed, every circumstance which marks its approach is duly celebrated and remembered; instance, the last night of our last encampment.

MILITARY ACADEMY,

WEST POINT, N.Y., Jan. 14, 1840.

My Dear Brother:

The examination is just over; the result is favorable toward me, as usual. In Engineering I am fourth in my class, in Geology and Rhetoric and Moral Philosophy each sixth; as to demerits I have also a respectable ' number, about one hundred. The studies and exercises will be for the remainder of the academic year exclusively military and important, and will engage us sufficiently to make the time pass pleasantly and rapidly. You may well suppose that we are all anxious for the arrival of June; the thoughts of graduation, the freedom from academic labors and restraints, already engross our minds and form the subjects of all our conversations and talks. Already have we given directions for a class ring, for graduating trunks, for swords, epaulettes, hats, chapeaux, and feathers, and in a couple of months the military tailor will be here from the city to take our measures for uniform dress and undress coats, cit's clothes, pants, etc., etc. Thus you see that by adding things of this nature, which will constantly keep the future before our minds, we break in upon and enliven our otherwise monotonous life.

What have you been doing all winter? Studying, or nothing? I am beginning to think that engineering is not the thing it is cracked up to be. It does not give constant employment to the engineer, who cannot, therefore, rely upon a sure and constant reward for his labors. His duties, whilst engaged, are exceedingly laborious and irksome, or of the other equally disagreeable extreme; beside these, the prosecution of the different improvements depends upon the States within which they lie, and there is but little doubt that the policy of most of the State governments will soon change in reference to their internal works, to paying more and borrowing less, and allow the improvements to grow with their wealth and population. By examining the public records you will see that the State debts are truly enormous, and if they attempt to pay them, they will undoubtedly stop all expenditures which are not absolutely necessary. I noticed in yesterday's paper that the governor of Pennsylvania vetoed six or seven bills granting money for different purposes, and returned them to the Legislature, assigning as a reason the absolute necessity of paying the debts. I have mentioned these things to you that you may reflect, while there is still time, of the propriety of selecting means to be resorted to in case of necessity. What more naturally suggests itself than a farm? Who can be more independent, more honest and honorable, who more sure of a full reward for his labor, who can bestow more benefits on his fellow-beings, and consequently be more happy, than an American farmer? If by any means you may be able to get some land in Ohio, Iowa, or Wisconsin, you should do so by all means, and more especially if it is partially improved. I do not mean for the purpose of speculation, but to make use of yourself.

Give my love to all the family, and oblige me by writing soon.

Your affectionate brother,

W. T. SHERMAN.

MILITARY ACADEMY,

WEST POINT, N.Y., March 7, 1840.

My Dear Brother: I acknowledged the receipt of your last in my letter to mother, since which time I have been waiting in hopes that something might turn up to write you about; but although the river has opened, and is alive with steamboats and sloops, still West Point appears as dull as ever; in fact, the only visitors we have had so far have been tailors, shoemakers, etc., etc., who prowl about us, knowing our inexperience and the necessity we are under of getting a full supply of clothing at their prices. The snow has entirely disappeared, and for the past three weeks the weather has been beautiful, and reminds me very much of sugar-making times at home, and I have no doubt, if your weather has been as fine as ours here, your farmers have not been idle in their camps. An evening at old Mr. Buchanan's or Wilson's sugar-camp would be great.

I presume the idea of your studying law has been decided upon by Mr. Reese and Taylor, so that it would be rather impertinent for me to object in the least; but for my part, it would be my last choice. Everybody studies law nowadays, and to be a lawyer without being exceedingly eminent — which it is to be hoped you will be some day—is not a sufficient equivalent for their risks and immense study and labor. However, if you decide upon anything, you should immediately commence to carry it into execution. As to me, I am already provided for. As soon as I graduate I am entitled by law to a commission in the army, and from my standing in the class to a choice of corps. To be stationed in the east or west, to be in the artillery, infantry, or dragoons, depends entirely on my choice. This choice will bo, unless war breaks out with England, the Fifth Regiment of Infantry, because it is stationed on the northwest frontier, a country which I have always felt a strong inclination to see; and if it meets my ideas, formed from descriptions of travellers and officers, it must be the finest spot on this continent. Also it is probable that the Indians will break out again, in which case I should have an opportunity of seeing some active service. Should war, however, be the consequence of this Maine difficulty, I should prefer the artillery, for the reason that it is stationed east of the mountains, which would be the seat of war, and it is an arm of service which I would prefer in a war against a civilized people. But as there is scarce a possibility of this, I have concluded to go to the west, and have accordingly ordered an infantry uniform. Whether I remain in the army for life or not is doubtful; but one thing is certain,—that I will never study another profession. Should I resign, it would be to turn farmer, if ever I can raise enough to buy a good farm in Iowa.... If I can spare money when I am at the city of New York, I intend to get one of Colt's patent rifles to shoot ten times in succession as fast as you can cook and pull the trigger. They cost from $40 to $60, more than, I fear, I can spare. I have been very well indeed all winter. Your affectionate brother,

W. T. SHERMAN.

His leave after graduation was passed in Ohio, where he seems to have reverted to his boyish days and amused himself generally. In one letter he writes as follows: —

"I'm glad to hear that you've got the coon. If it is no trouble, bring him when you come. Be sure to tie the chain to something, that he may not fool you the way he did me."

The following letters, from his first post, Fort Pierce, are descriptive, in answer to questions from home.

PORT PIERCE, P., March 30, 1841.

My Dear Brother:

The peninsula of Florida is of the latest geological formation, one mass of sand, with few rocks of the softest consistency, and, were it not for its delightful climate, would be as barren as the deserts of Africa. It is cut up by innumerable rivers, streams, and rivulets, which, watering the soil, nourish a rank growth of weeds and grass, which, continually decomposing, gives a rich soil, and gives rise in time to a heavy growth of live oak, palmetto, and scrub of every kind. These are the dreaded hummocks, the stronghold of the Indians, where he builds his hut, and has pumpkin and corn fields. The stream furnishes him with abundance of fish and alligators, the palmetto its cabbage. The thick growth conceals his little fire and hut, secures his escape, enables him to creep within a few yards of the deer or turkey feeding on the border, and drive his copper-headed, barbed arrow through the vital part. In a word, the deep streams, bordered by the dense hummock, have enabled the Indians thus far to elude the pursuit of our army.

The remainder of the country is so very level that water will not flow off, but collects in ponds until absorbed by the sand or evaporated. These ponds are met at every few yards, sometimes miles in extent and but few inches in depth, at other places narrow and boggy. All else is pine barren, and of course monotonous.

As to the history of the war, — the same as all our Indian wars. A treaty for the removal is formed by a few who represent themselves as the whole; the time comes, and none present themselves. The Government orders force to be used; the troops in the territory commence, but are so few that they all get massacred. The cowardly inhabitants, instead of rallying, desert their homes and sound the alarm-call for assistance. An army supposed to be strong enough is sent, seeks and encounters the enemy at a place selected by the latter, gets a few hundred killed. The Indians retreat, scatter, and are safe. This may be repeated *ad infinitum*. The best officer is selected to direct the affairs of the army, — comes to Florida, exposes himself, does all he can, gets abused by all, more than likely breaks down his constitution, and is glad enough to get out of the scrape. Treaties, truces, and armistices have been and are still being tried, with what success is notorious. The present mode of conducting things is to dispose the troops at fixed points, and require them to scout and scour the country in their vicinity,—about as good a plan as could be adopted, and one which would terminate the war if small columns of a hundred or a hundred and fifty men were to make excursions into the interior. We have from this post thoroughly expelled the Indians from this section of the territory, and have had the good luck to kill some and capture others, besides destroying and capturing boats, canoes, etc. The same has been done below and throughout that district where war prevails.

In the west, there is peace. General A— is buying them up, and, what is to be wondered at, has learned wisdom by experience. You doubtless know that he was most egregiously hoaxed last fall by them, but now he places all who come in under a strong guard, so they can't get off this time. Some flatter themselves that there is hope of the war's ending this summer, but I think there is no probability, as they have burnt their fields and hunting-grounds to the west and northwest of us, and Sam Jones and Coacoocher are still out, and have not the least notion of coming in whilst they are so strong.

We have just returned from a very pleasant scout, having been eight days out, examining several streams that empty south of us, without, however, accomplishing anything or seeing any sights except those left by a hunting party some ten or twelve days previous. We went to Jupiter, famous for the grab by General Jesup; from this place we went out to the battle-ground on the Locha Hatchee, where the Indians made a stand against General Jesup in 1838. It was a dense hummock on the stream called Locha Hatchee, where the army was to pass on the way to Jupiter. The trees were riddled with balls, and several of our men, who had been at the battle, pointed out the trees behind which Captain Such-a-one and Lieutenant Such, etc., etc., stood; the limb over which our men crossed to get at the enemy; how the general got his spectacles smashed by a ball, etc., etc.; how the volunteer militia, as usual, were seized with a panic, gathered together like sheep, presenting a sure target for the Indians, which of course was not allowed to pass unheeded. Your affectionate brother,

W. T. SHERMAN.

On January 16th, he writes from Fort Pierce: —

Upon all scouts or expeditions of danger, all the officers insist upon going, but as it is necessary that at least one should stay at the fort, this is done by rotation, and upon the expedition to the Hanlover, ninety miles distant, it fell to my share to remain. On the 4th instant the boats, seven in all, with four officers and forty-three men, left the fort, intending to travel by night and lay by by day; but not having a guide, and their map being incorrect, they could not find the way, so on the third day out they concluded it was best to hurry on by day, reach the point where they expected to find Indians, and lie concealed; but on the fourth morning they espied a little canoe in a cove, went ashore, found a trail, followed it, and soon came to a cluster of board and palmetto huts, which they rushed upon, but only found a negro family, —man, wife, and two children, as also an old squaw and papoose. They secured these, and learned that a party of Indians living at this place, and another which our party had previously destroyed, had gone up to the Hanlover or to the big swamp for oranges and—. The negro said he and his wife had been stolen four years previous, and had been with them ever since. He seemed quite rejoiced at his recapture and offered to act as guide. He was handcuffed, and a noose fixed about his neck as a gentle hint, then told to go on. On the 5th (Saturday) they reached the Hanlover, encamped at the Hanlover, and had the pleasure to receive the visit of a horse at daylight the next morning. They followed his track back for about a quarter of a mile, and came upon a temporary camp of the Indians. The dogs gave the alarm; they all rushed in, when you may well suppose there was a little scattering. Nearly all took to their canoes or the water, where, of course, they were pursued, and after half an hour's popping away and pursuing, they collected together, and found that they had killed two warriors, a woman, and a child; had captured three warriors, eight women, and fifteen children, two tolerably good boats, any quantity of canoes, pots and kettles, etc., corn, pumpkins, and dried fish, and bows and arrows, rifles, bullet-bags, leggins, moccasins, etc.; all this, too, on Sunday. Haying destroyed everything that could not be carried with ease, shot the horse, and secured the prisoners, they took to their boats and crossed the lagoon to the other side, from whence the next morning two of the officers and twenty men were sent over to the St. John's, to a place where, the negro said, a couple of families lived. They found it as he had said, but the dogs gave the alarm before they could be surrounded; but in escaping one warrior was shot, and two squaws and their two children, one warrior alone effecting his escape. Here they found two elegant canoes, one of mahogany large enough to carry twenty men, but were destroyed, not being able to bring them away. The houses were burnt, with all the corn, pumpkins, and household stuff. Thus, having captured all they could find in this quarter, and their provisions becoming scanty, they commenced their return, and reached this post after having been out ten days, exposed to some terrible showers, with hard rowing and little to eat, but were in good spirits from their success. They brought with them six boats and thirty-four prisoners. They are encamped here under charge of the guard until they can be sent to Augustine. I wish you could see the group in its savage state; although many have lost their husbands and fathers and wives and children, yet they show no grief. Several are very badly wounded; one little girl, with a ball through the back and coming out in the cheek, scarce utters a murmur; another woman, a buckshot through and through, bears it with the fortitude of a veteran soldier; there are several other wounds, given accidentally, of course, in the pell-mell of the fight and in the pursuit of the canoes.

I, of course, regretted very much not having been along, but consoled myself with the idea that I have a chance yet. In fact, I was on a scout some time ago, when we ran a large boat and canoe ashore, captured the boats, but the Indians escaped. To-night I start with fifteen men in three boats, my principal object being to capture an Indian for guide up the St. Lucie's River; expect to be gone five days. The boat has just arrived from the bar; it is the schooner *Frances* from Havana, bound to Augustine, so it will answer my purpose of sending this, though hurried.

I presume you have heard how Colonel Harney had been in the Everglades capturing eleven warriors, ten of whom he hung, and twenty-eight women and children. This boat brings the news that, seeing fires on the beach, about ten miles this side of Key Biscayne, ran in and fired a gun, which was answered from shore, and presently a small canoe came out, hailed, and four soldiers in them taken aboard. They were four of Colonel Harney's men, who said that it was Colonel Harney's camp; that they had gone on the 1st instant, with two hundred men, soldiers, and marines, in boats, with a guide, to Sam Jones' camp. They had found Sam much stronger in numbers than they had expected, and admirably posted, so that he could not have attacked him without receiving at least three deliberate shots from about one hundred warriors, so the Colonel decided to return for an accession to his force. He doubtless took a prudent course, though I think he should have attacked Sam. The secret of the matter is, I think, he felt no confidence in the marines and sailors, for he is no coward. He had, however, attacked a small party, capturing six and killing six.

Your affectionate brother,

W. T. SHEEHAN.

Through all the letters during the following spring, there appears great impatience at the nature and prolongation of the Indian wars. His promotion to the grade of first lieutenant, which came in 1842, was therefore very welcome, as it involved a change of station.

Poet Pierce, P., July 14, 1841.

My Dear Brother:

There is considerable talk up at St. Augustine that our regiment is going north in the fall, but I won't believe any such thing until the order comes 5 in fact, I want to stay till next spring, for I really believe that there is a shadow of hope of terminating this war in the coming winter, provided always no "treaties, truces, or talks."

Your affectionate brother,

W. T. SHERMAN.

POET PIERCE, P., Oct. 11, 1841.

My Dear Brother:

As to matters and things in Florida, they are as they have always been, — Indians plenty always coming, but none come, whilst the officer commanding flatters himself the war is just on the point of ending.

A short time ago a ship went ashore about sixty miles south of this, from *New* Orleans bound to Cowes, with a cargo of tobacco and Dutchmen (two hundred and odd). The latter went ashore, taking a tent and some beef and pork; but fortunately the steamboat that runs on the coast found them, and advised them to go aboard this vessel whilst she went in search of some wreckers (a species of pirates, who, for a high per cent, save portions of cargo and sometimes ship), who returned to her and luckily got her off the beach, it being calm; but it seems that whilst the steamboat was gone, some Indians came down on the beach and stole the things they had put ashore. As soon as we learned this, Major Childs, who commands here, immediately fitted out an expedition to look into matters and things down in that section. An old Spaniard we have here informed us that in rear of where the vessel had gone ashore there was a fine lake, and in all likelihood the Indians lived on it. As the object was to get on this lake in small open boats, this we effected by going an inland passage for forty miles, then hauled our boats over a narrow strip of land into the sea, launched our boats, and, going about ten miles further, landed, and hauled our boats again into the unexplored lake. We were here six days, searching the islands and bays, and though we found evidences of a great number of Indians and canoes, we were able to discover but two fellows, who escaped us. We got, however, plenty of roasting ears, sweet potatoes, sugarcane, and other Indian things. A great many fields, amounting in all to upwards of thirty acres, in very fine cultivation indeed, having, beside what I've already mentioned, beans, pumpkins, tobacco, and rice. So you see that Indians know, beside the use of their legs and the rifle, that of the hoe. But a few days ago a vessel belonging to the Government, and loaded with supplies for this post, ran ashore about thirty miles north of us. I was sent up with thirty men, and though I was unable to save the vessel, I succeeded in bringing off about $1000 worth of provisions and property....

Your affectionate brother,

W. **T. SHERMAN.**

PICOLATTO, F., Feb. 15, 1842.

My Dear Brother:

You doubtless saw my promotion announced in "Orders." I have been exceedingly fortunate, attaining a rank which generally requires five or eight years' service in the short period of seventeen months. This promotion separated me from the company to which I formerly belonged and from a garrison of officers to whom I had become much attached, yet I was of course rejoiced at being promoted to this company, which guards the road between St. Augustine and this place, — the road upon which so very many murders have been committed during the war. I command here a guard, have fine quarters, constant communication with the world, and although very little society, and no officers with me, I can mount my horse, and in a couple of hours can have both in the ancient city of St. Augustine, only eighteen miles distant. St. Augustine, you know, is the oldest town in the United States, nor does its appearance belie its age,—narrow, winding streets, close-built houses with the balconies meeting overhead, denoting its Spanish population. There are some few old English families, who remained when the Floridas were ceded to Spain, and together with the few Americans whom the delightful climate has enticed, constitute the best society. The Spaniards, or rather Minorcans, are very ignorant and have no desire to travel beyond their own circle. There is an old fort, built at enormous cost by the Spanish Government; but for want of appropriation, it is fast falling to decay.... The inhabitants still preserve the old ceremonies and festivities of old Spain. Balls, masquerades, etc., are celebrated during the gay season of the Carnival (just over), and the most religious observance of Lent in public, whilst in private they cannot refrain from dancing and making merry. Indeed, I never saw anything like it, — dancing, dancing, and nothing but dancing, but not such as you see at the north. Such ease and grace I never before beheld. A lady will waltz all the evening without fatigue, because it is done slowly, with grace; but it is in the Spanish dance they more especially excel, enchanting all who behold or participate. This, together with the easy and cordial hospitality all extend to officers, is what has captivated so many within the past few years.

In June, 1842, General Sherman was ordered to Fort Moultrie, S.C., where he remained for the next four years.

Fort Moultrie, S.C., May 28, 1843.

My Dear Brother:

Leaving the seasons to look after themselves, I'll try and give you an idea of how our days pass in a garrison like this. Here at Fort Moultrie we have about 250 soldiers, divided into four companies. These are quartered some inside the wall, some outside. All the unmarried officers — eight of us—live inside; all the married, five, outside. This being the headquarters of the regiment, we have the Colonel and his band of about fifteen instruments. Every morning at daylight all get up at reveille, attend a drill, either as infantry or artillery, at sunrise; breakfast at seven, have a dress parade at eight, and half an hour after the new guard takes the place of the old one,— a new officer relieving the old one. After that each one kills time to suit himself till reveille of next morning commences the new routine. Thus it is every fair day except Sunday, when we have an extra quantity of music, parade, and inspection in honor of the day and to keep our men in superfine order at church. Thus, you see that every day at nine o'clock and after we have nothing to do but amuse ourselves. Some read, some write, some loaf, and some go to the city. For the latter class a barge is in attendance, going and coming. Although six miles from a city, we have all its advantages, whilst separated from its annoying noises, taxes, and expenses... , During the past winter I have been at North Carolina twice, at Savannah once, and at Charleston some hundred times. The fact is, in the summer time we are so enveloped with citizens that we have to make acquaintances whether or no. When they move to Charleston and the country, they send invitations which must be accepted, or give offence. The consequence was that two or more of us had to go constantly as representatives of the whole, — always in rotation, unless duty or pleasure coincided, when a greater number would cross the water. These parties are very various, from the highly aristocratic and fashionable, with sword and epaulettes, or horse-racing, picnicing, boating, fishing, swimming, and God knows what not. A life of this kind does well enough for a while, but soon surfeits with its flippancy,—mingling with people in whom you feel no permanent interest, smirks and smiles when you feel savage, tight boots when your fancy would prefer slippers. I want relief, and unless they can invent a new Florida war I'll come back and spend a few months with you in Ohio. But as my visits have been, heretofore, in the spring and summer, I'll wait for the fall this time, when I hop© once more to see you all at home and Mansfield both.. .

Your affectionate brother,

W. T. SHERMAN.

In the autumn of 1843, General Sherman went on leave to Ohio. An account of his return is given in the following letter, also a description of those parts of Georgia which he afterwards visited with his army. The observations made on his first visit undoubtedly assisted him on his march.

PORT MOULTRIE, S.C., Jan. 19, 1844.

My Dear Brother: It was about the middle of November, and on one of those mornings so peculiar to your atmosphere, that I deposited my bones in the Chilicothe stage. I went to Portsmouth, thence down the Ohio to Cincinnati, where I remained with Lamp a couple of days, and then took my departure for St. Louis in the steamboat *Manhattan,,* loaded with every species of animal from men to Durham cattle. There were more than 200 souls on board a second-class boat, from which circumstance you can readily infer that the bodily comforts were not well cared for. Yet I was much pleased. Louisville, at which we stopped several hours, is a beautiful place; in fact, the whole river realized my wildest conceptions. In six days we reached St. Louis, which, you know, is trying to rival our queen city; but, although it has great merits and beauty beside a population of people, it has not that fixed and solid appearance that Cincinnati now wears as an established city of business and manufacture. I spent ten days in and near St Louis, after which I embarked in a new and very fine boat, called the *John Aull,* for New Orleans.... The trip cannot fail to interest one who has never been in the South, but, as I was familiar there, it could not produce its full effect. Imagine yourself, as I was, at the mouth of the Ohio in a heavy snowstorm, the shores clothed in ghost-like garb; the following day the snow is no longer seen, and before another day passes by the shores are clothed here and there in green corn and grass. Soon the oak appears with its green leaves, then the magnolia, orange, etc., and soon you find yourself down between the rich sugar-fields of Louisiana, the stalks ungathered and waving beautifully and luxuriantly in the breeze.... At Mobile I took a steamboat and ascended the Alabama River to a town called Montgomery. There, on a vehicle called a car on what was denominated a railroad to a town called Franklin, from which place I staged it over roads such as

20

you have about Mansfield, except the clay is slipperier, the hills shorter and steeper, and the drivers such as can be had nowhere else. Thus I went 120 miles to a town in Georgia called Griffin. Here I waited twenty-four hours for the cars, which had as usual run off the track. However, they came at last, and we started towards Macon, a distance of only sixty miles, which it took us twelve hours to accomplish. However, at Macon I found a well-finished railroad which led to Savannah, a distance of 190 miles, over which we passed in exactly the same time that it took us the day before to accomplish the sixty. From Savannah to Charleston I had the regular steamboat. Thus it has taken me the whole sheet to give you an outline of my journey, the details of which volumes would scarcely record. At last, on the 27th of December, after an absence of five months and two days, I stood once more in my old quarters at Ft. Moultrie. Since my return the weather has been so bright and delightful that I have almost renounced all allegiance to Ohio, although it contains all whom I love and regard as friends. I have been so busy of late that I have not even been to Charleston to see my old acquaintances, and could only steal time the other day to accept an invitation of some planters on an adjacent island to participate in a fox hunt and the consequent dinner and frolic.

On October 24th of the same year, with his hatred of politics and scorn of politicians, he learns that John has been stump-speaking. The letter shows a singular mingling of disapprobation and pride. As long as he has seen fit to seek political advancement, he is pleased with his success. The letters that follow from Fort Moultrie are descriptive of the life led on plantations about Charleston.

FORT MOULTRIE, S.C., Oct. 24, 1844.

My Dear Brother;... What in the devil are you doing? Stump speaking! I really thought you were too decent for that, or at least had sufficient pride not to humble and cringe to beg party or popular favor. However, the coming election will sufficiently prove the intelligence and patriotic spirit of the American people, and may deter you from committing a like sin again... For my part, I wish Henry Clay to be elected, and should rejoice in his success, for various reasons, but I do not permit myself to indulge in sanguine feelings when dependence has to be placed on the pitch-and-toss game of party elections.

Let me conclude by hoping that yon will now in the outset of life do all things in your power to advance your interest and fame, and to neglect no chance to better your fortune....

Your affectionate brother,

W. T. SHERMAN.

Smithville, *N.C.*, April 4, 1845.

My Dear Brother: I am going to return to Charleston to-night by sea, and expect to be turned wrong side out, as the wind is blowing a half gale. I have been to Wilmington in this State to stand by a young friend who exchanged the independence of the bachelor for the charms of Governor Dudley's daughter. We had a brilliant wedding, — dinner-parties and balls for three days, — when I came here to see a friend, and will now go home by the first steamboat that comes along.... I expect upon my arrival at Ft. Moultrie to find a letter from mother and yourself, and if I do not — good-by, for devil the word has reached me from Mansfield for four months. Love to all. Smithville is on the Cape Fear Fiver, near the outlet.

Your affectionate brother,

W. T. SHERMAN.

In the autumn of 1844 he was sent to Augusta Arsenal, Ga., on some special duty, remained there a few months, and then returned to his post.

At the first rumor of war with Mexico he shows the greatest anxiety and impatience to be sent to Texas. It was this anxiety that made him lose all chance and sent him to California instead.

AUGUST A ARSENAL, GA,, Aug. 29, 1845.

My Dear Brother:

I got back from Key West earlier than I anticipated by taking advantage of a small pilot boat that happened to be going to Charleston from Key West. In it we returned in four days, which contrasted somewhat with the passage out of eighteen days; but the Gulf Stream was favorable in the first instance, but not in the latter, A few days ago I was ordered here and assigned to duty with the company that occupies the arsenal, and on the same day an order arrived from Washington for one more company to sail for Arkansas Bay, Everybody supposed the Colonel would send the company to which I belonged, because we, its officers, are all young and unmarried, whereas the others were all differently situated; but in army affairs age has precedence of merit, and an older Captain Burke was sent, leaving us again behind. There are still two companies at Ft. Moultrie; and in case of a requisition for more men, we, or rather my old company, will certainly go, in which case I have the Colonel's promise that speedy notice will be given me, and I be ordered to go along. Also I am promised to go in case this company goes, thus securing two chances, which will inevitably enable me to go to Texas, in case more troops be required, and then most heartily will I give all the aid I can to further the views of Government to extend the "Area of Freedom."... As to Texas having been annexed for the sole purpose of extending slavery, I do not believe, Some politicians may do so, and abolitionists may act upon that decision and affect it; but if matters be permitted to take a natural course, the result will be as surely the reverse as water flows down hill. Your affectionate brother,

W. T. SHERMAN.

FORT MOULTRIE, S.C., Jan. 4, 1846.

My Dear Brother: I had to go to North Carolina on a wedding tour at Christmas time, and as soon as I got back I went to a plantation, not very far off, to spend the New Year. I am pretty well acquainted with all the rich people round about, and have from them enough invitations for the balance of the winter. It is a great relief occasionally to slip off from our monotonous drill and duty to ramble among the green and noble live oaks — the most magnificent evergreen in our forest. Then again, the planters have plenty to eat and drink, and can, without seeming inconvenience, entertain any number of straggling acquaintances. When we expect any assemblage large enough to dance, we take along four or five musicians from our band, which makes us doubly welcome during the Christmas holidays. The people here were not a little alarmed about war, for it would at once crush their prosperous rice and cotton trade—the only articles of trade here. Moreover, the English, in case of war, would doubtless do all they could to make the slaves rise and would supply them with the necessary arms and ammunition to make them really formidable. I have never seen the least sign of disaffection on the part of the negroes, and have seen them in the cotton field and rice ditches, met them hunting at all hours of day and on the road at night, without anything but "How d'ye, Massa? Please give me some bac." However, it is easy, no doubt, to make them believe they can own the fields and houses they now see, and to excite them to resort to means that would even astonish their provokers; but I have heard but one or two who in conversation would admit even such danger in case of war; but all admit that the price of negroes would so , fall as inevitably to destroy such as would be compelled to sell such, property, such as estates to be divided among children, etc. There would be no difficulty in taking Charleston—our fort is weak and has only about 100 men — it is not ditched or strengthened in such a way as to defy an assault A new fort is being built in the channel which, when done, will be very strong, but its walls are as yet barely out of water. The Charlestonians have such confidence in Mr. Calhoun, who is decidedly opposed to war, that since his arrival they have no apprehension. All here think that such resolutions as Mr. Hannigan introduced in the Senate, and such speeches as were made by Allen and Cass will cause immediate war for which no preparations are in progress, or even contemplated. If war takes place, I shall do all I can to better my future and rank, but if it slides by, as other rumors have, I must remain contented with my present commission....

Your affectionate brother,

W.T. SHERMAN.

In April, 1846, he writes: —

You may be surprised to learn that in a few days I will go to New York City and then to some place to me still unknown. Tell mother that she will have no more writing to Fort Moultrie for a long time, as I will, in all probability, be absent two years. I must be at New York on the 1st of May, and then shall learn my future station, which may possibly be at the West.

And later, still hoping to be sent to Texas, he writes: —

Direct a letter to me, if you want to write, at Fort Columbus, New York Harbor. It should reach there at or before the 1st of May or I won't get it. Tell me then whether your railroad is done from the lake, and what conveniences there are to reach Columbus, for it is in the reach of probability that I may receive orders for New Orleans or Texas, and be allowed to steer my own course, in which case I might give you a hasty call, if it wouldn't delay me too long....

On July 14th he sailed from New York, with one hundred and fifteen men and five officers, for California, on the *Lexington*, an old sloop-of-war. On November 10th he wrote a long letter to his sister Elizabeth, which was passed about in the family and finally found its place in John Sherman's letter-book.

UNITED STATES SHIP LEXINGTON AT SEA, Nov. 10, 1846.

My Dear Sister: The wind is now so strong and fair that we have hopes of reaching Valparaiso in about ten days, and, as our stay there will be too short to gratify curiosity and write letters too, I must prepare them beforehand. We sailed from Rio on the evening of the 21st of September, and ran down the coast of South America with nothing to disturb the usual monotony of a sea life till, on the twenty-first day out, we made Statenland, an island to the north and east of Cape Horn. It had become cold, and the bleak mountains, covered with snow, looked desolate enough. Soon they were sunken beneath the horizon, and our vessel felt the majestic swell of the Pacific. We were then in the sea so much dreaded by sailors, but a bright sun made us for the day think the dangers like most others, more imaginary than real. We were soon undeceived, for the southwest wind arose, driving us to the eastward amidst a conflict of waves such as I had never seen before. For twelve days we struggled with, the storm, snow, ice, and cold, and when the wind lulled, we found that no progress had been made. A favoring breeze then enabled us to reach Cape Horn, with its snow-capped rocks, and we passed quite near it, with a clear sky and bright sun overhead. We began to flatter ourselves that it was done with us, but we were again mistaken; for a northwester began and served us more rudely than its predecessor. For another twelve days it was one continued struggle for mastery, and really it seemed more than once as though the ship must be swamped. All hands were completely exhausted; our Captain Baily of the navy has made the passage some ten or twelve times, and the purser still oftener, and each say they never encountered so heavy a sea or such persevering head gales. Often our decks were covered with ice and snow, the rigging dangling with icicles, whilst the wind moaned and whistled as in our western woods. I will not attempt to give you an idea of the height or force of the waves, — words are inadequate to convey a true idea, and one must experience them to feel their full force. I trust, however, you may never have to seek such experience. Yesterday, however, the observation of the sun placed us in 54° 40' or north of Cape Horn, whose latitude is 55° G9, or we had been twenty-six days south of the Cape passing through a distance we might return in less than two. Our course on the chart is jagged and crooked enough; the farthest south latitude we made was 59°. Here it is now spring and the days very long. I have seen the sun rise before four in the morning and set after eight, with twilight extending nearly the whole night. Were we to remain here a month longer, we might see the sun throughout twenty hours out of twenty-four. Travellers always allude to the strangeness of seeing the sun to the north, new constellations in the sky, etc., hut education explains causes, removes mystery, and strips travelling of nearly all its ancient zest. The constellation of the Southern Cross is composed of four stars that are not very conspicuous. You may look up any night and see the same in any latitude. The Magellan clouds are three small patches of nebulae like the Milky Way. They are near the South Pole, and cannot, of course, be seen in the northern hemisphere. In no other respect does this part of the world differ from any other, for the sea, monotonous sea, is the same everywhere, differing only according to the freshness of the breeze. The little world, bounded by the walls of our ship, continues the same limited monarchy, with its grades and distinctions. The captain in his cabin, the officers in the wardrooms, and sailors and soldiers forward. Of the three, ours, being the middle rank, is doubtless the most pleasant, for it embraces eleven in number, with books, cards, and music. We are thrown into the most intimate contact, and thus far have not suffered from a feeling of jealousy that is very apt to arise among officers of different services. Strange, too, for it is an *impenum in imperio*. We are passengers, having our soldiers under one species of command—the naval officers are on duty with the sailors. We are bound to do nothing, but still do make one-fourth of our men stay on deck all the time to assist in working the ship, for the crew is very short. Such a mixture of duties seldom prospers, but here, by a good understanding on the part of the officers, we have had no trouble at all, all feeling our mutual dependence. Since we have been off the Cape it has been so cold that we have been compelled to wrap up and keep more to ourselves in our staterooms, sleeping or reading, the former having the preference—the better the sleeper the happier the man. Never was time more perfectly sacrificed, for we have been afloat near four months, and now, for the first time, we head towards our destination, after having sailed about nine thousand or ten thousand miles. If you hear about a subscription opening to dig a canal across the Isthmus of Panama, you may put me down any amount, for really I do not fancy a voyage of twenty-four thousand miles to accomplish a distance of less than two thousand. However, I do not permit myself to dream of a return to the United States for five or six years, when I hope to pass through Mexico. We are all most anxious to hear the state of the war. How many fights have been had, how the volunteers act, how General Kearny progresses, for we expect him to be in California this winter; yea, and a thousand other things that will be old before they reach our ears, for our own slow progress teaches us how slow and uncertain is communication by sea, to which we shall have mainly to rely for news and letters. The long, tedious time on board ship has given us ample time to reflect upon the past and make me feel a little astonished at my rapid movement from Pittsburgh. There I was well off, but, impelled by a feeling of shame at leading so quiet a life when my comrades were at war, I wrote to the Adjutant General, requesting him to order me upon any expedition,—the more hazardous, the more it would be to my liking. This letter was before him when Captain Tompkins, without my knowledge, made application for me. The coincidence produced the result, and I was ordered. My order reached Pittsburgh when I was absent of my own accord, so that when I reached Pittsburgh I found that the expedition would sail immediately; I started without regard to private risk or interest lest I should be too late and lose a reputation for prompt and willing obedience of dangerous orders. I wish, now I bad been more slow and made better preparations for so long an absence, but it is now too late and I must trust to fortune. I repeat these things that they may be known in case of accident to me.... I cannot imagine now how I was so hasty at Pittsburgh, except that then I had an idea that we were to land in California to act offensively with a battery instead of being planted to grow rusty and old in one place till Government be good enough to recall us. The only objects of life and curiosity in this region of earth are the whales and birds; the former do not show themselves often, but are known by the peculiar misty spout of water made as they rise to the surface for breath; but the birds are seen in a clearer element 5 they crowd in flocks all around the ship, following it for days and weeks, pouncing upon every piece of pork or bread that is thrown overboard. This greediness makes them an easy prey, for, with a baited hook and line, they are easily caught, and I don't know when I have had a more hearty laugh than at the simple idea of fishing for birds; but the idea is now a fact, having myself caught of all kinds. The most peculiar of them is the Cape pigeon, a beautiful, innocent bird exactly like a tame pigeon, except that it sits the water like a duck, and has webbed feet; but the albatross, the huge bird of the Cape, is more to my liking, and seems so perfectly indignant at being caught by stratagem. There are of these several varieties, the gray, the quaker (color) and white; the latter is the largest, measuring as much as twelve feet from wing to wing; their bodies are white and as large as a swan, and the spread of their wings great indeed. They soar about, scarcely moving a feather, just above the surface of the water, and, let the sea be as agitated as possible, they rise and fall with the huge waves, moving along them like a spirit upon the face

28

of the waters. To the soldier officers catching these birds, the sailors, ever superstitious, attribute our hard luck in passing the Cape....

We expected to have reached port ere this, but the sea is very uncertain, giving us a foul wind instead of fair; but now a strong south wind is carrying us straight towards Valparaiso. Already are they shortening sails, ready to lay to for morning, as soon as the lighthouse is made. It is Sunday, and the day has been remarkably beautiful; sailors, soldiers, and officers have crowded the spar deck to enjoy the warm sun and watch the varying shades of the distant Andes. They are distinctly visible, their sides and caps shining in their wintry garb, whilst the dark line of green at their base adds beauty to their cold, sterile magnificence. These mountains are from seventeen to twenty-two thousand feet in height, and may be seen at the distance of one hundred and fifty miles; but so accustomed have I been to read accounts of them and to see and dream pictures of snow-clad mountains, that these seem more like a representation than reality. I hope, however, to stroll as high up as possible, so as to realize all their magnitude and enjoy the splendid scenery grouped around them. Sixty-four days have now elapsed since we sailed from Rio, and you can easily conceive our anxiety to reach port. . There is a large fleet of English in harbor, but it seems that they have taken no steps to oppose our taking California. A lieutenant called upon our captain from the usual mark of politeness. I am officer of the day, and cannot go on shore, but will have the next three days to myself; then again Fll be officer of day, and will write to mother. Good-by. Your affectionate brother,

WT. SHERMAN

CHAPTER II

The date of the first letter from John Sherman in General Sherman's letter-book is May 2, 1847. At this time he was twenty-four years of age, and practising law in Mansfield, Ohio. As we have seen in General Sherman's letters, he had already "dabbled" in politics.

John Sherman was born in Lancaster, Ohio, May 10, 1823, the eighth child in a family of eleven. His father died when he was six years of age. At fourteen he had already begun to support himself, being a rodman on the Muskingum River Improvement Company. For a year he was engineer in charge, and was removed because he was a Whig. At seventeen he began the study of law in the office of his eldest brother, Charles, at Mansfield. In 1848 he was sent to the National Whig Convention at Philadelphia, and from that time his political life may be said to have begun. In 1851-1854 his intense interest in the excitement over the Missouri Compromise led to his election for Congress. From December, 1855, when he took his seat in the House of Representatives in Washington, his firm convictions and his earnestness in expressing them made him prominent. He was appointed by Congress on the Kansas Investigating Committee, a position of great personal danger. In 1861 he was elected Senator from Ohio, only a few weeks before the first shot was fired on Sumter.

He always took great interest in the financial questions of the day, thus preparing himself for the work he accomplished as Secretary of the Treasury under President Hayes. His first letter in this collection was written during the excitement of the Mexican War.

MANSFIELD, OHIO, May 2, 1847.

Dear Brother; Your letter of January 27th from Monterey, California, announcing your safe arrival at that port, was received by us a few days since. You have doubtless before this received letters from here, sent by way of Panama, at different times. I suppose you will get United States papers at Monterey West. They will keep you advised of all that is of importance in the history of the times. The battles of General Taylor, and particularly the recent one at Buena

Vista, have induced politicians to bring him forward as a candidate for the presidency. Politics are in a state of "hotch potch" The question of slavery in the newly conquered territory, the relative influences of the North and the South, the heroes of this Mexican War, who will demand high civil honors, will mingle in the political strife and will, in my opinion, break down the old parties and build up new ones, divided by different principles and led by different men.. ,.

We have heard, since I wrote the above, of General Scott's brilliant victory at Cerro Gordo, and the particulars of Donahue's battle at the Sacramento. Victory seems to follow our arms wherever they go. Nothing but a series of victories has sustained the administration in prosecuting the war; for there is no doubt but that a large majority of the people consider it an unjust aggression upon, a weak republic, excused by false reasons, and continued solely for the acquisition of slave territory.

Your old friend, Hull, I understand, is about to volunteer for the war and will probably be elected lieutenant. We sent two companies last year from this county. Next week another starts on the way, enlisted for the West, and there is no doubt that if the Government required it, a force of 100,000 men might be had to invade Mexico as readily as 10,000....

Your affectionate brother,

JOHN SHERMAN.

On landing in California, General Sherman was ordered to his station at Monterey, and writes from there.

MONTEREY, CAL., APRIL 18, 1848.

My Dear Brother:... We are here perfectly banished. Occasionally a vessel comes up from the Sandwich Islands and other parts in the Pacific, but now that the first excitement has worn off, California is fast settling into its original and deserved obscurity. Military law is supreme here, and the way we ride down the few lawyers who have ventured to come here is curious. We have no courts here but the Alcalde Courts, and no laws save the Articles of War and the

Regulations of Police, and yet a more quiet community could not exist. The lawyers are rampant; they came here to make money, and there are no courts, and the Governor won't make any, because the coming of lawyers to California is a bad omen....

Your affectionate brother,

W. T. SHERMAN.

In August, 1848, General Sherman writes of the excitement of the gold discovery. This letter was the first authentic account that reached Ohio, and was read to friends and neighbors for miles around.

I am on the point of despatching to San Francisco an express to carry up the news of peace which reached us last evening from La Paz, Lower California, all the way by land. This treaty leaves California with no military or civil government, discharges all the volunteers, and leaves no force in the country save two small companies of regulars—for our company has been reduced to a shadow by desertions caused by the high prices of labor. These are more exorbitant than any you have ever read of, for any laboring man can get (cash) one dollar an hour, and a tradesman would turn up his nose at anything less than fifteen or twenty dollars a day. The cause of all this is the recent discovery in the western slope of the Sierra Nevada, east of Sutter's, of beds of gravel mixed in such quantities with gold, that men wash out in tin pans and the rudest machines from one to six ounces daily. This is not a temporary delusion, but a stem reality. It was impossible to credit these stories, so a few weeks since Colonel Mason, the Governor, went thither to see with his own eyes. I went along, and t wish I could tell you all I saw. I will do so at some future time, but now I can only say that we saw enough to make us entertain the only fear that disturbs the bosoms of merchants here, that gold will be found in such quantities as seriously to diminish its value as a circulating medium. At present there are about four thousand people at work, and the amount of gold obtained daily cannot fall short of thirty or fifty thousand dollars daily. Many men are already become rich, and others are growing so fast. All have their pockets full of gold, and everybody gets more than ten dollars daily for Lis personal labor, save those in the employ of government—we are the sufferers, All prices Lave so advanced that we cannot possibly exist on our pay. We know not what to do, and, in spite of threats, our soldiers are all deserting us. But it is not of this I wish to write you now; all sorts of merchandise have risen three hundred per cent, and I have heard Colonel Mason say repeatedly that an invoice of $10,000 of the Hudson Bay or American Bur Companies' goods would sell here for $100,000. I believe it, for I have seen blankets worth one or two dollars in New York sell for $50. Shoes of the coarsest quality sell for $10 a pair, and the best of it is, all consumers are able to pay down in gold for these articles. If you can at once ship to San Francisco a cargo of the following articles you will make a splendid venture. Blankets highly colored or variegated; readymade clothing from the best to the worst qualities, principally stout, warm articles of clothing, pants and sack coats, shoes of all sizes and qualities, tobacco, beads, powder, lead, shot of all sizes, hats, caps, anything ready for immediate use. Cloth is of little value, as no one has time to make it up. Wagons, light and heavy with harness, a couple dozen of ordinary buggies, cotton handkerchiefs, and the like. If more than two or three ships have not sailed from the United States before you receive this with such cargoes, you will make your own prices, for a battalion of five hundred men have just arrived from Santa Be, are destitute, etc., will be discharged, will work at the mines all summer, winter until spring, when they will be in want of the articles I have mentioned. Gold is now sold in San Francisco for $11 the ounce. It is good gold, and by a courier soon to be despatched to the United States via Panama, I will send you a specimen. You may rely upon the above, as I am possessed of authentic information, in addition to what I have seen myself.

W. T. SHERMAN.

MONTEREY, CAL., Aug. 24, 1848.

My Dear Brother:... This gold is found in the beds of streams in dry places, in fact, mingled with the earth over a large extent of country, and the whole cannot be extracted in centuries. I have not the least doubt that five or six millions of dollars have already been extracted, and men are now getting, by their individual labor, from $5000 to

$3000 a month. This is not fiction; it is truth. I went with Governor Mason and saw the evidence of it myself, so if you can, even when you receive this, despatch a cargo of assorted articles ready for immediate consumption or use, you can realize more than a hundred per cent. Indian goods of all kinds command any price that is asked. A good supercargo should come over, as a man would not take charge and dispose of such business for less than twenty or thirty dollars a day. A laboring man can now get easily from $5 to $15 a day. A dollar an hour is the usual price....

Your affectionate brother,

W. T. SHERMAN.

The following letter, probably written to his friend, Major H. S. Turner, of St. Louis, is found in John Sherman's letter-book of this date. I insert it, as being more complete than those to his brother of the same date.

MONTEREY, CAL., AUG. 25, 1848

My Dear Friend: I wrote you last by Chouteau that probably I would soon be at Mazatlan, whence I would write to you; but events so transpired that Colonel Mason did not go there, but went to the Sacramento to examine into the truth of the rumors that were swelling each day the amount of gold found there. I, of course, accompanied him, and we had an agreeable tour by way of San Francisco. There we had our horses, and those of the escort, carried to the north side of the Bay of San Francisco, to Sousolito or Whaler's Harbor, whence we proceeded to Bodega. That is an old Russian port where the fur companies had located some families to raise wheat for the colony at Sitka, which is in too cold a region to raise wheat. The Russian company has broken up in California, and Bodega is in the hands of an enterprising American, named Smith, who, at great cost, has erected a steam saw-mill. It looked strange to see the puffing of an engine, and to witness once more its marvellous power. It is the only thing of the kind in this region of earth. Smith would have made his fortune by sawing lumber and grinding wheat, but the gold fever has stripped him of all his employees, and he himself was on the point of breaking up and going to the mines. From Bodega we crossed a range of hills into the valley of the Pataloma, which empties into the northwest corner of the Bay of San Francisco, and thence to Sonoma, which is on a stream of the same name. Each of these valleys are flat as a table and bounded by high hills.... The Sacramento, where we crossed it at Sutter's Fort, is a broad stream, with a current of two or three miles an hour; the banks are low, so that, when the rainy season sets in, the vast plain on the east side is one sheet of water, but at ordinary seasons the stream is confined within its banks of about three hundred yards wide. We crossed ourselves in a boat, but our horses and mules swam the river. Sutter's Fort stands about three miles back from the river, and about a mile from the American Fork, which also is a respectable stream. The fort encloses a space of about two hundred yards by eighty; the walls are built of adobe or sun-dried brick. All the houses are of one story, save one, which stands in the middle, which is two stories. This is the magazine, officers' mess-room, etc. It was in this that in former times Sutter held his state and issued orders amongst the tribes of Indians as peremptory and final as those of an emperor. This man Sutter has played a conspicuous part in the history of this country, and is likely to continue his onward career. His personal appearance is striking; about forty or fifty years of age, slightly bald, about five feet six inches in height, open, frank face, and strongly foreign in his manner, appearance, and address. He speaks many languages fluently, including that of all Indians, and has more control over the tribes of the Sacramento than any man living. We spent many days at Sutter's, and were at the first Fourth of July dinner ever given publicly at the fort. Sutter presided at the head of the table, Governor Mason on his right and I on his left. Almost fifty sat down to the table, mostly Americans, some foreigners, and one or two Californians. The usual toasts, songs, speeches, etc., passed off, and a liberal quantity of liquor disposed of, champagne, Madeira, sherry, etc.; upon the whole a dinner that would have done credit in any frontier town. I have no doubt it cost the givers $1500 or $2000. At Sutter's we began to see the full effect of the gold; rooms in the fort were rented at $100 a month, and one indifferent house at $500 a month. A small oxload, hauled some twenty-five miles, cost $60, and a trip of the *Lancet* to San Francisco was worth $600. The mechanics employed by Sutter got $10 a day the month round, and common laborers one dollar an hour. Horses that a few months ago were worth $15 and $20 were then worth $75 and now $100. From Sutter's we went up the American Fork twenty-five miles to the Mormon diggings. This is a half-formed island of sand and gravel where the Mormons first began to wash for gold. They got out a great deal at about the rate of $25 per man a day. The gold is in fine bright scales and is very pure. It is separated from the earth and gravel by washing in the pans by hand, but the better plan is in a kind of inclined trough with cleats nailed across the bottom. A grate is placed over the highest part of this trough, upon which the gravel is thrown, afterwards the water. The gold passes into the trough, the gravel and stones are removed, and by a constant dashing of water and rocking the machine, the earthy matter is washed off, leaving the gold mixed with black sand in the bottom of the machine. These are separated by drying them in the sun and blowing off the sand, leaving the gold pure. You would be astonished at the ease with which the precious metal is obtained; any man by common industry can make $25 a day. We visited a great many parties at work as high up the American Fork as Sutter's saw-mill, fifty miles above his fort, and there struck to the right and left into the mountains. In the bed of the stream the gold is in fine scales, whereas in the hollows and ravines it is of coarse and of irregular dimensions. I have seen a great many pieces as heavy as two or three ounces, one of six ounces, and have heard of one of six pounds. In the mountain ravine several men have made $8000 or $10,000 a month. Everybody is at perfect liberty to go where he will, but the gold occurs so plentifully that there is no quarrelling, no collisions. We saw a great deal of gold, and, as near as we could then estimate it, about four thousand people were at work getting out about $50,000 of gold daily. This gold occurs in the whole western slope of the Sierra Nevada north and south of Sutter's. Exploring parties not satisfied with $25 and $50 a day are looking for the pure metal unmixed with earth. Gold is so common that it can be bought for $8 or $9 the ounce, and it is worth in Valparaiso or the United States $16 or $18. The sudden development of so much wealth has played the devil with the country. Everybody has gone there, save women and officers. Our soldiers are deserting, and we can't stop it. A tailor won't work a day, nor a shoemaker, nor any other tradesman, — all have gone to the mines. The sailors desert their ships as fast as they come on the coast, and we have been waiting a month to send an express to the United States, but no vessel can get a crew to leave the coast. We remained up there among the mountains a few days, and saw enough gold to carry conviction of the truth of the most exaggerated accounts that had previously reached us. We hurried back to Monterey to despatch a courier to Washington, but no vessel has yet been able to leave the coast for want of a crew. We are now hourly expecting a small schooner from San Francisco, which is reported about to make an effort with three or four men to get to Valparaiso. When we were in the midst of despatches about the gold mines and mania, here comes the notice of the conclusion of the Treaty of Peace, and Great Jehovah, what a treaty I A conquering army, in the country of an enemy, making such terms! No wonder we could not impress the Mexicans with respect for us. Had we burned their capital, blown up San Juan d'Alloa, knocked down Mazatlan, and gone back to the United States, it would have been a better treaty than the present one. If we were at war, we should not have made apologies for it by paying fifteen millions and imposing on ourselves conditions that cannot be fulfilled. Every article of the treaty is just such a one as Mexico would have imposed on us had she been the conqueror. Mexico did not relinquish Lower California. It is many years since she has had more than a shadow of an authority here. But I have no doubt the treaty will be overhauled thoroughly by the papers at home. Peace increases our difficulties here tenfold. The Volunteers all have to be discharged, and in Upper California will not remain over a hundred soldiers at seven dollars per month. Of course, they are deserting as fast as they can, and in a very short time there will not be a dozen left, and we officers will be alone in this country, with heavy magazines and valuable stores unguarded. Peace, too, makes this American territory in which the military officers can exercise no constitutional authority. So that, at a critical moment, all force, civil and military, is withdrawn, and the country filled with the hardest kind of a population of deserters and foreigners.

All are now so intent upon getting plenty of gold that they cannot think of the danger that envelops us. The administration have left Colonel Mason in a tight place, with no troops and no civil powers. A government of some kind must exist here soon, or the devil will be to pay. Sonoma is the residence of General Guadelupa Vallejo, who was the great man of that section at the time of the change of flags. He is far better educated than any of his countrymen, lives in some comfort and style, and managed to secure some fifty or one hundred leagues of land in the olden time.

These people don't care a for a man who can't enforce his orders by soldiers. Two years ago they revolted at having garrisons in their towns, but now that these garrisons are about to be broken up, they beg and implore for protection, saying the Indians will ravage and destroy, steal their women, the horses and cattle. All this is true, but no human power or feeling will draw from the mines as heterogeneous a crowd as were ever crowded in a small comer of earth's surface. I suppose the official documents sent to the adjutant general will be called for by Congress, and will be printed. The maps accompanying are the best that have yet been compiled. Ord drew the large one, and I the small ones. If I have time I sketch you a sheet to show the position of the Gold District.

In January of 1850 General Sherman came home from California, bearing despatches to the War Department. In April he writes to his brother: —

The preparations for my wedding are complete, and will come off at the appointed time with much pomp! I shall leave next day, and hope to spend a few days with you.

He was married on the first day of May, 1850, to Ellen Boyle Ewing, daughter of the Hon. Thomas Ewing, Secretary of the Interior under General Taylor. In July he writes from Washington; —

Since my arrival here, the illness, death, and funeral ceremonies of President Taylor have so engrossed all minds and all attention that even I have not taken time to tell you how it affects me. All the

Cabinet have resigned, and will retire. Mr. Fillmore has appointed a new Cabinet, but it has not yet transpired who they are, but you will know by telegraph ere this reaches you. Mr. Ewing and family go to Ohio at once, or at least in a week, and I shall go along, but shall not tarry long, but early in August shall go to Jefferson Barracks.... Mr. Ewing turns over his office on Monday next, but his successor is not named.

I do not think Mr. Fillmore finds it easy to form a Cabinet, as so much time has been consumed in its formation. I hope the political history of the past year will make a strong impression on your mind not to seek honors or distinction through that channel.

ST. Louis, Mo., Jan. 14, 1851.

My Dear Brother:

I have nothing new at all here; am still expecting to be sent away in the spring, but where to is hard to tell. I ask no imprudent questions of the authorities at Washington, but leave them to act as the good of the service to them may seem fit.

We have had a bitter cold winter. The river closed in December, and is now closed, —not actually frozen over, but the floating cakes lodge in a narrow part, about eighty miles down the river, called a gorge; these cakes freeze together, and serve as a dam to all the ice up stream. Our mails have been entirely interrupted. I subscribe to a daily New York paper, but never receive them except occasionally twenty or thirty arrive at once.

There are the usual clamors against the administration, and all confess that the mails are worse than ever before.

Write me from Washington the political news, and again let me advise you to shun politics like poison, except it advance you in the profession of the law.

Affectionately your brother,

W. T. SHERMAN-.

The above advice, however good, was, it is needless to say, not taken.

In September of 1852 General Sherman went to New Orleans as a commissary to relieve Major Waggaman.

NEW ORLEANS, LA, NOV. 17, 1852

My Dear Brother:

I suppose at this time yon are cold enough. Here all is bright and sunshine; not a particle of frost yet, but some few days have been chilly, making a fire agreeable. Trees and grass are green. Some evergreens, oaks, and sycamores ornament Lafayette Square, upon which the building used for all the army offices fronts, and the verdant appearance of it is very agreeable.

There is evidence here of renewed prosperity. For some years New Orleans has been on the decline; but this year good crops of cotton, sugar, corn, wheat, everything, give great animation to business. Think of cotton alone from this place shipped annually to the value of sixty millions of dollars I More than the California gold mines yield. Add to this the sugar and up-river produce, and you can form some conception of the commerce of a place six miles long by a mile deep, the whole river front being occupied with steamers and ships of all kinds

By the way, I suppose you are now effectually and forever cured of politics. You were born of the wrong party, and should now be content to follow your profession, and leave the democracy to their power and subsequent defection and downfall.

Shortly after General Sherman's arrival at New Orleans, he received notice of his appointment as partner in the banking firm of Lucas, Turner & Co. He therefore resigned from the army, and went to San Francisco to inaugurate a branch, of the firm there. Before leaving, he wrote as follows: —

NEW ORLEANS, LA., March 4, 1853.

My Dear Brother: I suppose you have heard of my proposed departure for California. It is proper you should have distinct information on this head. I start on Sunday, 6th instant, in the *Pampero,* for San Juan, taking the Nicaragua route for novelty. I go as a member of the banking house of Lucas & Turner, a branch of that of Lucas & Simonds of St. Louis. Turner is a particular friend of mine, and is already in California; he is quite wealthy. Lucas is decidedly the richest property-holder in St. Louis, and has credit unlimited. Now I, of course, could not have better associates in business, if I am ever to quit the army, and in these prosperous times salaried men suffer. Nevertheless, I was unwilling to resign, and have procured leave of absence for six months, at the end of which time I can best determine what to do. You may depend on it that I will not throw away my present position without a strong probability of decided advantage. I can see that the parties are very anxious to get me permanently with them. I had fixed upon the 22d of March for my departure, but Mr. Lucas came down from St. Louis to expedite my departure.

Consequently he started with his family for San Francisco by way of Nicaragua early in March. The following letter is the first he received from John after landing: —

MANSFIELD, OHIO, April 25, 1853.

My Dear Brother: I designed writing to you and sending you a package of newspapers by Captain Hull of San

Francisco, but he left home sooner than I anticipated. California is so far away, and it requires so long a time for a letter to go, that it seems like writing for futurity. This, with the press of engagements, will account for me not answering sooner your letter from New Orleans.

In your new undertaking, you encounter some risks, but I think from the statement of your letter I should have had no hesitation in adopting your course. The spirit of the age is progressive and commercial, and soldiers have not that opportunity for distinction which is the strongest inducement in favor of that profession. From your business habits and experience, you ought in a few years to acquire a fortune which will amply compensate you for the loss of the title of colonel. Besides, officers of the army must either be in large cities, where their pay is insufficient to meet current expenses, or on the borders of civilization, where their families must either be separated from them or share their banishment.

If we can do anything to advance your business, of course you can command us in any way.

Your affectionate brother,

JOHN SHERMAN.

In the following letters General Sherman describes the changes that have taken place in San Francisco during his absence, and discusses the question of slavery, already beginning to give cause for alarm.

SAN FRANCISCO, CAL., June 3, 1868.

My Dear Brother:

This is the most extraordinary place on earth. Large brick and granite houses fill the site where stood the poor, contemptible village $ wharves extend a mile out, along which, lie ships and steamers of the largest class, discharging freight in a day that used to consume with scows a month. Yet amid all this business and bustle there is more poverty than in New York. Not a day without distressed individuals ask for money.

My business here is the best going, provided we have plenty of money. Without it, I stick to Uncle Sam, most emphatically.

Your brother,

W. T. SHEEHAN.

The following eighteen months were passed quietly and without incident by General Sherman, while in December of 1855, John Sherman entered upon the six exciting years preceding the war, in the events of which he took a leading part. In March of 1856 General Sherman writes to his brother: —

97 BANKING HOUSE OE LUCAS, TURNER & Co., SAN FRANCISCO, CAL., NOV. 30, 1854.

My Dear Brother: I have seen by the papers that you are elected to Congress. I suppose you feel entitled to the congratulations of all the family, and I should not have been so late in giving you mine, only I expected that you would announce by letter the fact of your plans. To be elected is of course a higher honor than to occupy a seat in the

House of Representatives; yet that must be the school for those who are ambitious for higher honors. The Senate is, in my opinion, the only body which reflects an honor upon its members, and should you aspire to a seat there, I should be proud to learn of your success. As a young member I hope you will not be too forward, especially on the question of slavery, which it seems is rising more and more every year into a question of real danger, notwithstanding the compromises. Having lived a good deal in the South, I think I know practically more of slavery than yon do. If it were a new question, no one now would contend for introducing it but it is an old and historical fact that you must take as you find it. There are certain lands in the South that cannot be inhabited in the summer by the whites, and yet the negro thrives in it—this I know. Negroes free won't work tasks of course, and rice, sugar, and certain kinds of cotton cannot be produced except by forced negro labor. Slavery being a fact is chargeable on the past; it cannot, by our system, be abolished except by force and consequent breaking up of our present government. As to restraining its further growth, the North have a perfect right to their full vote, and should, as a matter of course, use it. The Nebraska bill was a mistake on the part of the South, a vital mistake that will do them more harm than all the violent abolitionists in the country. Let slavery extend along the shores of the Gulf of Mexico, but not in the high salubrious prairies of the West. It was a mistake to make Missouri a slave State j but it was done long ago, and now there is no remedy except in the State itself. Slavery can never exist here or north of us, so the North now has the power and can exercise it in prudence and moderation. Of all the follies of our government, that of the purchase of the Ladslen line excelled any, — the land embraced in that line would not sell at auction for a thousand dollars, and yet it cost ten millions. My idea is to leave our present limits alone until we have more population, and then to make other adjacent territories pay for coming into the Union. The Sandwich Islands and Cuba, as long as held by Spain, or are independent, are more useful to us than if annexed as territory. If we had a colonial system like England, whereby we could govern them absolutely, it would be good property, but to admit the

Kanakas of the Pacific and mixed Creoles of Cuba on a par with ourselves, would not exalt them, but would degrade us....

Your affectionate brother,

W. T. SHERMAN.

Happily, General Sherman lived to see the freed slaves work, and realized with his friends in the South the consequent improved condition of the Southern commerce.

BANKING HOUSE OF LUCAS, TURNER & Co., SAN FRANCISCO, March 20, 1856.

My Dear Brother: I see you are placed on the Committee of Foreign Relations, which is deemed a compliment. Since you are embarked in politics, I shall watch your course with deep interest, and of all things, I shall expect you to avoid localism and to act as a representative of a great developing nation rather than a mere emblem of the freaks and prejudices of a small constituency. The slavery question is forced on you in spite of yourself. Time and facts are accomplishing all you aim at, viz the preponderance of the free over the slave States. This is so manifest that the politicians and people of the South feel it, and consequently are tetchy and morose. Of course, you will vote as you think right; but should you have occasion to speak, do not imitate Giddings or Seward, but avoid the subject as a dirty black one. The repeal of the Compromise was unfortunate, but being done, to repeal it would only produce feeling and no good. Kansas will be a free State, so will Missouri and Kentucky in time; but the way to accomplish that is to let things go on as now, showing the eminent prosperity of the free States, whilst the slave States get along slowly. Self-interest is the great motor, and the Kentuckians and Missourians, seeing the land and property of adjoining free States commanding a high and ready price in consequence of the influx of white men, will feel that they have other interests beside slave property, and this cause is now telling, and will go on increasing. Therefore, to accomplish any political end, no provoking speeches are necessary, but on the contrary defeat the object in view. I think you may do yourself credit and a public good by aiding California and the Pacific coast, which is poorly represented. There are now Indian wars going on to the north of us that will appeal to you. Don't meddle in it. Let Oregon and Washington Territories have reasonable help; but they should help themselves, as Congress has donated to them liberally in the way of land, and these wars are doubtless provoked by the indiscriminate robbery of the Indians, who, driven from the valleys, find no alternative but to steal and kill.

All the Pacific slope is mountainous, and the valleys are limited in extent. Prom these the Indians have been expelled, and of right they resist. The settlements have pushed forward more than the extent of the white population warrants, and they cannot be restrained, save by the danger of Indians, a proper and necessary restraint.

The time for the great national railroad has not yet come. The surveys thus far made do not settle the question of the best route; but my opinion is the old emigrant route from Port Leavenworth or Council Bluffs is the best one. But the movement now on foot to open a good wagon road is very timely. Its cost will be comparatively small, as California will make one or more good roads across the Sierra Nevada, Some four or five military posts with settlements around them, some bridges and free ferries, will be all that is needed. Advocate the wagon road with all the zeal you possess, and you will do a good thing. A stage will use the wagon road as soon as the wants of the people demand. The great object to be accomplished is to afford convenient resting places, where the emigrant can buy a mule or ox and can have his wagon repaired at moderate cost. This post should be fortified in the strongest manner possible, and supplied in advance of any necessity with all the munitions of war. The engineer in chief will have made the necessary estimates, and you will be safe in advocating whatever he may recommend.

Independent of gold, California is of great value to the Union by affording so good a harbor and point of commerce, from which we can trade with the Pacific Islands, with Mexico, and the Asiatic continent. The navy yard and docks now in process of building should be finished as soon as possible. I throw out these ideas to you, as I suppose you will admit my means of judging.

Your affectionate brother,

W. **T. SHERMAN.**

Almost at the same time, March 28, John writes his brother: "I have been appointed on a committee of three of the House to go to Kansas to investigate, etc.," and in answer to the General's letter of the 20th, he says: —

Washington, June 29, 1856.

My Dear Brother: Your letter of March 20ᵗʰ has been received by me upon my return from Kansas. Your notions about the slavery question are in common with my own. In accepting the appointment to go to Kansas, I was left free to follow my own judgment and form my own opinions about the disturbances there. These opinions are embodied in the Report of the Committee, all of which I wrote, a copy of which I will send to you as soon as it is printed. You will see that the condition of affairs in that territory are far worse than you anticipated. Please give me your opinion frankly as to the character of the report.

I do not think that the Pacific Railroad will pass this Session. A liberal appropriation will be made, I think, to construct a wagon road. This will be the best plan for the present, and I will therefore cordially support it.

I saw your name connected with the disturbances in San Francisco. Please inform me all about it. I shall feel disposed to favor appropriations to California, Oregon, and Washington, and especially to make communications between them and older States, but the sums you ask rather startle our economical notions.

Affectionately your brother,

JOHK SHERMAN.

The following group of letters, treating of the Vigilance Committee, and including the one to Mr. Ewing, referred to in John Sherman's letter of July 15, explain very fully the General's opposition to the committee. The former rather sympathizes with it, because of his recent experience in Kansas, which the General asserts to have been different.

SAN FRANCISCO, CAL., July 7, 1858.

My Dear Brother: The steamer sails to-day, and will bring you news of the same character as the two past. The Vigilance Committee is in full blast, still exercises entire control, has Judge Terry in their power, and had the man Hopkins died, they would have hung him. Now the probabilities are they will send him away. Where the matter is to end, I cannot imagine, but I think the community is getting sick and disgusted with their secrecy, their street fools, and parades, and mock trials, — worse, far worse, than the prompt, rapid executions of a mob or lynch court.

Since my resignation I have kept purposely aloof from all parties, either one way or the other; being in a business where large interests are at stake, I cannot act with that decision otherwise that would suit me. I do not think there is any necessity for the interference of the federal authorities, but that before we can hear from Washington the matter will be over and forgotten.

SAN FRANCISCO, CAL., Aug. 3, 1856.

My Dear Brother:

Here in this country the Democratic — a mob — element prevails to such a degree that, as you will have observed, the influence of governor, mayor, and all the executive authority has been utterly disregarded. For three months here we have been governed by a self-constituted committee, who have hung four men, banished some twenty others, arrested, imprisoned, and ironed many more, and who now hold a judge of the Supreme Court in their power.... There is no doubt we have a bad administration of law here, and more than a fair share of rowdies; but I think the Committee itself no better, and if we are to be governed by the mere opinion of the Committee, and not by officers of our own choice, I would prefer at once to have a Dictator. The Committee is now in a bad fix. The man whom Terry stabbed is now well. The Executive Committee of Vigilance are now willing to acquit him, but before they can act in such a matter by their by-laws, they must submit the case to a Board of Delegates, composed of three from each of their military companies. This Board of Delegates, of course, want action, and they insist that Terry shall resign his office and go away, or be hung. There is a sloop-of-war here, the *John Adams,* whose commander says that he will intercept any ship that attempts to carry Terry off so that it will be difficult for them to banish Terry, and it is not impossible that they may yet hang Terry to save themselves the consequences of his return to the Bench. If there is not an entire revolution and withdrawal from, the Union, then all these acts of violence must come up before our courts on actions for civil damages, and it is likely, if Terry returns to the Bench, he will have some feeling against the men who have kept him imprisoned some two months, with daily expectation of death or banishment. We are waiting to hear what President Pierce will do in the matter. I doubt whether he will interfere as long as these men do not try to bring about an absolute revolution, which I do not think they have yet contemplated. My own opinion is, the committee is tired of its position, but find it difficult to withdraw from the complications in which they are involved.

Affectionately your brother,

W. T. SHERMAN.

Washington, July 15, 1850.

My Dear Brother: Your letter to Mr. Ewing and the accompanying letters were carefully read by me and then sent to Mr. Ewing. I do not see how your conduct can be assailed. I had watched with a very great deal of anxiety your movements, and had carefully preserved every extract of a paper which related to it, fearing at the time a collision between the Vigilant Committee and your authority. I must confess that, except as you were personally interested in the contest, my sympathies were all with the committee. The same class of characters who were so infamous in this city and in election frauds have controlled the cause of Law and Order in Kansas, and there committed such calamities with the direct sanction of the authorities that it seemed to me just and right to organize and to enforce a higher law. The early movements of the people meet the cordial approval of all good men here, and this feeling was deepened by the

48

act of your representative, Herbert, in killing the Irish waiter. If the proclamation of the governor had been equally obeyed by the committee, all would have been satisfied; but their continued action subverts all law and authority, and it seems to me ought not to be tolerated. At first I was surprised that you had taken part in the strife, and especially against the committee; but the newspapers have contained such full information as to your movements that it was manifest that you did right in accepting the authority you did, and under the circumstances you could do nothing but resent what they did. The papers here take the same view of it, and approve the course you pursued, and generally condemn General Johnson that he did not observe more moderation in dealing with the committee. As it seems to exercise its novel authority wisely and promptly, I hope they will expel the worst of their prisoners without further violence, and then gradually dissolve, and allow the constituted authorities to resume their usual course. The lesson taught them may be of service.

Affectionately your brother,

JOHN SHERMAN.

SAN FRANCISCO, CAL,, Aug. 19, 1856.

My Dear Brother: I have received your letter. The difference between the Kansas case and this is that in Kansas the efforts came from the slavery party to restrain the free emigration, and to stuff the vote, so as to nullify the numbers of free voters. Here the ballot-box stuffing was partly imaginary, the famous box being a humbug, used at the primary elections to secure the nominations, and never used at the public polls. One was positively illegal, the other was simply irregular, and the Legislature of the State had already decided that the judges of election should he appointed by five well-known gentlemen of this city, — a remedy ample and conclusive for future elections, which was an admission on the part of the State that the former judges of election were not trustworthy. Again, in Kansas it was doubtful who was the legal governor. Here there is no question that Johnson was duly and fairly elected, for if any illegal votes were cast, they were against him. The city of San Francisco, where all these alleged frauds were committed, voted against

Johnson. If murder had not been punished heretofore, it was not the fault of the judges, but of the juries, the merchants, and those who are of the Vigilance Committee, having avoided jury duty as much as possible. I remember when Cora's jury was empanelled, there was a universal answer that it was a good jury, and the judge charged strongly for murder j but the jury did not agree, and those who voted for Cora's acquittal were of the Vigilance Committee. Same of Hothington's trial

Tour affectionate brother,

W. T. Sherman.

In August, 1856, General Sherman, who has evidently been watching with concern and anxiety the trouble brewing in the House of Representatives, says: —

Unless people, both. North and South, learn more moderation, we'll see sights in the way of civil war. Of course, the North have the strength, and must prevail, though the people of the South could and would be desperate enough. I hope in Congress you will resolve yourself into the fighting branch and work off some of the surplus steam that is threatening to blow up the Union.

Again, in December, he urges the necessity of a road to California.

I wish you would make it your business to advocate the wagon road to California, one road along the usually travelled emigrant way. Let the railroad alone; it will cost so much money that it will break down any administration that adopts it as a party measure. Such a road is for the future, not the present. Give us a good wagon road, costing, say, a million or two, with bridges, wells, and stations. Also, more particularly, I wish you would use your private efforts to procure the passage of a bill granting the usual proportion of public land to the Sacramento Valley Railroad. This road is already built at heavy expense from Sacramento City east to the foot of the mountains.

Your affectionate brother,

W. T. SHERMAN.

In May, 1857, General Sherman removed with his family to New York, and shortly after returned to Ohio. The general panic in California, attendant upon the failure of the gold mines, rendered the banking business perilous in the extreme, so that Lucas, Turner & Co. wound up their affairs in San Francisco. Shortly after General Sherman had opened a branch house in New York, the parent firm in St. Louis failed, and, after closing the bank in the former city, he returned to Ohio to again start out in the world. In December, 1857, he writes: —

I think rather than be idle or to undertake any new indefinite scheme, I would return to my old business (the army), for which I am better qualified than any other. There will be great press for the higher appointments of Colonel, Lieutenant-Colonel, and Major: still, I have very many friends among the higher officers, and think by vigorous efforts I might get one of them.

The army was not increased, as he hoped it would be, so he failed to secure his reinstatement. In January General Sherman finally decided to become a lawyer, and entered into partnership with his brothers-in-law, Hugh and Thomas Ewing, in Leavenworth, Kansas.

In writing to John at this time he foretells some things that have come true, and another war that may still come to us, though far from probable.

I think in the next ten years we will have plenty to do in the war line — Mormon war, civil broils and strife, contests for political power, growing out of slavery and other exciting topics, and last a war with Spain, resulting in the conquest of Cuba,

Much of his work was done in surveying roads, and upon being asked to draw up a map of the supposed gold region in Kansas, he writes: —

It is very dangerous to attempt to draw lines by any old maps, for, like Benton, you will have ideal, wide, beautiful valleys, where awful mountains stand and won't get out of the way. Again, it is not safe to locate roads along valleys, because these valleys are not like the valleys of Ohio or the Alleghanies, for in California I have seen valleys with almost perpendicular sides of 1500 to 2500 feet, -which is a smooth country, 'tis said, to that about Shasta. I think that this memorandum of mine will answer your questions; whether satisfactorily or not, I don't know.

On Dec. 19, John Sherman writes from Washington:—

Dear Brother: Your letter of the 8th came opportunely, as it gives me a good opportunity to make a request which it may be a pleasure to grant. I have heretofore opposed the Pacific Railroad, or rather its aid by the government, principally because its construction within the ten years will be premature and will be subject to interruptions by the Indians, and because our knowledge of the country was not sufficient to enable the best route to be chosen. I have fought against all grants to railroads because of the change it made in the settled policy of the government in regard to settled lands. I have favored the "Pre-emption and Homestead Lines," and have steadily opposed either grants or sales except to actual settlers and for settlement. Within a few days, in a conference with polite friends and rather in deference to the general demand for a Pacific Railroad, I have agreed to support a bill containing the following as its leading features: 1st. Authority to the President to contract fox the transportation of the mails, etc., by railroad company between Big Sioux and Kansas River; thence between latitude 27° and 43° to San Francisco. 2d. A grant of alternate sections of public lands for twenty miles on each side of roads to be sold within five years after the completion of each section of the road of twenty-five miles; to be subject, however, to pre-emption by actual settlers at not over $2,50 per acre, and the remaining sections to be granted to actual settlers under the Homestead Bill. 3d. A payment by the government of $10,000 a mile, to be paid as each section of twenty-five miles is completed, with proper reservations to secure completion of the contract.

The details of this measure are a compound of Giddings and other railroad bills. I do not think any bill will pass this session. I may wish to speak upon it, and what I want to ask of you is a full statement of your ideas, pro and con, with liberty to use what you write. You must have a general knowledge of the routes, etc., etc., and if you take time to do as I ask, I hope you will be so full and yet so guarded in your statements that I may quote them and implicitly insist upon their entire accuracy.

I have here ample opportunities and facilities for information, but I have not time to wade through the immense volumes of exploration, etc.

I have talked with Stevens (your old friend) and Larder and others, but they are enlisted in. some war scheme. To aid you I will send you the exploration in eight quarto volumes, but all I have are in Mansfield. You shall, however, have a full set in the spring. You had better keep posted in this Pacific Railroad, for who knows but you may be connected with it some day.

In your statement, answer me these questions:

Why should government build a railroad so much in advance of settlements? Why is the central road to be chosen rather than any other? What is the best mode for the government to do it? By its own agents? By its contracts with corporations or individuals? Shall it be with lands, money, etc.? What are the difficulties to be overcome, and how? Indians, timber, water, transportation, mountains, elevation, and face of the country?

It is a magnificent project and I fear the greatness of the task will lure our people into a premature attempt to build it. We like great and splendid schemes, and sometimes forget they do not pay.

Affectionately yours,

JOHN SHERMAN.

P.S. — You are mistaken about the Republican party; there are no signs of division in its ranks. It is now the most compact and by far the strongest political element in our politics.

I think that I met Mr. Williams in New York. I was at a party given by Governor Morgan, the governor-elect of New York, and met nearly all the leading capitalists and bankers of the State, and I am pretty sure he was among them. By the way, a good many of them had waded through a financial speech I made last spring and so got the idea that I know ten times more about "Finance" than I do.

The request made (in the letter of December 19th) was granted and highly approved of by John Sherman. In acknowledging it, he calls it the "best statement of the arguments pro and con and the difficulties to be overcome" that he had seen. In the same letter he says: "While I like the excitement of political life, it will make me an old man before my time," a prophecy happily unfulfilled. In writing of the admission of Kansas as a free or slave State, General Sherman writes: —

For many years the Southern politicians have struggled to maintain that equal representation in the Senate, long since lost in the House, and when, as now also, a majority is obtained in the Senate beyond chance of alteration, then the question is settled and all angry controversy might and ought to cease. The South, with a minority of representation in both branches, and with the presence of three millions of slaves in their midst, are weak and in the power of the North; so that it seems to me that the Northern representatives can afford to lay low and let events develop the solution of the dangerous political problem. If Congress do admit Kansas as a slave State, her people will forthwith abolish it, and the South will never again attempt to coerce their Southern ideas upon any new territory so illy adapted to slave labor. To taunt them with their want of success and weakness can do no good.

Affectionately your brother,

W. T. SHERMAN.

And later, in writing to congratulate John on his reelection, he urges moderation in the coming discussions and strife with the Southern members.

I see by the papers that you are re-elected; I took that for granted. It seems to be the impression that we are to have a Republican candidate, or rather President, in 1860. I hope, if you have a hand in it, you will be as moderate as possible. I don't fear the South flying off for any such cause; but there is a reasonable middle ground on which all educated Americans may stand.

In April of 1869 John Sherman sailed on the *Vanderbilt* for a short trip abroad. Just at this time Kansas became the scene of gold discoveries, or rumors of such. General Sherman seems destined to lead a life of excitement, His arrival seems to herald some human upheaval. He writes to John of these new excitements.

Leavenworth City, Kansas, April 80, 1869,(Finished May 1.)

Dear Brother:... I would like very much to be with you and make the trip, although my tastes might lead me to traverse fields and places which have no interest to you; hut Europe, being now the concentrated history and civilization of our time, has in every part interest enough for all men. I wish, therefore, you to tell me of your progress and observations....

At this moment we are in the midst of a rush to Pike's Peak. Steamboats arrive in twos and threes each day, loaded with people for the new gold region. The streets are full of people buying flour, bacon, and groceries, with wagons and outfits, and all around the town are little camps preparing to go west. A daily stage goes west to Port Riley, 135 miles, and every morning two spring wagons, drawn by four mules and capable of carrying six passengers, start for the Peak, distance six hundred miles, the journey to be made in twelve days. As yet the stages all go out and dor't return, according to the plan for distributing the carriages; but as soon as they are distributed, there will be two going and two returning, making a good line of stages to Pike's Peak. Strange to say, even yet, although probably 25,000 people have actually gone, we are without authentic advices of gold. Accounts are generally favorable as to words and descriptions, but no positive physical evidence comes in in the shape of gold, and I will be incredulous until I know some considerable quantity comes in in the way of trade.

In telling John his political convictions at this time, he says: —

I keep along still, and shall not even vote till some organization arises that is more in accordance with my personal convictions, which are more and more strong. My idea is that the Southern States should be more likened to a man having a deformity, like the fox who lost his tail and wanted all others to cut theirs off. They think they are best off, or at least are bound to think so and instead of thrusting the fact before them all the time, I would indulge them in their delusion with all the philosophy and complacency of a strong man. If they attempt to abolish the law about slave trade, vote them down without unnecessary debate. If they and committee frame a bill to restrain territorial legislation from restricting slavery, vote them down. They have not the physical or political power to oppress the free States, nor can they afford to disperse their slaves any more. Already they have Florida, Arkansas, Texas, and large parts of Alabama and Mississippi, with less population per area than Mexico or Central America. There is no outlet for the negroes of our country; we have no right to displace the population of Mexico to put slaves there. Slavery must stay pretty much in its present boundaries by the constitution and laws as they now are.

Whether in the midst of moving battalions, in rattling towns, amid the towering Alps, or in sunny Italy, you must think of us out here on the pampas of Kansas.

Your affectionate brother,

W. T. SHERMAN.

In writing to John Sherman, travelling abroad in May, 1859, General Sherman shows the most glowing interest in the Italian war, and bemoans his inability to go to the scene of conflict. His short epitome of the possibilities and probabilities of the outcome of the trouble is curious in its accuracy as well as in its mistaken idea of the chief actor.

Of course we are all expectation here to read news of the war in Italy. Our latest accounts are simply that the Austrians, after entering Piedmont, have manoeuvred without any definite plan, giving full time for the Sardinians to organize, and for France to pour into Italy her well-equipped armies by every avenue of approach. We know, too, that the Emperor of Austria has gone to control the operations of his army, that the King of Sardinia is also his own generalissimo, and that Napoleon had sailed from Marseilles for Genoa, whence, I take it, he promptly crossed to Turin, and that he, too, will command in person.

I should like of all things to be in your stead, and I think ere this I would be near the Lake of Maggiori, within a circuit of thirty miles of which, I feel satisfied, will be or have been fought several great battles. So rapid now are movements of troops, so well-equipped are they, and so glowing with a desire to battle, that I doubt not ere this some actions have been fought that will give a clue to the result. If Napoleon can drive the Austrians out of all Italy, even from Venice and Triest, and from thence north of the Styrian Alps, and then gradually surrender the power thus acquired to a federation of states, retiring to France, he would be the most celebrated man of this or any age. He can do so. The elder Bonaparte could not, as he was never cordially recognized by other governments; but Napoleon III. is so firmly fixed, to all appearance, in France, that he can moderate his plans, and cease conquest the moment his aim is accomplished. So few ambitious men, however, have been able to stop at the right place that fortune seems to tempt them beyond human depth into ruin; still, so wilful, silent, and determined has he shown himself that I expect that he will force the Austrians back from Italy, and then allow some form of government to control the Italian kingdoms, states, and republics. Austria, however, will not relinquish Triest, Dalmatia, and Venice without a death struggle, and it may be that the war now begun may spread and make as many dynastic changes as those wars which followed the French Devolution. I wish I were there to watch the operations and changes j but alas! I am in Kansas.

As ever,

Your brother,

W. T. SHERMAN.

While the soldier brother was in the wilds of Kansas, pining to hear the clash of great armies, the statesman brother was in London, burning to suggest new measures in the House of Commons, to fight another kind of battle.

Paris, June 19, 1859.

My Dear Brother: You will perceive from the date of this letter that I am in the capital of gaiety, and such I have found it. This city is a striking contrast to any I have ever seen. If there are unhappy people here, I have not seen them. The streets are alive with people, and bands are playing in the gardens and palaces. Croups are gathered around singing-stalls, the cafes and restaurants are filled, and the broad promenades are encroached upon by persons sitting in front of the cafes, sipping coffee, etc. I have now been here eight days, and if I was to select a happy city, judging only from appearances, there could be no rival with Paris.

I know very well, from the history of the Parisians, that a sudden impulse would change them into tigers, and that the gayest spots have been the scenes of frightful cruelties, but surely they seem happy now. I have been constantly contrasting the people of Paris with the English: the conclusion is all in favor of the Parisians.

I -was in Great Britain seven -weeks; went into England, Ireland, Scotland, and Wales. I saw all I was allowed to see, without prejudice, with, a sincere desire to improve my limited time. As a matter of course, I could not give you reasons or ideas on facts gathered on the way. The mere journal of places, men, and sights seen would be a very poor guide-book. My conclusions are all against the British Government.... When Englishmen hereafter talk about their rights, I will know what they mean. They do enjoy a limited liberty of speech and of the press, and then you have said all. It is a government of the aristocracy, more exclusive, repelling, and narrow than I conceived of. The House of Commons is the only pretended representation of the people, and that is but a mere pretence. The representation is so glaringly unequal that it is a surprise to me that the people will submit to it. As the members are not paid, and none can vote without property, it is a mere representation of money and not of men. Every regulation of the government, the rules of caste, the combined insolence and obsequiousness of all classes with whom I came in contact, were so unpleasant to me that, while my visit there was a constant enjoyment and a school, I would not live under the British Government for any consideration. Without this detail, this is my idea of the British Government, and if time and space united allowed, I could state the facts and observations that, little by little, led to this conclusion; but I will leave that for some long talk when time is not so precious.

The cultivated scenery of England fully met my expectations. I can imagine nothing more beautiful than their hawthorn-hedge fields, their cattle and sheep, and indeed everything that depends on care and cultivation. The idea that all this stock and property belonged to a few, that the great mass of the people merely labored for others, and that the whole government was conducted and a system of laws passed simply to continue and intensify this state of things, and that the favored class had the possession of all the powers of government, securely hedged about, made me a rebel from the beginning.

I was present at the great debate in the House of Commons, when the ministry was overthrown upon questions utterly insignificant, and I could not but wish that I was a member of that body for ten years, with full power to introduce and discuss several measures of reform, to bring to the people of England equal representation, based upon men and not upon property or boroughs, a law against entailment, and a law of descent and distribution, which would divide property among children equally. The discussion of such radical measures could not but convince intelligent men. But what then? Neither the intelligence nor population of England is represented in Parliament, and a favored class have never yielded power except to revolution or the fear of it.

The French government is much more tolerable. Louis Napoleon is emperor by usurpation, but I really think that the government is not only for the good, but is the choice of the people and others. There is the greatest personal liberty and equality here, and the institutions tend to advance equality and give a fair chance to merit. It is true that through the press people cannot discuss politics, except on one side. In private life, and indeed in the saloons and public places, there seems no restraint. The administration of the law seems well conducted. Taxes, as compared with England, are light, and the Frenchman has no restraint, either by caste or law, from doing what he wishes, except that he must not write against the government. His equality with his neighbor is recognized. There is more freedom, if I might say so, more mixing of all classes of people here, and on terms of kindliness and equality, than you will find even in America.

The blouses, the uniforms, and the black coats all sit and eat and chat together. On the whole, they have much more claim to be a "free people" than the English, and hereafter I will know how to appreciate an English account of French tyranny.

But enough of this. I received two of your letters with great pleasure. Through friends and the papers to be found here, in many places, I am kept well advised of the American matters.

My travels have given me a fund of information that I could get in no other way. I think I will never regret the trip. I leave Paris tomorrow for Milan and the seat of war; thence we visit Switzerland and the Rhine, returning here in time to take the boat leaving Havre August 3d for New York. I regret to return so soon, but business demands it.

CHAPTER III

In August of 1859, General Sherman was appointed superintendent of a military school in Louisiana. At that time great attention was paid in the South to the military education of the young men; and it is singular, in the knowledge of after events, that General Sherman should have gone to teach the art of war to the youth of the South.

While there, or about that time, he received an offer from a banking firm to open a branch office in London; but after consulting John, he decided not to leave this country and his school, in which he was greatly interested. It was not long, however, before his relations with the school became strained, owing to his Northern ideas. In September, 1859, he wrote to John from Lancaster, Ohio, where he stopped on his way to Louisiana. slaves, and probably always will and must, and whose feelings may pervert every public expression of yours, putting me in a false position to them as my patrons, friends, and associates, and you as my brother, I would like to see you take the highest ground consistent with your party creed.

Throughout all the bitterness in the House of Representatives before the war, General Sherman urged upon his brother John to maintain a moderate course; but even then the General thought him too severe on the South, and writes in October, 1859, as follows: —

Each State has a perfect right to have its own local policy, and a majority in Congress has an absolute right to govern the whole country; but the North, being so strong in every sense of the term, can well afford to be generous, even to making reasonable concessions to the weakness and prejudices of the South. If Southern representatives will thrust slavery into every local question, they must expect the consequences and be outvoted; but the union of States and general union of sentiment throughout all our nation are so important to the honor and glory of the confederacy that I would like to see your position yet more moderate.

In December, John Sherman, being the Republican candidate for Speaker of the House, his brother, who was greatly excited and anxious as to his election, writes: —

New Orleans, Dec. 12, Sunday.

Dear Brother: had it not been for your signing for that Helper's Book. Of it I know nothing, but extracts made copiously in Southern papers show it to be not only abolition but assailing. Now I hoped you would be theoretical and not practical, for practical abolition is disunion, civil war, and anarchy universal on this continent, and I do not believe you want that.... I do hope the discussion in Congress will not be protracted, and that your election, if possible, will occur soon. Write me how you came to sign for that book. Now that you are in, I hope you will conduct yourself manfully. Bear with taunts as far as possible, biding your time to retaliate. An opportunity always occurs.

Your affectionate brother,

W. T. SHERMAN.

The following letters, relating to the Helper Book," explain themselves: —

Washing-ton, D.C., Dec. 24, 1860.

My Dear Brother: Your letter was duly received, and should have been promptly answered but that I am overwhelmed with calls and engagements.

You ask why I signed the recommendation of the Helper Book. It was a thoughtless, foolish, and unfortunate act. I relied upon the representation that it was a political tract to be published under the supervision of a committee of which Mr. Blair, a slave-holder, was a member. I was assured that there should bo nothing offensive in it, and so, in the hurry of business of the House, I told Morgan, a member of last Congress, to use my name. I never read the book, knew nothing of it, and now cannot recall that I authorized the use of my name. Everybody knows that the ultra sentiments in the book are as obnoxious to me as they can be to any one, and in proper circumstances I would distinctly say so, but under the threat of

Clark's resolution, I could not, with self respect, say more than I have.

Whether elected or not, I will at a proper time disclaim all sympathy with agrarianism, insurrection, and other abominations in the book.

In great haste,

Your affectionate brother,

JOHN SHERMAN.

SEMINARY, ALEXANDRIA, LA., Jan. 16, 1860.

Dear Brother: I received your letter explaining how you happened to sign for that Helper Book. Of course, it was an unfortunate accident, which will be a good reason for your refusing hereafter your signature to unfinished books. After Clark's resolution, you were right, of course, to remain silent. I hope you will still succeed, as then you will have ample opportunity to show a fair independence.

The rampant Southern feeling is not so strong in Louisiana as in Mississippi and Carolina. Still, holding many slaves, they naturally feel the intense anxiety all must whose property and existence depend on the safety of their property and labor. I do hope that Congress may organize and that all things may move along smoothly. It would be the height of folly to drive the South to desperation, and I hope, after the fact is admitted that the North has the majority and right to control national matters and interests, that they will so use their power as to reassure the South that there is no intention to disturb the actual existence of slavery.

Yours,

W. T. SHERMAN.

Through, all General Sherman's letters of this date one can hear the thunder crash before the storm. His ardor for peace and the avoidance of trouble are reassuring in a man of great military longings and ambitions. In [February, 1860, he writes: —

If Pennington succeeds, he will of course give you some conspicuous committee, probably quite as well for you in the long run as Speaker.

I don't like the looks of the times. This political turmoil, the sending commissions from State to State, the organization of military schools and establishments, and universal belief in the South that disunion is not only possible but certain, — axe bad signs. If our country falls into anarchy, it will be Mexico, only worse. I was in hopes the crisis would have been deferred till the States of the Northwest became so populous as to hold both extremes in check. Disunion would be civil war, and you politicians would lose all charm. Military men would then step on the tapis, and you would have to retire. Though you think such a thing absurd, yet it is not so, and there would be vast numbers who would think the change for the better.

I have been well sustained here, and the Legislature proposes further to endow us well and place us in the strongest possible financial position. If they do, and this danger of disunion blow over, I shall stay here but in case of a breach, I would go North.

Yours,

W. **T. SHERMAN.**

Later, when things look more peaceful for the country, he writes: —

The excitement attending the Speakership has died away here, and Louisiana will not make any disunion moves. Indeed, she is very prosperous, and the Mississippi is a strong link, which she cannot sever. Besides, the price of negroes is higher than ever before, indicating a secure feeling.

I have seen all your debates thus far, and no Southern or other gentleman will question their fairness and dignity, and I believe, unless you are unduly provoked, they will ever continue so. I see you are suffering some of the penalties of greatness, having an awful likeness paraded in Harper's, to decorate the walls of country inns. I have seen that of Harper, and as the name is below, I recognize it. Some here say they see a likeness to me, but I don't.

The following letters, relating to John Sherman's speech in New York, explain themselves.

WASHINGTON, March 26, 1860.

My Dear Brother: Yours of the 12th instant was received when I was very busy, and therefore I did not answer in time for you at Lancaster. I sent Gales and Seaton the six dollars for the paper.

Your estimate of the relative positions of Speaker and Chairman of Ways and Means Committee is not accurate. The former is worth struggling for; it is high in dignity, influence, and when its duties are well performed it is an admirable place to gain reputation. I confess I had set my heart upon it and that I could have discharged its duties.... My present position is a thankless, laborious one. I am not adapted to it. It requires too much detailed labor and keeps me in constant conflict; it is the place of a schoolmaster with plenty of big boys to coax and master. I will get along the best I can.... You need not fear my caution about extreme views. It is my purpose to express my political views in the State of New York in April, and to avoid hasty expressions, I will write it out in full for publication.

Affectionately yours,

JOHN SHERMAN.

LOUISIANA STATE SEMINARY OF LEARNING AND MILITARY ACADEMY, ALEXANDRIA, LA., April 4, 1800.

Dear Brother:

I know that some men think this middle course absurd, but no people were ever governed by mere abstract principle. All governments are full of anomalies, — English, French, and our own; but ours is the best because it admits of people having their local interests and prejudices, and yet living in one confederacy. I hope you will send me your speech, and if national, I will have it circulated.

I see you have reported nearly all the appropriation bills early in the session. This has been referred to in my presence repeatedly as evidence of your ability and attention to business; so, whether you feel suited to the berth or no, it will strengthen your chances in the country.

Your brother,

W. T. SHERMAN.

Washington, D.C., April 18, 1860,

I sent you a copy of my speech in New York. I delivered it with credit and to a very large and kind audience. Upon looking it over, I perceive a good deal of bitterness, natural enough, but which you will not approve. It is well received here.

Affectionately yours, John Sherman.

ALEXANDRIA, LA., May 8, 1860.

Last night I got the copy of the speech and read it.... There is one point which you concede to the Southern States, perfect liberty to prefer slavery if they choose; still, you hit the system as though you had feeling against it. I know it is difficult to maintain perfect impartiality. In all new cases, it is well you should adhere to your conviction to exclude slavery because you prefer free labor. That is your perfect right, and I was glad to see that you disavowed any intention to molest slavery even in the District. How, so certain and inevitable is it that the physical and political power of this nation must pass into the hands of the free States, that I think you all can well afford to take things easy, bear the buffets of a sinking dynasty, and even smile at their impotent threats. You ought not to expect the Southern politicians to rest easy when they see and feel this crisis so long approaching, and so certain to come absolutely, at hand.

But this year's presidential election will be a dangerous one; may actually result in civil war, though I still cannot believe the South would actually secede in the event of the election of a Republican.

Your affectionate brother,

W. T. SHERMAN.

As the year goes on, General Sherman's anxiety increases, and his position becomes almost too strained for comfort. In his intense longing for the preservation of peace, he favors the nomination of Seward rather than of Lincoln, believing him to be less inimical to the South. In June of 1860, he writes: —

66

I think, however, though Lincoln's opinions on slavery are as radical as those of Seward, yet Southern men, if they see a chance of his success, Will say they will wait and see. The worst feature of things now is the familiarity with which the subject of a dissolution is talked about. But I cannot believe any one, even Yancey or Davis, would be rash enough to take the first step. If at Baltimore to-day the Convention nominate Douglas with unanimity, I suppose if he gets the vote of the united South he will be elected. But, as I apprehend will be the case, if the seceders again secede to Richmond, and there make a Southern nomination, their nomination will weaken Douglas' vote so much that Lincoln may run in. The real race seems to be between Lincoln and Douglas.... Now that Mr. Ewing also is out for Lincoln, and it is strange how closely these things are watched, it is probable I will be even more "suspect" than last year. All the reasoning and truth in the world would not convince a Southern man that the Republicans are not abolitionists. It is not safe even to stop to discuss the question: they believe it, and there is the end of the controversy.... Of course, I know that reason has very little influence in this world: prejudice governs. You and all who derive power from the people do not look for pure, unalloyed truth, but to that kind of truth which jumps with the prejudice of the day. So Southern politicians do the same. If Lincoln be elected, I don't apprehend resistance; and if he be, as Mr. Ewing says, a reasonable, moderate man, things may move on, and the South become gradually reconciled. But you may rest assured that the tone of feeling is such that civil war and anarchy are very possible.

The following letter, written by John Sherman to his brother shortly after the election of Lincoln, is full of the intensest feeling and is a complete statement of the Republican sentiment of the time: —

MANSFIELD, OHIO, Nov, 26, 1860.

My Dear Brother: Since I received your last letter I have been so constantly engaged, first with the election and afterwards in arranging my business for the winter, that I could not write you.

The election resulted as I all along supposed. Indeed, the division of the Democratic party on precisely the same question that separates the Republican party from the Democratic party made its defeat certain. The success of the Republicans has no doubt saved the country from a discreditable scramble in the House. *No* doubt the disorders of the last winter and the fear of their renewal induced many good citizens to vote for the Republican ticket. With a pretty good knowledge of the material of our House, I would far prefer that any one of the candidates be elected by the people rather than allow the contest to be determined in Congress. Well, Lincoln is elected. *No* doubt, a large portion of the citizens of Louisiana consider this a calamity. If they believe their own newspapers, what is far worse, the lying organs of the Democratic party in the free States, they have just cause to think so. But you were long enough in Ohio and heard enough of the ideas of the Republican leaders to know that the Republican party is not likely to interfere directly or indirectly with slavery in the States or with the laws relating to slavery; that, so far as the slavery question is concerned, the contest was for the possession of Kansas and perhaps New Mexico, and that the chief virtue of the Republican success was in its condemnation of the narrow sectionalism of

Buchanan's administration and the corruptions by which he attempted to sustain his policy. Who doubts but that, if he had been true to his promises in submitting the controversy in Kansas to its own people, and had closed it by admitting Kansas as a free State, that the Democratic party would have retained its power? It was his infernal policy in Kansas (I can hardly think of the mean and bad things he allowed there without swearing) that drove off Douglas, and led to the division of the Democratic party and the consequent election of Lincoln.

As a matter of course, I rejoice in the result, for in my judgment the administration of Lincoln will do much to dissipate the feeling in the South against the North by showing what are the real purposes of the Republican party. In the meantime, it is evident we have to meet in a serious form the movements of South Carolinian Disunionists. These men have for years desired this disunion; they have plotted for it. They drove Buchanan into his Kansas policy; they got up this new dogma about slave protection; they broke up the Charleston

Convention merely to advance secession; they are now hurrying forward excited men into acts of treason without giving time for passion to cool or reason to resume its sway. Grod knows what will be the result. If by a successful revolution they can go out of the Union, they establish a principle that will break up the government into fragments. Some local disaffection or temporary excitement will lead one State after another out of the Union. We will have the Mexican Republic over again, with a fiercer race of men to fight with each other. Secession is revolution. They seem bent upon attempting it. If so, shall the government resist? If so, then comes civil war, a fearful subject for Americans to think of.

Since the election I have been looking over the field for the purpose of marking out a course to follow this winter, and I have, as well as I could, tested my political course in the past. There has been nothing done by the Republican party but merits the cordial approval of my judgment. There have been many things said and done by Republican leaders that I utterly detest. Many of the dogmas of the Democratic party I like, but their conduct in fact in administering the government, and especially in their treatment of the slavery question, I detest. I know we will have trouble this winter, but I intend to be true to the moderate conservative course I think I have hitherto undertaken. Whatever may be the consequences, I will insist on preserving the unity of the States, and all the States without exception and without regard to consequences. If any Southern State has really suffered any injury or is deprived of any right, I will help redress the injury and secure the right. They must not, merely because they are beaten in an election, or have failed in establishing slavery where it was prohibited by compromise, attempt to break up the government. If they will hold on a little while, they will find no injury can come to them unless, by their repeated misrepresentation of us, they stir up their slaves to insurrection. I still hope that no State will follow in the wake of South Carolina. If so, the weakness of her position will soon bring her back again or subject her to ridicule and insignificance.

It may be supposed by some that the excitement in the South has produced a corresponding excitement in the North. This is true in financial matters, especially in the cities. In political circles, it only strengthens the Republican party. Even Democrats of all shades say, The election is against us; we will submit and all must submit. Republicans say, The policy of the government has been controlled by the South for years, and we have submitted: now they must submit. And why not? What can the Republicans do half as bad as Pierce and Buchanan have done?

But enough of this. You luckily are out of politics, and don't sympathize with my Republicanisms any way; but as we are on the eve of important events, I write about politics instead of family matters, of which there is nothing new.

Affectionately yours,

JOHN SHERMAN.

This is followed by a letter from General Sherman, in which one can see that already he fully realizes the inevitable outcome of the attempted dissolution of the Union and the strength of the South. Some months later he demanded 75,000 men to defend Kentucky, which required in the end more than twice that number to defend it, and he was in consequence called and believed to be insane. It was his knowledge, obtained through his singular position in the South, that enabled him to judge more accurately than others the immense proportions of the coming war.

LOUISIANA STATE SEMINARY OF LEARNING AND MILITARY ACADEMY,

Alexandria, Dec. 1, 1800.

Dear Brother:

The quiet which I thought the usual acquiescence of the people was merely the prelude to the storm of opinion that now seems irresistible. Politicians, by hearing the prejudices of the people and running with the current, have succeeded in destroying the government. It cannot be stopped now, I fear. I was in Alexandria all day yesterday, and had a full and unreserved conversation with Dr. S. A. Smith, State senator, who is a man of education, property, influence, and qualified to judge. He was during the canvass a

Breckinridge man, but, though a Southerner in opinion, is really opposed to a dissolution of our government. He has returned from New Orleans, where he says he was amazed to see evidences of public sentiment which could not be mistaken.

The Legislature meets December 10 at Baton Rouge. The calling a convention forthwith is to be unanimous, the bill for army and State ditto. The Convention will meet in January, and only two questions will be agitated, —Immediate dissolution, a declaration of State independence, and a General Convention of Southern States, with instructions to demand of the Northern States to repeal all laws hostile to slavery and pledges of future good behavior.... When the Convention meets in January, as they will assuredly do, and resolve to secede, or to elect members to a General Convention with instructions inconsistent with the nature of things, I must quit this place, for it would be neither right for me to stay nor would the Governor be justified in placing me in this position of trust; for the moment Louisiana assumes a position of hostility, then this becomes an arsenal and fort.

Let me hear the moment you think dissolution is inevitable. What Mississippi and Georgia do, this State will do likewise.

Affectionately,

W. T. SHERMAN-.

In the next letter, of December 9th, General Sherman, after reasserting his belief that "all attempts at reconciliation will fail," and realizing that Louisiana will undoubtedly follow South Carolina and Georgia, laments personally this, his fourth change in four years, and "each time from calamity/—California, New York, Leavenworth, and now Louisiana, which must be admitted was discouraging to any man. On December 15th John Sherman urges his brother to leave Louisiana at once, while the General waits, hoping against hope for peace.

I am clearly of the opinion that you ought not to remain much longer at your present post. You will in all human probability be involved in complications from which you cannot escape with honor. Separated from your family and all your kin, and an object of

71

suspicion, you will find your position unendurable. A fatal infatuation seems to have seized the Southern mind, during which any act of madness may be committed.... If the sectional dissensions only rested upon real or alleged grievances, they could be readily settled, but I fear they are deeper and stronger. You can now close your connection with the seminary with honor and credit to yourself, for all who know you speak well of your conduct, while by remaining you not only involve yourself but bring trouble upon those gentlemen who recommended you.

It is a sad state of affairs, but it is nevertheless true, that if the conventions of the Southern States make anything more than a paper secession, hostile collisions will occur and probably a separation between the free and the slave States. You can judge whether it is at all probable that the possession of this capital, the commerce of the Mississippi, the control of the territories, and the natural rivalry of enraged sections can be arranged without war. In that event, you cannot serve in Louisiana against your family and kin in Ohio. The bare possibility of such a contingency, it seems to me, renders your duty plain, to make a frank statement to all the gentlemen connected with you, and with good feeling close your engagement. If the storm shall blow over, your course will strengthen you with every man whose good opinion you desire; if not, you will escape humiliation.

When you return to Ohio, I will write you freely about your return to the army, not so difficult a task as you imagine.

The following short extracts from letters at this time show the gradual approach of war. General Sherman writes from Louisiana: —

Events here seem hastening to a conclusion. Doubtless you know more of the events in Louisiana than I do, as I am in an out-of-the-way place. But the special session of the Legislature was so unanimous in arming the State and calling a convention that little doubt remains that Louisiana will, on the 23d of January, follow the other seceding States. Governor Moore takes the plain stand that the State must not submit to a black Republican President. Men here have ceased to reason; they seem to concede that slavery is unsafe in a confederacy with Northern States, and that now is the time; no use of longer delay. All concessions, all attempts to remonstrate, seem at an end.

A rumor says that Major Anderson, my old captain (brother of Charles Anderson, now of Texas, formerly of Dayton and Cincinnati, Lary, William and John, all of Ohio), has spiked the guns of Port Moultrie, destroyed it, and taken refuge in Sumter. This is right. Sumter is in mid-channel, approachable only in boats, whereas Moultrie is old, weak, and easily approached under cover. If Major Anderson can hold out till relieved and supported by steam frigates, South Carolina will find herself unable to control her commerce, and will fee], for the first time in her existence, that she can't do as she pleases.

A telegraph despatch, addressed to me at Alexandria, could be mailed at New Orleans, and reach me in three days from Washington.

WASHINGTON, D.C., Jan. 6, 1861.

Dear Brother:

I see some signs of hope, but it is probably a deceptive light. The very moment you feel uncomfortable in your position in Louisiana, come away. Don't for God's sake subject yourself to any slur, reproach, or indignity. I have spoken to General Scott, and he heartily seconds your desire to return to duty in the army. I am not at all sure but that, if you were here, you could get a position that would suit you. I see many of your friends of the army daily.

As for my views of the present crisis, I could not state them more fully than I have in the enclosed printed letter. It has been very generally published and approved in the North, but may not have reached you, and therefore I send it to you.

Affectionately your brother,

JOHN SHERMAN.

Following is the letter referred to: —

Washington, Dec. 22, 1800.

Gentlemen: Tour note of the 15th inst., inviting me to attend a public dinner in your city, on Friday evening next, was duly received.

I remember with pleasure the kindness shown me during the recent canvass by our political friends at Philadelphia; and would gladly avail myself of the proposed celebration; to mingle my personal thanks with your rejoicings over the recent triumph of our political principles. Other engagements and duties, however, will not allow me that pleasure.

No State can dispute with Pennsylvania the honor of this triumph. Her own son was upon trial, and her voice of condemnation was emphatic and decisive. The election of Governor Curtin foreshadowed her decision, and strengthened our cause in every State where freedom of election is allowed to the people. Her verdict in November reconsidered and reaffirmed her verdict in October. And now, since the victory is won, let us not lose the fruits of it.

Fidelity to principle is demanded by the highest patriotism. The question is not whether this or that policy should prevail, but whether we shall allow the Government to be broken into fragments, by disappointed partisans, condemned by four-fifths of the people. It is the same question answered by General Jackson in his proclamation of 1833. It is the same question answered by Henry Clay in the Senate in 1850. It is the same question answered by Madison and Jefferson, and recently by Wade and Johnson. It is a question which, I feel assured, every one of you will answer, in the patriotic language of General Jackson—"The Union, it must be preserved."

Such would be the voice of the whole country, if the Government was not now administered by those who not only permit treason but actually commit it, by turning the powers of the Government against itself. They kill the Government they have sworn to maintain and defend, because the people, whose agents they are, have condemned them. In this spirit we have seen a Secretary of the Treasury, charged with the financial credit of the Government, offering for sale the bonds of the Government, and at the same moment declaring that it will be overthrown, and that he would aid in overthrowing it. We see other high officers receiving PAY for services to the Government and yet, at the same moment, plotting its destruction. We see the Treasury robbed by subordinate officers amid the general ruin. Stranger still, we see the President of the United States acknowledging his duty to execute the laws, but refusing to execute them. He admits that the Constitution is the supreme law; that neither a State nor the citizens of a State can disregard it; and yet, armed as he is with all the executive power, he refuses even to protect the property of the United States against armed violence. He will not hear General Cass, the head of his cabinet. He will not heed General Scott, the head of the army. He has transferred to Southern States more than one hundred thousand arms, of the newest pattern and most effective calibre, to be turned against the Government.

The American people are now trembling with apprehension lest the President allows our officers and soldiers to be slaughtered at their posts for want of the aid which he has refused, or what is far more disgraceful, shall' order the flag of the Union to be lowered without resistance to lawless force.

Treason sits in the councils, and timidity controls the executive power. The President listens to, and is controlled by threats. He theorizes about coercing a State when he should be enforcing the laws against rebellious citizens. He admits that the States have surrendered the power to make treaties, coin money and regulate commerce, and yet we will probably have the novel and ridiculous farce of a negotiation between the President and a State for the surrender of forts and arsenals and sovereignty. Congress can do nothing, for the laws now are sufficient, if executed. Impeachment is too slow a remedy. The Constitution provided against every probable vacancy in the office of President, but did not provide for utter imbecility.

The people, alarmed, excited, yet true to the Union and the Constitution, are watching with eager fear, lest the noble Government, baptized in the blood of the Revolution, shall be broken into fragments, before the President elect shall assume the functions of his office.

What pretext is given for this alarming condition of affairs? for every treasonable act has its pretext. We are told that the people of the Southern States *apprehend* that Mr. Lincoln will deprive them of their constitutional rights. It is not claimed that, as yet, their rights have been invaded, but upon an *apprehension* of evil, they will break up the most prosperous Government the providence of God ever allowed to man.

We know very well how groundless are their apprehensions, but we are not even allowed to say so to our fellow citizens of the South. So wild is their apprehension, that even such statesmen as Stephens, Johnson, Hill, Botts, and Pettigrew, when they say, "wait, wait, till we see what this Republican party will attempt," are denounced as Abolitionists, — Submissionists. You know very well that we do not propose to interfere in the slightest degree with slavery in the States. We know that our leader, for whose election you rejoice, has, over and over again, affirmed his opposition to the abolition of slavery in the District of Columbia, except upon conditions that are not likely to occur; to any interference with the inter-State slave trade; and that he will enforce the constitutional right of the citizens of the slave States to recapture their fugitive slaves when they escape from service into the free States. We know very well that the great objects which those who elected Mr. Lincoln expect him to accomplish will be to secure to free labor its just right to the Territories of the United States; to protect, as far as practicable, by wise revenue laws, the labor of our people; to secure the public lands to actual settlers, instead of to non-resident speculators; to develop the internal resources of the country by opening new means of communication between the Atlantic and the Pacific, and to purify the administration of the Government from the pernicious influences of jobs, contracts and unreasonable party warfare.

But, some of you may say, all this is very well, but what will you do to save the Union? Why don't you compromise?

Gentlemen, remember that we are just recovering from the dishonor of breaking a legislative compromise. We have been struggling, against all the powers of the Government, for six years, to secure practically what was expressly granted by a compromise. We have succeeded. Kansas is now free. The Missouri restriction is now practically restored by the incipient Constitution of Kansas, and safer yet by the will of her people. The baptism of strife through which she has passed has only strengthened the prohibition. There let it stand.

But, our political opponents, who have dishonored the word "compromise," who trampled, without a moment's hesitation, upon a compromise, when they expected to gain by it, now ask us to again compromise by securing slavery south of a geographical line. To this we might fairly say: There is no occasion for compromise. We have done no wrong; we have no apologies to make, and no concessions to offer. You chose your ground, and we accepted your issue. We have beaten you, and you must submit, as we have done in the past, and as we should have done if the voice of the people had been against us. As good citizens you must obey the laws, and respect the constituted authorities. But we will meet new questions of administration with a liberal spirit. Without surrendering our convictions in the least, we may now dispose of the whole Territorial controversy by the exercise of unquestioned Congressional power.

The only Territory, south of the line, except that which, by treaty with Indian tribes, cannot be included within the jurisdiction of a State, is New Mexico. She has now population enough for admission as a State. Let Congress admit her as a State, and then she has the acknowledged right to form, regulate, change or modify her domestic institutions. She has now a nominal slave code framed, and urged upon her by Territorial officers. Practically, slavery does not exist there. It never can be established there. In a region where the earth yields her increase only by the practice of irrigation, slave labor will not be employed. At any rate, it is better to settle all questions about slavery there, by admitting the Territory as a State. While a Territory, it is insisted that slavery shall be protected in it. We insist that Congress may prohibit it; and that the people have an undisputed right to exclude slaves. Why not, by terminating their Territorial condition, determine this controversy? The same course might now properly be adopted with all the Territories of the United States.

In each of the Territories there are now small settlements scattered along the lines of transit. Within five years, the least populous will contain sufficient population for a representative in Congress. Dacotah, Washington, Nevada and Jefferson are destined soon to be as familiar to us as Kansas and Nebraska. It is well worthy the consideration of the old States, whether it is not better to dispense with all Territorial organizations — always expensive and turbulent — and, at once, to carve the whole into States of convenient size for admission. This was the Jeffersonian plan, which did not contemplate Territories, but States. It was also sanctioned by General Taylor, and, but for his death, would have been adopted.

This is an easy, effectual remedy, within the power of Congress, and in its nature an irrevocable act. There is no necessity of an amendment to the Constitution. It is not at all probable that two-thirds of both Houses of Congress and three-fourths of the States can agree to any amendments. Why attempt it, unless to invite new conquests, new acquisitions, to again arouse sectional animosities? We know that if Mexico is acquired, the South will demand it for slavery, and the North for free institutions. We must forego, for the present, new conquests, unless the love of acquisition is stronger than the love of domestic peace.

Suppose it to be conceded that the Constitution should be amended, what amendment will satisfy the South? Nothing less than the protection of slavery in the Territories. But our people have pronounced against it. All who voted for Mr. Lincoln or Mr. Douglas — over three million three hundred thousand citizens—voted against this claim. Less than a million voted for it. Should the great majority yield to a meagre minority, especially under threats of disunion? This minority demand that slavery be protected by the Constitution. Our fathers would not allow the word "slave" or "slavery" in the

Constitution, when all the States but one were slaveholding. Shall we introduce these words when a majority of the States are free, and when the progress of civilization has arrayed the world against slavery? If the love of peace, and ease, and office, should tempt politicians and merchants to do it, the people will rebel. I assure you, whatever may be the consequence, they will not yield their moral convictions by strengthening the influence of slavery in this country. Recent events have only deepened this feeling. The struggle to establish slavery in Kansas; the frequent murders and mobbings, in the South, of Northern citizens; the present turbulence and violence of Southern society; the manifest fear of the freedom of speech and of the press; the danger of insurrection; and now the attempt to subvert the Government rather than submit to a constitutional election — these events, disguise it as you may, have aroused a counter irritation in the North that will not allow its Representatives to yield, merely for peace, more than is prescribed by the letter and spirit of the Constitution. Every guarantee of this instrument ought to be faithfully and religiously observed. But when it is proposed to change it, to secure new guarantees to slavery, to extend and protect it, you awake and arouse the anti-slavery feeling of the North to war against slavery everywhere.

I am, therefore, opposed to any change in the Constitution, and to any compromise that will surrender any of the principles sanctioned by the people in the recent contest. If the personal-liberty bills of any State infringe upon the Constitution, they should at once be repealed. Most of them have slumbered upon the Statute-book for years. They are now seized upon by those who are plotting disunion as a pretext. We should give them no pretext. It is always right and proper for each State to apply to State laws the test of the Constitution.

It is a remarkable fact that none of the border free States — New Jersey, Pennsylvania, Ohio, Indiana, Illinois, nor Iowa — have any such upon their Statute-books. The laws of these States against kidnapping are similar to those of Virginia and Kentucky. The laws of other States, so called, have never operated to release a single fugitive slave, and may be regarded simply as a protest of those States against the harsh features of the fugitive slave law. So far as they infringe upon the Constitution, or impair, in the least, a constitutional right, they are void and ought to be repealed.

I venture the assertion, that there have been more cases of kidnapping of free negroes, in Ohio, than of peaceable or unlawful rescue of fugitive slaves in the whole United States. It has been shown that the law of recapture and the penalties of rescue have been almost invariably executed. Count up all the cases of rescue of negroes in the North, and you can find in your newspapers more cases of unlawful lynching and murder of white men in the South. These cases have now become so frequent and atrocious, as to demand the attention of the General Government. The same article of the Constitution that secures the recapture of fugitives from service and justice also secures the rights of citizens of Pennsylvania and Ohio to all the immunities and privileges of citizens of the several States. No law has been passed by Congress to secure this constitutional right. No executive authority interposes to protect our citizens, and yet we hear no threats of retaliation or rebellion from Northern citizens or Northern States. So, I trust, it may ever be.

The great danger that now overshadows us does not arise from real grievances. Plotters for disunion avail themselves of the weakness of the Executive to precipitate revolution. South Carolina has taken the lead. The movement would be utterly insignificant if confined to that State. She is still in the Union, and neither the President nor Congress has the power to consent to her withdrawal. This can only be by a change in the Constitution, or by the acquiescence of the people of the other States. The defence of the property of the United States and the collection of the revenues need not cause the shedding of blood, unless she commences a contest of physical force. The increase, in one year, of our population is greater than her entire population, white and black. Either one of several Congressional districts in the West has more white inhabitants than she has. Her military power is crippled by the preponderance of her slaves. However brave, and gallant, and spirited her people may be, and no one disputes these traits, yet it is manifest she is weak in physical force. This great Government might well treat with indulgence paper secession, or the resolves of her Convention and Legislature, without invoking physical force to enforce the laws among her citizens.

Without disrespect to South Carolina, it would be easy to show that Shays's rebellion and the whiskey insurrection involved the Government in greater danger than the solitary secession of South

Carolina. But the movement becomes imposing when we are assured that several powerful States will very soon follow in the lead of South Carolina; and when we know that other States, still more powerful, sympathize with the seceding States, to the extent of opposing, and perhaps resisting, the execution of the laws in the seceding States.

In this view of the present condition of public affairs it becomes the people of the United States seriously to consider whether the Government shall be arrested in the execution of its undisputed powers by the citizens of one or more States, or whether we shall test the power of the Government to defend itself against dissolution. Can a separation take place without war? If so, where will be the line? Who shall possess this magnificent capital, with all its evidences of progress and civilization? Shall the mouth of the Mississippi be separated from its sources? Who shall possess the Territories? Suppose these difficulties to be overcome; suppose that in peace we should huckster and divide up our nationality, our flag, our history, all the recollections of the past; suppose all these difficulties overcome, how can two rival Republics, of the same race of men, divided only by a line or a river for thousands of miles, with all the present difficulties aggravated by separation, avoid forays, disputes and war? How can we travel our future march of progress in Mexico, or on the high seas, or on the Pacific slope, without collision? It is impossible. To peaceably accomplish such results, we must change the nature of man. Disunion is war! God knows, I do not threaten it, for I will seek to prevent it in every way possible. I speak but the logic of facts, which we should not conceal from each other. It is either hostilities between the Government and the seceding States; or, if separation is yielded peaceably, it is a war of factions— a rivalry of insignificant communities, hating each other, and contemned by the civilized world. If war results, what a war it will be! Contemplate the North and South in hostile array against each other. If these sections do not know each other *now*, they will *then*.

We are a nation of military men, naturally turbulent because we are free, accustomed to arms, ingenious, energetic, brave and strong.

The same qualities that have enabled a single generation of men to develop the resources of a continent, would enable us to destroy more rapidly than we have constructed. It is idle for individuals of either section to suppose themselves superior in military power. The French and English tried that question for a thousand years. We ought to know it now. The result of the contest will not depend upon the first blow or the first year, but blood shed in civil war will yield its baleful fruits for generations.

How can we avert a calamity at which humanity and civilization shudder? I know no way but to cling to the Government framed by our fathers, to administer it in a spirit of kindness, but in all cases, without partiality to enforce the laws. Ho State can release us from the duty of obeying the laws. The ordinance or act of a State is no defence for treason, nor does it lessen the moral guilt of that crime. Let us cling to each other in the hope that our differences will pass away, as they often have in times past. For the sake of peace, for the love of civil liberty, for the honor of our name, our race, our religion, let us preserve the Union, loving it better as the clouds grow darker. I am willing to unite with any man, whatever may have been his party relations, whatever may be his views of the existing differences, who is willing to rely on the Constitution as it is for his rights, and who is willing to maintain and defend the Union under all circumstances, against all enemies, at home or abroad.

Pardon me, gentlemen, for writing you so fully. I feel restrained, by the custom of the House of Representatives, from engaging there in political debate; and yet I feel it is the duty of every citizen to prepare his countrymen for grave events, that will test the strength and integrity of the Government.

Believing that our only safety is in a firm enforcement of the laws, and that Mr. Lincoln will execute that duty without partiality, I join my hearty congratulations with yours that he is so soon to be the President of the United States. With great respect, I remain, very truly Your obedient servant,

JOHN SHERMAN.

MESSES. WM. READ, D. J. **COCHRAN, L. S. FLETCHER,**

H. E. WALLACE, CHARLES O'NEILL, *Committee.*

Governor Moore of Louisiana took possession of the Arsenal at Baton Rouge, January 10, 1861. General Sherman comments upon this in a letter written to his brother, January 16, and regarding it as a declaration of war, sends in his resignation January 18, a copy of which he encloses to John Sherman in a letter written the same day.

ALEXANDRIA, Jan. 16th, 1861.

My Dear Brother: I am so much in the woods here that I can't keep up with the times at all. Indeed, you in Washington hear from New Orleans two or three days sooner than I do. I was taken aback by the news that Governor Moore had ordered the forcible seizure of the Forts Jackson and St. Philip, at or near the mouth of the Mississippi; also of Forts Pike and Wood, at the outlets of Lakes Bogue and Pontchartrain. All these are small forts, and have rarely been occupied by troops. They are designed to cut off approach by sea to New Orleans, and were taken doubtless to prevent their being occupied, by order of General Scott. But the taking the arsenal at Baton Rouge is a different matter. It is merely an assemblage of store-houses, barracks, and dwelling-houses designed for the healthy residence of a garrison, to be thrown into one or the other of the forts in case of war. The arsenal is one of minor importance, yet the stores were kept there for the moral effect, and the garrison was there at the instance of the people of Louisiana. To surround with the military array, to demand surrender, and enforce the departure of the garrison, was an act of war. It amounted to a declaration of war and defiance, and was done by Governor Moore without the authority of the Legislature or Convention. Still, there is but little doubt but that each of these bodies, to assemble next week, will ratify and approve these violent acts, and it is idle to discuss the subject now. The people are mad on this question.

I had previously notified all that in the event of secession I should quit. As soon as a knowledge of these events reached me, I went to the vice-president, Dr. Smith, in Alexandria, and told him that I regarded Louisiana as at war against the Federal Government, and that I must go. He begged me to wait until some one could be found to replace me. The supervisors feel the importance of system and discipline, and seem to think that my departure will endanger the success of this last effort to build up an educational establishment.... You may assert that in no event will I forego my allegiance to the United States as long as a single State is true to the old Constitution.

Yours,

W. T. SHERMAN.

LOUISIANA STATE SEMINARY OF LEARNING AND MILITARY ACADEMY, ALEXANDRIA, Jan. 18, 1861.

Dear Brother: Before receiving yours of the 7th, I had addressed a letter to Governor Moore at Baton Rouge, of which this is a copy: —

Meaning the letter of the 6th.

"Sir: As I occupy a quasi military position under the laws of the State, I deem it proper to acquaint you that I accepted such position when Louisiana was a State in the Union and when the motto of this seminary was inscribed in marble over the main door: 'By the liberality of the General Government. The Union Esto perpetua.' Recent events foreshadow a great change, and it becomes all men to choose. If Louisiana withdraw from the Federal Union, I prefer to maintain my allegiance to the old constitution as long as a fragment of it survives, and my longer stay here would be wrong in every sense of the word. In that event I beg that you will send or appoint some authorized agent to take charge of the arms and munitions of war here belonging to the State or advise me what disposition to make of them. And furthermore, as President of the Board of Supervisors, I beg you to take immediate steps to relieve me as superintendent the moment the State determines to secede; for on no earthly account will I do any act or think any thought hostile to or in defiance of the United States.

"With respect, etc.

"W. T. SHERMAN."

I regard the seizure by Governor Moore of the United States Arsenal as the worst act yet committed in the present revolution. I do think every allowance should be made to Southern politicians for their nervous anxiety about their political power and the safety of slaves. I think that the constitution should be liberally construed in their behalf, but I do regard this civil war as precipitated with undue rapidity.... It is inevitable. All the legislation now would fall powerless on the South. You should not alienate such States as Virginia, Kentucky, Tennessee, and Missouri. My notion is that this war will ruin all politicians, and that military leaders will direct the events.

W. T. S.

In the following letter of February 1st, the General quotes the handsome note from Governor Moore accepting his resignation: —

I have felt the very thoughts you have spoken. It is war to surround Anderson with batteries, and it is shillyshally for the South to cry "Hands off! Ho coercion!" It was war and insult to expel the garrison at Baton Rouge, and Uncle Sam had better cry Cave! or assert his power. Fort Sumter is not material, save for the principle; but Key West and the Tortugas should be held in force at once, by regulars if possible, if not, by militia. Quick! They are occupied now, but not in force. Whilst maintaining the high, strong ground you do, I would not advise you to interpose an objection to securing concessions to the middle and moderate States, —Virginia, Kentucky, Tennessee, and Missouri. Slavery there is local, and even if the world were open to them, its extension would involve no principle. If these States feel the extreme South wrong, a seeming concession would make them committed. The cotton States are gone, I suppose. Of course, their commerce will be hampered.

But of myself. I sent you a copy of my letter to the Governor. Here is his answer: —

"*Dear Sir:* It is with the deepest regret I acknowledge the receipt of your letter of the 18th instant. In the pressure of official business I can now only request you to transfer to Professor Smith the arms, munitions, and funds in your hands whenever you conclude to withdraw from the position you have filled with so much distinction. You cannot regret more than I do the necessity which deprives us of your services, and you will bear with you the respect, confidence, and admiration of all who have been associated with you.

"Very truly, your friend and servant,

"THOS. D. MOORE."

This is very handsome, and I do regret this political imbroglio. I do think it was brought about by politicians. The people in the South are evidently unanimous in the opinion that slavery is endangered by the current of events, and it is useless to attempt to alter that opinion. As our government is founded on the will of the people, when that will is fixed, our government is powerless, and the only question is whether to let things slide into general anarchy, or the formation of two or more confederacies, which will be hostile sooner or later. Still, I know that some of the best men of Louisiana think this change may be effected peacefully. But even if the Southern States be allowed to depart in peace, the first question will be revenue.

Now, if the South have free trade, how can you collect revenues in the eastern cities? Freight from New Orleans to St. Louis, Chicago, Louisville, Cincinnati, and even Pittsburgh, would be about the same as by rail from New York, and importers at New Orleans, having no duties to pay, would undersell the East if they had to pay duties. Therefore, if the South make good their confederation and their plan, the Northern confederacy must do likewise or blockade. Then comes the question of foreign nations, So, look on it in any view, I see no result but war and consequent changes in the form of government.

In March of 1861 General Sherman started north by the Mississippi River. On the way, and after reaching Ohio, he heard discussions as to the advisability of coercion. Whereas in the South there was absolute unanimity of opinion and universal preparation for war, in the North there was merely argument and apathy. After leaving his family at Lancaster, he went to Washington, still uncertain as to his next move. While there, he called on Mr. Lincoln, and stated his fears and convictions as to war and the gravity of it. Mr. Lincoln treated all he said with some scorn and absolute disregard, and remarked, "Oh, well, I guess we'll manage to keep house." This, with the general unconcern regarding the necessity of military interference, discouraged General Sherman, and, greatly dispirited, he returned to Ohio, and took his family to St. Louis after ascertaining from friends that, in all probability, Missouri would stick to the Union. In writing at this time he says: —

Lincoln has an awful task, and if he succeeds in avoiding strife and allaying fears, he will be entitled to the admiration of the world; but a time has occurred in all governments, and has now occurred in this, when force must back the laws, and the longer the postponement, the more severe must be the application.

On April 8th General Sherman writes to his brother: —

Saturday night late I received this despatch: "Will you accept the Chief Clerkship in the War Department? We will make you Assistant Secretary when Congress meets. —M. Blair." This morning I answered by telegraph: "I cannot accept."

In writing to explain his refusal, he does not state the real reason, which was undoubtedly that he preferred active service. John Sherman's letter of April 12th approves of the determination, and states more fully his reasons for advising it. It is interesting to see, from the very first, John Sherman's belief in his brother's talents as a soldier, and conviction that he will rise to a high position in the army in the event of war. Through all of General Sherman's letters of that time there are evidences of very sincere distrust of himself and deprecation of John's flattering belief.

WASHINGTON, April 12, 1861.

Dear Brother: I was unexpectedly called here soon after receiving your letter of the 8th, and at midnight write you. The military excitement here is intense. Since my arrival I have seen all the heads of departments except Blair, several officers, and many citizens. There is a fixed determination now to preserve the Union and enforce the laws at all hazards. Civil war is actually upon us, and strange to say, it brings a feeling of relief: the suspense is over. I have spent much of the day in talking about you. There is an earnest desire that you go into the War Department, but I said this was impossible. Chase is especially desirous that you accept, saying that you would be virtually Secretary of War, and could easily step into any military position that offers.

It is well for you seriously to consider your conclusion, although my opinion is that you ought not to accept. You ought to hold yourself in reserve. If troops are called for, as they surely will be in a few days, organize a regiment or brigade, either in St. Louis or Ohio, and you will then get into the army in such a way as to secure promotion. By all means take advantage of the present disturbances to get into the army, where you will at once put yourself in a high position for life. I know that promotion and every facility for advancement will be cordially extended by the authorities. You are a favorite in the army and have great strength in political circles. I urge you to avail yourself of these favorable circumstances to secure your position for life; for, after all, your present employment is of uncertain tenure in these stirring times.

Let me now record a prediction. Whatever you may think of the signs of the times, the Government will rise from this strife greater, stronger, and more prosperous than ever. It will display energy and military power. The men who have confidence in it and do their full duty by it may reap whatever there is of honor and profit in public life, while those who look on merely as spectators in the storm will fail to discharge the highest duty of a citizen, and suffer accordingly in public estimation....

I write this in a great hurry, with numbers around me, and exciting and important intelligence constantly repeated, even at this hour; but I am none the less in earnest. I hope to hear that you are on the high road to the "General" within thirty days.

Affectionately your brother,

JOHN SHERMAN.

From the time of General Sherman's conversation with Mr. Lincoln he distrusted the preparations of the administration, which savored greatly of militia and raw recruits. "With this army General Sherman was unwilling to cast his lot, believing that he was worthy of a better command if of any. In April he writes to John: —

But I say volunteers and militia never were and never will be fit for invasion, and when tried, it will be defeated, and dropt by Lincoln like a hot potato.

And in the same letter: —

The time will come in this country when professional knowledge will be appreciated, when men that can be trusted will be wanted, and I will bide my time. I may miss the chance: if so, all right; but I cannot and will not mix myself in this present call.

The first movements of the government will fail and the leaders will be cast aside. A second or third set will rise, and among them I may be, but at present I will not volunteer as a soldier or anything else. If Congress meet., or if a National Convention be called; and the regular army be put on a footing with the wants of the country, if I am offered a place that suits me, I may accept. But in the present call I will not volunteer.

Note. — Fort Sumter, situated in mid-channel at the entrance to Charleston harbor, was the commanding point in the defences of the harbor, and was occupied at the time of its bombardment by a garrison of less than 100 men under Major Robert Anderson. The first shot of the war was fired against it by General Beauregard early on the morning of April 12, 1861.

Washington, Sunday, April 14, 1861.

Dear Brother;

The war has really commenced. You will have full details of the fall of Sumter. We are on the eve of a terrible war. Every man will have to choose his position. You fortunately have the military education, prominence, and character, that will enable you to play a high part in the tragedy. You can't avoid taking such a part. Neutrality and indifference are impossible. If the government is to be maintained, it must be by military power, and that immediately. You can choose your own place. Some of your best friends here want you in the War Department; Taylor, Shires, and a number of others talk to me so. If you want that place, with a sure prospect of promotion, you can have it, but you are not compelled to take it; but it seems to me you will be compelled to take some position, and that speedily. Can't you come to Ohio and at once raise a regiment? It will immediately be in service. The administration intend to stand or fall by the Union, the entire Union, and the enforcement of the laws. I look for preliminary defeats, for the rebels have arms, organization, unity; but this advantage will not last long. The government will maintain itself or our Northern people are the veriest poltroons that ever disgraced humanity.

For me, I am for a war that will either establish or overthrow the government and will purify the atmosphere of political life. We need such a war, and we have it now.

Affectionately yours,

JOHN SHERMAN.

OFFICE ST. LOUIS RAILROAD CO., St. LOUIS, April 22, 1861.

I know full well the force of what you say. At a moment like this the country expects every man to do his duty. But every man is not at liberty to do as he pleases. You know that Mr. Lincoln said to you and me that he did not think he wanted military men. I was then free, uncommitted.... I approve fully of Lincoln's determination to use all his ordinary and extraordinary powers to maintain and defend the authority with which he is clothed and the integrity of the nation, and had I not committed myself to another duty, I would most willingly have responded to his call.

The question of the national integrity and slavery should be kept distinct, for otherwise it will gradually become a war of extermination, — a war without end. If, when Congress meets, a clearly defined policy be arrived at, a clear end to be accomplished, and then the force adequate to that end be provided for, then I could and would act with some degree of confidence, not now.

I take it for granted that Washington is safe; that Pickens can beat off all assailants; that Key West and Tortugas are strong and able to spare troops for other purposes; that, above all, Fort Monroe is full of men, provisions, and warlike materials, and that the Chesapeake is strongly occupied. Then the first thing will be the avenues of travel. Baltimore must be made to allow the free transit of troops, provisions, and materials without question, and the route from Wheeling to the Belay House kept open. Here there must be some fighting, but a march from Brownsville to Frostburg would be a good drill, via Hagerstown, Frederick, and the Potomac.

From present information I apprehend that Virginia will destroy the road from Harper's Ferry west, and maybe the Marylanders will try the balance; but, without an hour's delay, that line should swarm with troops, who should take no half-way measures.

Affectionately,

W. T. SHERMAN.

Through all the spring months, while nominally only president of a street-car company, General Sherman's mind is engaged in defending the country, building forts, occupying positions of importance, and possessing railroads. His letters are full of military suggestions, some of which John Sherman showed the Secretary of War, Mr. Cameron, who, as it will appear, acted upon them.

Although the Confederate government had been organized and its officers chosen in February, 1861, still the border slave States, and among them Virginia, had taken no active or open part in the secession. Sumter decided them, and from that time Virginia was enrolled among the Confederate States. She seceded April 17th.

OFFICE ST. LOUIS RAILROAD CO.,

Dear Brother: ST. LOUIS, April 25, 1801.

Virginia's secession influences some six millions of people. Ho use in arguing about it at all, but all the

Virginians, or all who trace their lineage back, will feel like obeying her dictates and example. As a State, she has been proud, boastful, and we may say overbearing; but, on the other hand, she, by her governors and authority, has done everything to draw her native-born back to their State.

I cannot yet but think that it was a fatal mistake in Mr. Lincoln not to tie to his administration by some kind of link the Border States. Now it is too late, and sooner or later Kentucky, Tennessee, and Arkansas will be in arms against us. It is barely possible that Missouri may yet be neutral.

It is pretty nearly determined to divert the half million set aside for the July interest for arming the State. All the bankers but one have consented, and the Governor and legislature are strongly secession. I understand today the orders at the custom-house are to refuse clearance to steamboats to seceding States. All the heavy trade with groceries and provisions is with the South, and this order at once takes all life from St. Louis. Merchants, heretofore for peace and even for backing the administration, will now fall off, relax in their exertions, and the result will possibly be secession, and then free States against slave,—the horrible array so long dreaded. I know Frank Blair desired this plain, square issue. It may be that sooner or later it is inevitable, but I cannot bring myself to think so. On the necessity of maintaining a government, and that government the old constitutional one, I have never wavered, but I do recoil from a war, when the negro is the only question.

I am informed that McClellan is appointed to command the Ohio militia, — a most excellent appointment; a better officer could not be found.

WASHINGTON, May 30, 1861.

My Dear Brother: Your recent letters have been received. One of them I read to Secretary Cameron, and he was much pleased with some of your ideas, especially with your proposition about Fort Smith and the island off Mobile. The latter is probably now in possession of the government.

It is probable that no movements will be made into the cotton States before winter. A regular plan has been formed by General Scott, and is daily discussed and reconsidered by him and other officers. The movements now occurring are merely incidental, rather to occupy public attention and employ troops than to strike decisive blows. In the meantime it is becoming manifest that the secessionists mean to retreat from position to position until they concentrate sufficient force to strike a decisive blow. I have a fear not generally shared in that now a rapid concentration is taking place and that we will, within a few days, have a terrible battle near Washington. Indeed, I don't see how it can be avoided. General Butler at Norfolk, General McClellan at Grafton, General Patterson at Charlesborough, and General Scott here, all concentrating, will surely bring on a fight in which I fear the Virginians will concentrate the largest mass. I have been all along our lines on the other side, and confess that we are weaker than I wish. Every day, however, is adding to our mass and strengthening our position....

What think you of Fremont and Banks as Major-Generals of Volunteers and Schenck as Brigadier? They are all able men, though I know you don't like volunteers. These appointments are generally satisfactory, even to the regular officers, many of whom say that they had rather serve under able citizens than old-fogy officers. The old army is a manifest discredit. The desertion of so many officers (treachery I had better say), the surrender on parole in Texas of so many officers where all the men were true to their allegiance, has so stained the whole regular course of officers that it will take good conduct on their part to retrieve their old position.

You are regarded with favor here. It will be your own fault if you do not gain a very high position in the army.

Affectionately yours,

JOHN SHERMAN.

On May 3, 1861, John Sherman writes from Philadelphia: —

The time is past for expedients. They must either whip us or we will whip them. A threat of secession is idle. Missouri can't secede, nor can Virginia secede.... Those Dutch troops in St. Louis will have enough backing. Thank God, the arms in the arsenal were not stolen. I am now acting as volunteer aide to Major-General Patterson. Porter, Belger, Beckwith, Patterson, Price, and others are on his regular staff.

In John Sherman's letter-book is a copy of a letter, which General Sherman wrote to Secretary Cameron in 1861, giving his reasons for not enlisting sooner. Upon receipt of this, it was decided at Washington to make him colonel of three battalions of regulars, or major-general of volunteers.

OFFICE St. LOUIS RAILROAD Co., St. LOUIS, May 8, 1861.

Hon. S. Cameron, Secretary of War:

> *Dear Sir:* I hold myself now, as always, prepared to serve my country in the capacity for which I was trained.

I did not and will not volunteer for three months, because I cannot throw my family on the cold support of charity, but for the three years' call made by the President an officer could prepare his command and do good service. I will not volunteer, because, rightfully or wrongfully, I feel myself unwilling to take a mere private's place, and having for many years lived in California and Louisiana, the men are not well enough acquainted with me to elect me to my appropriate place. Should my services be needed, the Record or the War Department will enable you to designate the station in which I can render best service.

> Yours truly,

> **W. T. SHERMAN.**

Before leaving St. Louis, General Sherman was the unintentional witness of the first fighting in the West, of which he gives the following account: —

OFFICE ST. LOUIS RAILROAD CO., ST. LOUIS, May 11, 1861.

Dear Brother: Very imprudently I was a witness of the firing on the people by the United States Militia at Camp Jackson yesterday. You will hear all manner of accounts, and as these will be brought to bear on the present Legislature to precipitate events, maybe secession, I will tell you what I saw.

My office is up in Bremen, the extreme north of the city. The arsenal is at the extreme south. The State camp was in a pretty grove directly west of the city, bounded by Olive Street and Laclede Avenue. I went to my house on Locust, between Eleventh and Twelfth, at 3 p m., and saw the whole city in commotion, and heard that the United States troops were marching from the arsenal to capture the State camp. At home I found

Hugh, and Charley Ewing and John Hunter so excited they would not wait for dinner, but went out to see the expected battle. I had no such curiosity and stayed to dinner, after which I walked out, and soon met a man who told me General Frost had surrendered. I went back home and told Ellen, then took Willy to see the soldiers march back. I kept on walking, and about 5.30 b m. found myself in the grove, with soldiers all round, standing at rest. I went into the camp till turned aside by sentinels, and found myself with a promiscuous crowd, men, women, and children, inside the grove, near Olive Street. On that street the disarmed State troops, some eight hundred, were in ranks. Soon a heavy column of United States Regulars followed by militia came down Olive Street, with music, and halted abreast of me. I went up and spoke to some of the officers, and fell back to a knoll, where I met Hugh and Charley and John Hunter. Soon the music again started, and as the Regulars got abreast of the crowd, about sixty yards to my front and right, I observed them in confusion, using their bayonets to keep the crowd back, as I supposed. Still, they soon moved on, and as the militia reached the same point a similar confusion began. I heard a couple of shots, then half a dozen, and observed the militia were firing on the crowd at that point, but the fire kept creeping to the rear along the flank of the column, and, hearing balls cutting the leaves of trees over my head, I fell down on the grass and crept up to where Charley Ewing had my boy Willy. I also covered his person. Probably a hundred shots passed over the ground, but none near us. As soon as the fire slackened, I picked Willy up, and ran with him till behind the rising ground, and continued at my leisure out of harm's way, and went home.

I saw no one shot, but some dozen men were killed, among them a woman and little girl. There must have been some provocation at the point where the Regulars charged bayonets and where the militia began their fire. The rest was irregular and unnecessary, for the crowd was back in the woods, a fence between them and the street. There was some cheering of the United States troops and some halloos for Jeff Davis.

I hear all of Frost's command who would not take the oath of allegiance to the United States are pxisoners at the arsenal. I suppose they will be held for the orders of the President. They were mostly composed of young men who doubtless were secessionists. Frost is a New Yorker and was a graduate of West Point, served some years in the army, and married a Miss Graham here, a lady of great wealth and large connections. He was encamped by order of the Governor; and this brings up the old question of State and United States authority. We cannot have two kings: one is enough; and of the two the United States must prevail. But in all the South, and even here, there are plenty who think the State is their king.

As ever, yours affectionately,

W. T. SHERMAN.

OFFICE ST. LOUIS RAILROAD CO., ST. LOUIS, May 20, 1861.

Dear Brother:... The greatest difficulty in the problem now before the country is not to conquer but so conquer as to impress upon the real men of the South a respect for their conquerors. If Memphis be taken, and the army move on South the vindictive feeling left behind would again close the River. And here in Missouri it would be easy to take Jefferson City, Lexington, and any other point, but the moment they are left to themselves the people would resume their hatred. It is for this reason that I deem Regulars the only species of force that should be used for invasion. I take it for granted that Virginia will be attacked with great force this summer, and that the great problem of the war— Mississippi — will be reserved for the next winter....

In the war on which we are now entering paper soldiers won't do. McClellan is naturally a superior man and has had the finest opportunities in Mexico and Europe. Even his juniors admit his qualifications.

Yours affectionately,

W. T. SHERMAN.

OFFICE ST. LOUIS RAILROAD CO., ST. LOUIS, May 22, 1861.

My Dear Brother: I received your despatch last evening stating I would be appointed Colonel of one of the new 3 Battalion Regiments, this was I suppose an answer to my own despatch to Adjutant General asking if such would be the case. The fact is so many persons had written to me and spoken to me, all asserting they had seen or heard I was to have one of the new Regiments, that I thought the letter to me had been misdirected or miscarried.... I shall promptly accept the Colonelcy when received and I think I can organize and prepare a regiment as quick as anybody. I prefer this to a Brigadier in the Militia, for I have no political ambition, and have very naturally more confidence in Regulars than Militia. Hot that they are better, braver or more patriotic, but because *I know* the people will submit with better grace to them than to Militia of any particular locality....

I think Missouri has subsided into a quiescent state. There will be no attempting to execute the obnoxious and unconstitutional Militia Law. A prompt move on Little Rock from here and Cairo and recapture of Fort Smith from Kansas would hold Arkansas in check. A movement which could be made, simultaneous with that on Richmond. I hope no men or time will be wasted on Norfolk; it is to one side and unimportant. The capture of Richmond would be fatal to Virginia, and the occupation of Cumberland, Hagerstown and Frederick by the Pennsylvanians, whilst troops threaten Winchester from Washington would make the further occupation of Harper's Ferry useless. But after all the Mississippi is the great problem of the Civil War, and will require large forces and good troops.

Affectionately your brother,

W. T. SHERMAN.

On May 14th General Sherman received a despatch from his brother Charles in Washington, telling him of his appointment as Colonel of the 13th Regular Infantry, and that he was wanted in Washington at once. The following letter was written while he was preparing to leave St. Louis for Washington, and the next one (June 8) from Pittsburgh on his way East: —

OFFICE ST. LOUIS RAILROAD Co.,

ST. LOUIS, May 24, 1861.

Dear Brother: I have already written you so much that more would be a bore. Yours of the 21st is at hand and I can act with promptness and sufficient vigor when the occasion arises. You all overrate my powers and abilities and may place me in a position above my merits, a worse step than below. Eeally I do not conceive myself qualified for Quartermaster General or Major General. To attain either station I would prefer a previous schooling with large masses of troops in the field, one which I lost in the Mexican War by going to California. The only possible reason that would induce me to accept my position would be to prevent its falling into incompetent hands. The magnitude of interest at issue now, will admit of no experiments....

I have still my saddle, sword, sash and some articles of Uniform which will come into immediate play. But look out — I want the regular Army and not the 3 year men....

Yours affectionately,

W. T. SHERMAN.

Pittsburgh, Sunday, June **8,** 1861.

Dear Brother:... Should I on my arrival find the Secretary determined to go outside the Army, and should he make advances to me, of course I shall accept. In like manner if he tenders me a brigade, I will do my best, or if a colonelcy — ditto. I still feel that it is wrong to ask for anything and prefer that they should make their own choice of this position for me. You are with Gen. Patterson. There are two A Ho. I men there, George H. Thomas Col. Second Cavalry and Cap. Sykes 3 Infantry. Mention my name to both and say to them that I wish them all the success they aspire to, and if in the varying chances of war I should ever be so placed, I would name

98

such as them for high places. But Thomas is a Virginian from near Norfolk and say what we may he must feel unpleasantly at leading an invading Army. But if he says he will do it, I know he will do it well. He was never brilliant but always cool, reliable and steady, maybe a little slow. Sykes has in him some dashing qualities.... If possible I will try and see you in your new capacity of soldier before I make another distinct break. If you please you may telegraph, to Mr. Chase simply that I have come to Washington on Taylor's call, but I cannot wait long, and if the Administration don't want my services, to say so at once emphatically.

Yours affectionately,

W. T. SHERMAN.

Washington, June 20, 1861.

Dear Brother: **At last the order is out and I am Colonel 13 Infantry. I have been asking for orders and am this moment informed for the present, that inasmuch as Lt. Col. Burbank may enlist my Regiment, and as my personal services here are needed, I will forthwith consider myself on duty here attached to Gen. Scott's staff as Inspector General. I did not dream of this, but it really does well accord with my inclinations and peculiar nature. My duty will be to keep myself advised of the character and kind of men who are in Military service here near Washington and to report to General Scott in person. Porter can tell you what these duties will amount to.... I suppose you will soon be here, for from Col. Burnside I hear all of Patterson's army is on the Maryland side of the Potomac, and no possible movement will be attempted before Congress meets....**

In haste,

Your Brother,

W. T. SHERMAN.

CHAPTER IV

GENERAL SHERMAN remained on duty with General Scott only ten days (June 20-30), and then was given command of one brigade of McDowell's army, which was to move from the defences of Washington. He assumed command June 30, and went to work at once to prepare his brigade for the general advance.

CAMP OPPOSITE GEORGETOWN, July 16, 1861.

Dear Brother: We start forth to-day, camp to-night at or near Vienna, to-morrow early we attack the enemy at or near Fairfax C.H., Germantown and Centerville, thereabouts we will probably be till about Thursday, when movement of the whole force, some 35,000 men on Manassas, turning the position by a wide circuit. You may expect to hear of us about Aquia Creek or Fredericksburg (secret absolute)....

If anything befall me, my pay is drawn to embrace June 30, and Ellen has full charge of all other interests. Good bye. Your Brother,

W. T. SHERMAN.

After Bull Run, Sherman's brigade remained encamped at Port Corcoran, a part of the Washington defences. He was made a brigadier-general of volunteers, and in his next letters explains his transfer to the West.

He was relieved in his command by General Fitz-John Porter, and started for Cincinnati on one of the last days in August to meet General Anderson.

At this time John Sherman was in Ohio, and his letters from there to his brother require no explanation.

PORT CORCORAN, Aug. 19, 1861.

My Dear Brother: I have been here ever since yon left, hardly taking off my clothes at night. McClellan is so confident that Beauregard will attack that I try to be prepared at all times. Our forts are in pretty good condition, but whether the volunteers can serve the guns or not is to be tested. It does seem to me strange that when all know that if Beauregard get Washington, the Southern Confederacy will be an established fact that they should leave volunteers to hold the most important point in the world. Out of my seven regiments three are in a state of mutiny, and I have been compelled to put about 100 men as prisoners on board a man-of-war. And yesterday I had my Regulars all ready with shotted guns to fire on our own troops, some of whom not only claim their discharge, but threaten to spike our guns. They claim to be only 3 months men, whereas the War Department claims their services for 3 years. Even some of the 3 years men say the President had no right to call for 3 years men and that the subsequent legislation of Congress was ex-post facto....

Bull **BUR** is a small stream about thirty miles southwest from Washington, and here the first great battle of the war was won by the rebel army of about 32,000 men under Generals Beauregard and J. E. Johnston, on July 21, 1861.

General McDowell commanded the Union army of about 28,000 men, and Sherman, then a colonel, commanded a brigade in this army.

A few days since Gen. Robert Anderson sent for me to meet him at Willard's. I found him with Senator Johnson, a Mr. Maynard, and several other members from Kentucky and Tennessee. They told me the President had resolved to send assistance to the Union men of Kentucky and Tennessee, that Anderson being a Kentuckian to him was given the lead, and that he was allowed to select three Brigadiers, that he had chosen me first and Burnside and Thomas next. The President agreed, but McClellan would not spare me till the danger in his front was lessened. It was then agreed to wait a week, when if nothing happens here I am to be ordered into Kentucky. As I understand we are to go there in person, mingle with the people, satisfy ourselves of their purpose to oppose the Southern Confederacy and then to assist in the organization there of a force adequate to the end in view, that when Kentucky is assured in her allegiance that we then push into East Tennessee. I feel well satisfied that unless Kentucky and Tennessee remain in our Union it is a doubtful question whether the Federal Government can restore the old Union....

There is no time to be lost and I will not spare my individual efforts, though I still feel as one groping in the dark. Slowly but surely the public is realizing what I knew all the time, the strong vindictive feeling of the whole South.

Your Brother,

W. T. SHERMAN.

Cincinnati, Sept. 9, 1861.

Dear Brother: I am still here. Gen. A. went quietly over to Frankfort last Thursday, and I hear from him that things are progressing favorably. The time seems to have passed in this country when the voice of the

People is considered the voice of God. Notwithstanding the large vote for the Union and the controlled majority in the Legislature, there is still a doubt whether that state will go for the Union....

I think it of vast importance and that Ohio, Indiana and Illinois must sooner or later arm every inhabitant, and the sooner the better. I hardly apprehend that Beauregard can succeed in getting Washington, but should he, it will be worse to us than Manassas; but supposing he falls back, he will first try to overwhelm Rosecrans in Western Virginia and then look to Tennessee. We ought to have here a well appointed Army of a hundred thousand men. I don't see where they are to come from, but this is the great centre. I still think that Mississippi will be the grand field of operations. Memphis ought to be taken in all October, even if we have to fortify and hold it a year. I think it of more importance than Richmond. It may be that the Southern leaders have made such tremendous calls upon their people and resources, that if we remain on the defence they will exhaust themselves, but upon the first manifest symptoms of such a result we should follow it up. Here we have no means of offence and but little of defence, and if you are full of zeal you could not do better than to raise your voice to call the young and middle-aged men of Ohio to arms. If they can't get muskets then let. them get such arms as can be gathered together, or if not that, then let them organize in companies in every township and be ready to collect together and move on short notice. I am amazed to see here and everywhere such apparent indifference when all know that Rebels threaten the Capital and are creeping around us in Missouri and Kansas. If they are united, and we disunited or indifferent, they will succeed. I knew this reaction was natural and to be expected, but it is none the less to be deplored....

Affectionately,

W. T. SHERMAN.

MANSFIELD, OHIO, Sept. 12, 1861.

My Dear Brother: Enlistments in this part of the State now go on rapidly. Dickey's regiment is nearly full, and companies have formed for cavalry and artillery regiments organizing in other parts of the State. It is also manifest a better feeling prevails among the people, a more hopeful and hearty support of the War and a readiness to bear its burdens. When you remember that all these regiments are formed by voluntary enlistments, and for the war and under the shadow of defeat, it is wonderful so large a force is raised. As winter approaches more will enlist, for employment in civil pursuits will be out of the question. Want is as good a recruiting sergeant as patriotism. If, however, voluntary enlistments fail, then drafting must be resorted to. It is the fairest and best mode, for it makes all classes contribute alike. I have been at a loss what to do with myself this fall.

I dislike the idea of being idle in these stirring times. My relations with Gov. Dennison are not such as will justify me in asking the organization of a regiment, and I will not undertake it without *carte blanche* as to officers. I notice from the papers that he has adopted somewhat such a plan of enlistment as I suggested to him. If he asks me to assist to execute it, I will do so at once and actively, but I presume he will not do so. As to making speeches through the State, it is very irksome. And this is not all. Speeches from me unless I enlist or am in the service myself will not come with a good grace.

My speeches would be regarded as political. There is no disposition this fall to gather in mass meetings to hear speeches. It is probable I will take some part in the canvass for the Union Ticket, but after the election I will go to Washington and seek some active employment until after Congress meets. The delay in Kentucky appears ominous. The whole character of the State is reversed in this contest. The Kentuckians have always had the reputation of being ready fighters, and as Kentucky has taken position for the Union I should think they would at once take arms. Eastern Kentucky is the loyal part. All the counties between Ohio and East Tennessee have been considered thoroughly loyal. If civil war does break out in Kentucky, it seems to me that it must be in the Western part of the State, and then Paducah, Madison, Ind., and Louisville will be the place for you....

Affectionately Yours,

JOHN SHERMAN.

MANSFIELD, OHIO, Sept. 28, 1801.

Dear Brother: I am at last engaged in recruiting. I have received an order from Gov. Dennison to raise two regiments of Infantry, one squadron of Cavalry, and a battery of artillery, and I am now hard at work executing the order. I want a good Colonel, an educated, brave, reliable officer. I must have him. The orders of the Governor give me the utmost latitude in the selection of the officers of this force and I am determined it shall be well commanded if proper officers can be obtained. Can you name me one as Major, and one as Lieutenant Colonel? They will receive promotion upon the meeting of Congress, when I shall resign the nominal place of Colonel. In the multiplicity of your important duties I trust you can name such officers as I wish. I would like it all the better if one at least of them may be a Kentuckian, as this force is intended for Kentucky.

Affy. Your Brother,

J. S.

General Sherman found Generals Anderson and Thomas at Cincinnati, and Anderson decided to send him to Indianapolis and

Springfield to confer with the governors of Indiana and Illinois, and to General Fremont, who was in command at St. Louis, to get help to resist the threatened invasion of Kentucky. While at St. Louis General Sherman was summoned hastily back to Louisville, and on his arrival was sent by General Anderson with such troops as were available, to secure a position on Muldraugh's Hill, before General Buckner with his invading force could get there. The next letter is written from there.

MULDRAUGH'S HILL,

40 miles from Louisville, Oct. 5, 1861.

Dear Brother:... I'm afraid you are too late to save Kentucky. The young active element is all secession, the older stay-at-homes are for Union and Peace. But they will not take part. In the meantime the Southern Confederacy looking forward to this very condition of things has armies organized, equipped, &c., and have the Railroads so disposed that by concentration they can overwhelm any part. There was one Camp south and East of Lexington formed by Lt. Nelson, U. S. Navy, now commanded by Brig. Gen. Thomas, and an army under Zollicoffer of Tennessee is advancing on it. Gen. Anderson at Louisville, Ky., has sent in that direction all the regiments from Ohio. Here the secessionists secured several trains of cars and locomotives, moved them South and broke up the bridges so that they are safe. We came out here hastily to secure Muldraugh's Hill, a kind of chain which separates the waters of Salt Creek from Green River. We are at one part of this chain where the Railroad from Louisville to Nashville crosses it, but it is by no means a strong point. I have examined the country all around, but every strong defensible position is devoid of water, and our absolute dependence on that element forces me into a position which upon being surrounded by vastly superior forces will be a complete ambush. The people are all unfriendly. Their trade and relations have been with the South, and there their feelings lie, so that when Buckner sees fit he can come up from Green River where he now is with from to 15,000 men. We have 5,000, and the Railroad behind is guarded by three more, but this road can be cut at a hundred different points which would starve us out or force me to strike out and live on a country which produces only beef and corn. I have Col. Gibson's Ohio Regt., 3 Indiana Regts. and 2 of Kentucky, but I must say that these latter were made up in Louisville and over in Indiana and [are] composed most of strangers to Kentucky. It will require near one hundred thousand men in Kentucky, and where they are to come from I don't know.

If I am reinforced as promised I will advance to a place called Moline where the ground is better for a desperate fight....

I see they are falling back from Washington. I hope McClellan will press forward and keep them all engaged; in like manner the forces in Missouri should be employed without a minute's delay, and for that reason I am sorry to see a change of plans....

If the Confederates take St. Louis and get Kentucky this Winter you will be far more embarrassed than if

Washington had fallen into their possession, as whatever nation gets the control of the Ohio, Mississippi and Missouri Rivers will control the Continent. This they know and for this they will labor. You of the North never fully appreciated the energy of the South. My health is good, but as you perceive I am far from easy about the fate of Kentucky.

Affectionately,

W. T. Sherman, Brig. Gen'l.

On the 8th of October, 1861, General Anderson, worn out by the cares of his position, resigned, and Sherman' naturally was forced into the command until he could be relieved. He continued so until the middle of November, when General Buell was sent to relieve him, and Sherman was ordered to report to General Halleck, then in command in Missouri.

In a letter to Adjutant-General Thomas, dated Louisville, October 22, General Sherman wrote: —

You know my views, that this great centre of our field was too weak, far too weak, and I have begged and implored till I dare not say more.

The two following letters show clearly how weak Sherman considered his position, and how hard he tried to better it by acquiring more men and better arms: —

HEADQUARTERS, DEPARTMENT OF THE CUMBERLAND, LOUISVILLE, KEN., Oct. 26, 1861.

Dear Brother: I am just in receipt of your letter and am glad the Secretary remembered my remark, that to accomplish the only purposes for which Kentucky can be used there should be a force here of 200,000 men. My force is ridiculously small and I think to [augment] it by driblets. Look at the fact—we know the South is all arms and prepared and must have Kentucky; for it they will struggle. They see us under-valuing their force. They have already invaded the state with five times my forces and are gradually preparing for an onset. I know their leaders and their designs, and feel that I am to be sacrificed. The Western part of the state is now in their possession. They have about 6000 men in the Valley of the Big Sandy, 6000 or 7000 at Cumberland Gap and Ford, and I doubt not at least 35,000 in front of me, with nothing between us but Green River, now fordable, and about 23 miles of intervening country. Indiana is devoid of arms, so is Ohio and the North-West, and to my crying demand for arms they send me a few hundreds of condemned European muskets, whilst the people ask for rifles. We have called on the Kentuckians to form regiments and they are responding slowly to be sure but when they come for arms I can only answer I have none, or such as they won't touch. I tell you, and warn you of the danger so far as my power goes. I cannot promise to prevent the enemy reaching the Ohio river at a hundred different points. Our camps are full of their spies and the people here all prefer their Southern connections.... I am compelled to distribute them [troops] on three weak lines all dependent on railroads which may at any moment be interrupted, also on telegraphs which are daily cut. A reverse to any one of these might be fatal to all, yet I cannot do otherwise. The forces up Sandy must be driven or threatened from the direction of Paris. Those at Cumberland Gap from Dick Robinson, and those over Green River from here; this is the most important point and the most in danger. The Southern army wants it with its mills, foundries, shops, and all the affairs of a city, besides the control of the river....Yours,

HEADQUARTERS, DEPARTMENT OP THE MISSOURI,
LOUISVILLE, KENTUCKY, NOV. 21, 1861.

Dear Brother: Your letter was received yesterday. I know that others than yourself think I take a gloomy view of affairs without cause. I hope to God tis so. All I know is the fact that all over Kentucky the people are allied by birth, interest, and preference to the South. Their trade points that way and in spite of all efforts letters pass to and fro daily. Applications come by hundreds asking protection which cannot be granted, and all know the fact that we have not the power to prevent it. Again the men who have come here by regiments are exposed to not only the chances of war but of interruption to the railroad which I have guarded thus far successfully, but a child or man with a crowbar may destroy it. How that Buell is in command I might divest myself of all care on this score. We have been out to camp inspecting the troops and he has entered upon his duties and I have delayed here simply to give him information. I have not been instrumental in bringing troops here, and I will give no advice on the subject....

They have sent here old condemned European [muskets], and have sent no arms for Cavalry, and when I bought pistols wherewith to arm some scouts the accounts have been disallowed at Washington because I had not procured authority beforehand. Troops come from Wisconsin and Minnesota without arms and receive such as we have here for the first time, and I cannot but look upon it as absolutely sacrificing them. I see no hope for them in their present raw and undisciplined condition, and some terrible disaster is inevitable....

For myself I will blindly obey my orders and report to Gen. Halleck in Missouri, but till I can see daylight ahead I will never allow myself to be in command.

Affectionately, W. T. Sherman.

It is interesting to remember how completely the future carried out Sherman's prediction with regard to Kentucky. Later, Burnside was cornered there as Sherman always believed his successors must be, and he (Sherman) was sent to his relief.

After being relieved of his command in Kentucky and reporting to Halleck in St. Louis, Sherman went to his old home in Lancaster, Ohio, for a short leave, and on his return was sent to take command of the camp of instruction at Benton Barracks near St. Louis and to get the troops there into condition for immediate use.

On December 24 he writes from Benton Barracks: —

... In Missouri I find things black enough. All my old friends are now against us, not openly but really. We have possession of St. Louis and the railroads but the Secessionists have possession of the country. They have destroyed the North Missouri railroad and will in time the others. These railroads are the weakest things in war; a single man with a match can destroy a bridge and cut off communications, and no one seems to apprehend the danger by laying in supplies accordingly....

And two weeks later he wrote: —

I have received your letter and will give you what you ask: the reason why I ordered Gen. Thomas to fall back from London towards Danville or Kentucky River. Thomas had his advance in Front of London, Shorpf's brigade at London and he was at Crab Orchard. All the stores for the command had to be hauled from Nicholasville. The country was very barren of forage and roads beyond Crab Orchard were very bad. Thomas reported that General Zollicoffer had obstructed the roads to East Tennessee, and had moved westward as far as Jacksboro, and I knew he would make his appearance in front of Somerset which he did, uniting his force of about 5,000 to Stanton's of about 2,500, giving him a column of 7,500 men on a good road leading north to Lexington. It was necessary to move Thomas to check this. Had Zollicoffer alone to have been watched the movement would have been directed to Somerset, but at the same time I had information that Gen. Hardee had left Bowling Green with his division of 3000 men, with a full supply of country wagons to the East toward Columbia from which point there is a good road to Lexington. I inferred their plan to be, as I doubt not it was, to join these two columns on the Lexington road, and therefore Thomas' force was required at some point common to the two roads, viz.: about Stamford, Danville or the Kentucky River Bridge, where he could act on the defense or offense as the case might be. The lines of operation from Nicholasville were long and weak, and there was at all times danger that a superior force would interpose between Thomas and his base, and I was satisfied that our enemies had at Bowling Green enough to send such a force, and we had not enough to make detachments from the Louisville line. The fact was our force in Kentucky was ridiculously weak for such an extent of country. My orders to Thomas pointed out the danger of this force getting between him and Lexington and for him to fall back to some point near Danville, and afterwards I notified him of my information that the anticipated movement had been reported from Columbia.

The distance was not great, but it so happened that the weather was very bad and the retrograde was made too rapidly. Of course I do not wish to throw on Thomas any blame but must bear it myself. That this movement on Lexington was contemplated then, I am well satisfied, and that some cause interposed I am also well satisfied....

By giving up command in Kentucky I acknowledged my inability to manage the case, and I do think Buell can manage better than I could, and if he succeeds he will deserve all honor, but I do think it is wrong to push him on that line, whilst the army at Washington remain comparatively inert....

Now Halleck has in Missouri about 80,000 men on paper and there are not in organized shape more than 10,000 or 20,000 opposed to him, yet the country is full of Secessionists, and it takes all his command to watch them. This is an element which politicians have never given full credit to. These local Secessionists are really more dangerous than if assembled in one or more bodies, for then they could be traced out and found, whereas now they are scattered about on farms and are very peaceable, but when a bridge is to be burned they are about....

I wish I could take another view of this war, but I cannot. It thrusts itself upon me from every side, and yet I hope I am mistaken....

Halleck has been successful thus far and I hope may continue, but he cannot by mere written papers cope with Price who is in the field bothered by no papers or accounts, taking what he can lay his hands on. I think he has orders to move down the river, but the moment he moves a man from the interior to go to Cairo, Price will return. That is his game. And in that way with a comparatively small force he holds in check five times his number....

Affectionately,

W. T. SHERMAN.

HEADQUARTERS, CAMP OF INSTRUCTION,

BENTON BARRACKS (near St. Louis, Mo.), Feb. 3, 1862.

I am still her© at the Barracks doing my best to organize, equip, and prepare regiments for the coming Spring....

I believe an attempt will be made on the Forts on the Tennessee and Cumberland Rivers in co-operation with Buell who finds with his 120,000 men he still needs help. I rather think they will come up to my figures yet. Halleck is expected to send them from 30,000 to 50,000 men. Had this been done early and promptly, the Confederates could not have made Bowling Green and Columbia next to impregnable. Until these places are reduced it will not do to advance far into Tennessee and I doubt if it will be done. East Tennessee cannot exercise much influence on the final result. West Tennessee is more important, as without the navigation of the Mississippi all commercial interests will lean to the Southern cause. If the Southern Confederacy can control the navigation of the lower Mississippi, and European nations from the mouths of the Mississippi, what can Missouri and Kentucky do? These are, however, questions for the future....

Affectionately,

W. T. SHERMAN.

While General Sherman was in command of the camp of instruction at Benton Barracks, the movement up the Tennessee began. Grant and Foote took Fort Henry. Before Fort Donelson was taken Sherman was ordered to go at once to Paducah, Ky., to take command of that post and expedite the operations up the Tennessee and Cumberland. The day after his arrival (February 16), there came the news of the capture of Fort Donelson.

WASHINGTON, Feb. 15, 1862.

Dear Brother:

I was infinitely rejoiced to see in this morning's paper the announcement that you were to command at Cairo. I sincerely hope it is true. If so, you will have a noble opportunity to answer those who have belied you. Take my advice, be hopeful, cheerful, polite to everybody, even a newspaper reporter. They are in the main, clever, intelligent men, a little too pressing in their vocation.

Above all things, be hopeful and push ahead. Active, bold, prompt, vigorous action is now demanded. McClellan is dead in the estimation of even military men....

Do not the cheers with which our gun-boats were received in Tennessee and Alabama show you what I have always contended, that this rebellion is a political one, managed by "Southern gentlemen" and not grounded in the universal assent of the people? Johnson has now more adherents in Tennessee than Jeff. Davis. Let our leading army officers who have been educated to defend the nation catch the spirit of our people, a generous, hopeful, self-sacrificing spirit. Let them go ahead and you will find the Union restored and strengthened by its trials....Affectionately yours,

JOHN SHERMAN.

On Feb. 23, 1862, General Sherman wrote from Paducah, Kentucky:—

Don't get to war with McClellan. You mistake him if you underrate him. He must begin to move soon and I think he will. If he can threaten Richmond and cause Johnston to fall back from Manassas, he will relieve the Capital, which is the reason why foreign Governments talk of acknowledging the Southern Independence.

On March 10th Sherman, under orders from Halleck, embarked his division at Paducah, steamed up the river beyond Port Henry, met General C. P. Smith three days later, and was ordered by him to push on and break up the Memphis and Charleston R.R. between Tuscumbia and Corinth. March 19th found Sherman encamped about three miles from Corinth, where he remained until the battle of Shiloh, April 6th and 7th. The following letters from General Sherman are devoted chiefly to explaining the series of events at Shiloh, and to defending the army from the unjust charges which were circulated throughout the country before the official reports of the battle were made public.

[DICTATED.]

CAMP SHILOH NEAR PITTSBURGH, TENN., April 16, 1862.

Hon. **JOHN SHERMAN,** Washington, D.C.

Dear Brother:

My division is made up mostly of new regiments, some of which behaved well and others badly, but I hope by patience to make it as good as any other division in the Army.

Since the battle I have been up to Chickasaw, from which point I caused the destruction of the Charleston and Memphis Railroad at its crossing over Bear Creek, a valuable piece of service.

My right hand is temporarily disabled by inflammation from a wound, but with good luck will be all right in a week.

I believe that our hardest fighting is yet to be done, but I have absolute faith in Generals Halleck, Buell, and Grant.

Affectionately your Brother,

W. T. SHERMAN.

SENATE CHAMBER, WASHINGTON CITY, April 20, 1862.

Dear Brother: I heartily and with great pride in you congratulate you on your escape and for the high honors you won in the battle of the 7th and the 8th. Cecilia and I have watched with the most anxious interest your course and have read every word that was accessible in regard to the battle. I need not say that it has been with the highest satisfaction. The official report of Generals Halleck and Grant leave nothing to desire except that the information as to your wound in the hand is indefinite. From your subsequent operations I infer it is not so serious as to disable you. It is a fearful battle, and I cannot yet conceive how a general rout was avoided. The first accounts gave an exaggerated account of the surprise, of whole regiments killed or captured in their tents, and of inexcusable carelessness in guarding against surprise. More recent accounts modify the extent of the surprise, but still there is an impression that sufficient care was not taken. That pickets were not far enough advanced or of sufficient force, and that General Grant should have been nearer his command. I sincerely hope he will be relieved from all blame. I enclose you a note to General Patterson.

The general tone of public sentiment is very hopeful.

This arises partly from the changed tone of our foreign news, and perhaps from the comparative ease of money matters under our enormous expenditures.

The great drawback is on account of McClellan's position. Military men of the highest character as well as all civilians think he is in a position from which he cannot retreat, and where he must fight under very great disadvantage. Still the general feeling is hopeful of the success of our arms and the preservation of the Union.

I still adhere to my conviction that we will demonstrate the strength, unity and prosperity of a Republican Government for fifty years to come. Notwithstanding your reluctance to mingle in the stirring events of the time, it will be your fate to do so and I have entire confidence that it will be with success and distinction.

Affectionately yours,

JOHN SHERMAN.

HEADQUARTERS, CAMP SHILOH, April 22, 1862.

Dear Brother: My hand is still very sore but I am able to write some. The newspapers came back to us with accounts of our battle of the 6th and 7th inst. as usual made by people who ran away and had to excuse their cowardice by charging bad management on the part of leaders. I see that we were surprised, that our men were bayoneted in their tents, that officers had not had breakfast, &c. This is all simply false. The attack did not begin until 7 34 a m. All but the worthless cowards had had breakfast. Not a man was bayoneted in or near his tent. Indeed our brigade surgeon, Hartshorn, has not yet seen a single bayonet wound on a living or dead subject. The regiments that profess to have been surprised lost no officers at all, and of the two that first broke in my division 53 and 57 Ohio, the 53 lost no officers and only 7 men, the 57 two officers and 7 men. Some of my Ohio regiments that did fight well lost as many as 49 and 34, but not a bayonet, sword or knife wound, all cannon and musket ball. Those of my brigade held our original position from 7 3-4 a m. when the attack began, until 10 h. 10 m. when the enemy had passed my left and got artillery to enfilade my line when I ordered them to fall back. We held our second position until 4 P M. and then fell back without opposition to the third and last position, more than a mile from the river.

As to surprise, we had constant skirmishes with the enemies' cavalry all the week before, and I had strong guards out in front of each brigade, which guards were driven in on the morning of the battle, but before the enemy came within cannon range of my position every regiment was under arms at the post I had previously assigned to them. The cavalry was saddled and artillery harnessed up, unlimbered, and commenced firing as soon as we could see anything to fire at.

On Saturday I had no cavalry pickets out because I had no cavalry in my division. General Grant had made a new assignment of cavalry and artillery on Friday. The Ohio Fifth which had been with me was ordered to Hurlburt, and eight companies of the fourth, III., Colonel Dickey, assigned to me did not get into camp till near Saturday night and I ordered them into the saddle at midnight.

I occupied the right front, McClernand was to my rear, and on his left in echelon with me was Prentiss. I watched the Rondy road and main Corinth, Prentiss the Ridge Corinth road....

The enemy did not carry either of my roads until he had driven Prentiss and got in on my left....

Whether we should have been on this or that side of the Tennessee river is not my business. I did not apprehend an attack from Beauregard because I thought then and think now he would have done better if he could have chosen ground as far back from our stores as possible. We are bound to attack him, and had we run out of cartridges or stores or got stampeded twenty miles back from the Tennessee the result would have been different from now. But we knew the enemy was in our front, but in what form could not tell, and I was always ready for an attack. I am out of all patience that our people should prefer to believe the horrid stories of butchery, ridiculous in themselves, gotten up by cowards to cover their shame, than the plain natural reports of the officers who are responsible and who saw what they describe. My report with all the subordinate reports of Brigadiers and Colonels with lists of killed and wounded and missing went to General Grant on the 11th.

The enemy is still in our front, we can get a fight the hour and minute we want it. Halleck, Buell, Grant all in authority are now here and responsibility cannot be shifted. The common soldiers and subordinates ran away and now want to blame the commanders....

Your affectionate brother,

W. **T. SHERMAN.**

CAMP EIGHT MILES FRONT OP CORINTH, May 7, 1862.

My Dear Brother:

The scoundrels who fled their ranks and left about half their number to do their work have succeeded in establishing their story of surprise, stuck with bayonets and swords in their tents and all that stuff.

They were surprised, astonished and disgusted at the utter want of respect for life on the part of the confederates, whom they have been taught to regard as inferior to them, and were surprised to see them approach with banners fluttering, bayonets glistening and lines dressed on the centre. It was a beautiful and dreadful sight and I was prepared for and have freely overlooked the fact that many wilted and fled, but gradually recovering, rejoined our ranks. But those who did not recover, their astonishment has to cast about for a legitimate excuse; and the cheapest one was to accuse their officers, and strange to say, this story is believed before ours who fought two whole days....

In this instance the scamps will soon learn their mistake. Those who ran and cried "surprise," "cut up," &c., expected all who stood to their work to be killed, but all were not killed and enough remained as witnesses, after the public are satisfied with the horrid stories of men butchered, &c....

For two days they hung about the river bank filling the ears of newspaper reporters with their tales of horrid surprise. Regiments all cut up, *they* the only survivors and to our utter amazement we find it settling down as history....

Every battery (three) was harnessed up in position before called on to fire and cavalry (only 250 in my whole division) was in the saddle at daylight, and the attack did not begin until the sun was two hours high....

Prentiss was not surprised, for I sent him word an hour before the enemies' infantry began to appear, and he was not made prisoner until after 3 p m....

I confess I did not think Beauregard would abandon his railroads to attack us on our base (when he knew that by waiting a short time we should be forced to advance) where he would most assuredly have been beaten.

I am on the extreme right and we are in contact with the enemies' pickets. Some fierce struggle must soon follow,

but that the war is ended or even fairly begun I do not believe.

Affectionately your brother,

W. T. SHERMAN.

WASHINGTON CITY, May 10, 1862.

My Dear Brother: I received jour recent letter in which you mention your position on the morning of Sunday very opportunely.

It arrived on the morning I had to make a speech on Ohio volunteers. The imputations, whether just or unjust, upon our regiments make it necessary in the opinion of our delegation that someone should speak, and I did so. I was exceedingly anxious for your report and went or sent to the Adjutant General's office daily for several days, but was informed that none of the details or division reports had come, although several were published in the newspapers. I collected all the information I could and made my speech. Whether I am in a mile of the truth is mere chance, but I believe my statement is more accurate than any made. Read it and let me know. You will see from Harlan's remarks there is much feeling against Grant and I try to defend him, but with little success. Why is not your report sent in? Pray hereafter have a copy sent to me of all future reports....

I never spoke under greater embarrassment than I did yesterday. It was a delicate subject, upon which my constituents were sensitive, and yet I was in ignorance how far your reply would overthrow me....

As to your personal position you need not fear. Halleck's opinion about your action of Sunday is the opinion of the country. You are as likely to be abused on my account as on your own. I am so accustomed to storms of factious opposition as to be perfectly serene under it. I hope you will become so.

Affectionately,

JOHN SHERMAN.

HEADQUARTERS 5TH DIV., May 12, 1862.

CAMP BEFORE CORINTH.

My Lear Brother:... I was gratified on Monday when I came in contact with my old Kentucky command. They gathered around me and were evidently pleased to meet me again, officers and men. I think Mr. Lincoln is a pure minded, honest and good man. I have all faith in him....

I think it is a great mistake to stop enlistments. There may be enough soldiers on paper, but not enough in fact. My aggregate, present and absent, is 10,452. Present for duty, 5,298; absent sick, 2,557; absent wounded, 855. The rest are on various detached duties, as teamsters or hospital attendance, embracing about 600 sick in camp.

About this proportion will run through the whole army. I have not really one thorough soldier in my whole army. They are all green and raw....

Last evening I had to post my own pickets and come under the fire of the enemies pickets. Came near being hit. Of course, being mounted and ahead, I and staff always get an undue share of attention.

I made my official report on the battle of the 6th and 7th on the 11th of April, sent it to Grant, and he to Halleck. It has not been published and it is none of my business. An officer ought not to publish anything. His report is to the Government, may contain confidential matters, and the War Department alone should have the discretion to publish or not, according to the interests of Government....

I have been worried to death by the carelessness of officers and sentinels; have begged, importuned, and cursed to little purpose; and I will not be held responsible for the delinquencies of sentinels fresh from home, with as much idea of war as children. All I know is, we had our entire front, immediate guards and grand guards, and I had all my command in line of battle well selected before we had seen an infantry soldier of the enemy. We had been skirmishing with the cavalry for several days, and we could not get behind them. All we could see was the head of their column, and that admirably qualified by familiarity of the country for the purpose of covering an approach.

Grant had been expecting Buell a whole week before he arrived. We all knew the enemy was in our front, but we had to guess at his purpose. Now that it is known, all are prophets; but before, we were supposed to be a vast aggressive force sent by an intelligent Government to invade the South, and for us to have been nervous on the subject would have indicated weakness. Beauregard then performed the very thing which Johnston should have done in Kentucky last October.

My force was divided; he could have interposed his, attacked McCook at Nolin and Thomas at London, and would have defeated us with perfect ease. The secessionists would then have had Kentucky and Missouri both. Why he did not is a mystery to me. And Buckner told me that Johnston's neglect on that occasion was so galling to him that he made him give a written order not to attempt to manoeuvre....

We are now encamped six miles from Corinth, pickets about one mile and a half in advance. I am on the extreme right, McClernand is in my rear and guards off to the right. The roads are again pretty good and I don't bother myself about the plans and aims of our generals. I will do all I can with my division, but regret that I have not better discipline and more reliable men. Too many of the officers are sick of the war and have gone home on some pretence or other. I am in pretty good health and keep close to my work. The success of our arms at Norfolk and Williamsburg are extraordinary and may result in peace sooner than I calculated. All I fear is that though we progress we find plenty of push everywhere. Weather begins to be hot.

Affectionately yours,

SENATE CHAMBER, WASHINGTON, May 19, 1862.

Dear Brother: Your official report was so complete and satisfactory that it has settled forever all the absurd stories about the battle of the 6th and 7th. It also shows me that with all my care to be right I made several mistakes, especially as to the volunteers of the 6th and 7th.

Deep anxiety is felt here as to your position. I talked with the President on Saturday about the general state of the war. He evidently fears the accumulation of forces under Beauregard and said he had and would again telegraph Halleck not to move forward until he was certain to win. If the Mississippi is clear of the enemy and we get Richmond, it is thought that will secure the border States and we can afford to wait. In the mean time, even under terrible financial pressure and drain of active war, the country is flourishing. Our bonds are above par, trade is active and produce bears a good price. Much of this may be induced by the inflation of paper money, but gold is abundant, foreign importations active, and foreigners are making investments here heavily. In my experience in public affairs I have never known times more easy. If the war could only be brought to a close upon the basis of the unity and integrity of the Government, we should have a rebound of national prosperity that would soon heal all the losses and burdens of the war. As to politics now, lines are being drawn. Radicals and Conservatives are taking sides without regard to party reasons. If the rank Secessionists would only give up their insane attempt at division they could easily secure every reasonable right. They must, however, lay aside the insolence and dogmatism with which they have domineered over our better men. If they do not abandon their cause, events will force a war in the cotton States between the whites and blacks. Hunter has already invited it, but his inconsiderate proclamation will be set aside. However, delay, defeat or a much longer continuance in the barbarity of rebel warfare will prepare the public mind in the North for a warfare that will not scruple to avail itself of every means of subjection.

In the course of business I have received many kind messages for you from your many friends, among others from Swords, Van Vleit, Garesche and others.

Affectionately yours,

JOHN SHERMAN.

After Shiloh, Sherman was made a major-general.

Corinth was evacuated and burned by the rebels on the night of May 29th, and was occupied by the Northern army on the following day.

The following order issued by Sherman to his division was found in his letter-book, and is inserted here: —

HEADQUARTERS 5TH DIV. ARMY OP THE TENN., CAMP BEFORE CORINTH, May 31, 1862.

ORDERS No. 30.

The General commanding 5th Division Right Wing takes this occasion to express to the officers and men of his command his great satisfaction with them for the courage, steadiness and great industry displayed by them during the past month. Since leaving our memorable camp at Shiloh we have occupied and strongly entrenched seven distinct camps in a manner to excite the admiration and high commendation of General Halleck. The division has occupied the right flank of the Grand Army, thereby being more exposed and calling for more hard work and larger guard details than from any other single division, and the Commanding General repeats that his officers and men have promptly and cheerfully fulfilled their duty, have sprung to the musket or spade according to the occasion, and have just reason to claim a large share in the honors that are due the whole army for the glorious victory terminating at Corinth on yesterday, and it affords him great pleasure to bear full and willing testimony to the qualities of his command that have achieved this victory, a victory none the less decisive because attended with comparatively little loss of life.

But a few days ago a large and powerful rebel army lay at Corinth with outposts extending to our very camp at Shiloh. They held two railroads extending North and South, East and West across the whole extent of their country, with a vast number of locomotives and cars to bring to them speedily and certainly their reinforcements and supplies. They called to their aid all their armies from every quarter, abandoning the sea coast and the great river Mississippi that they might overwhelm us with numbers in the place of their own choosing. They had their chosen leaders, men of high education and courage, and they dared us to leave the cover of our iron clad gunboats to come and fight them in their trenches, and the still more dangerous ambuscades of their Southern swamps and forests. Their whole country from Richmond to Memphis and from Nashville to Mobile rang with their taunts and boastings, as to how they would immolate the Yankees if they dared to leave the Tennessee River. They boldly and defiantly challenged us to meet them at Corinth. We accepted the challenge and came slowly and without attempt at concealment to the very ground of their selection, and they had fled away. We yesterday marched unopposed through the burning embers of their destroyed camps and property, and pursued them to their swamps till burning bridges plainly confessed they have fled and not marched away for better ground. It is a victory as brilliant and important as any recorded in history, and any officer or soldier who has lent his aid has just reason to be proud of his part. No amount of sophistry or words from the leaders of the Rebellion can succeed in giving the evacuation of Corinth under the circumstances any other title than that of a signal defeat, more humiliating to them and their cause than if we had entered the place over the dead and mangled bodies of their soldiers. We are not here to kill and slay, but to vindicate the honor and just authority of that Government which has been bequeathed to us by our honored fathers, and to whom we would be recreant if we permitted their work to pass to our children marred and spoiled by ambitious and wicked rebels. The General commanding while thus claiming for his division their just share in this glorious result, must at the same time remind them that much yet remains to be done, and all must still continue the same vigilant patience, industry and obedience till the enemy lay down their arms and publicly acknowledge that for their supposed grievances they must obey the laws of their country and not attempt its overthrow by threats, by cruelty and by war. They must be made to feel and acknowledge the power of a just and mighty nation.

This result can only be accomplished by a cheerful and ready obedience to the orders and authority of our own leaders in whom we now have just reason to feel the most implicit confidence. That the fifth division of the right wing will do this, and that in due time we will all go to our families and friends at home, is the earnest prayer and wish of your immediate commander.

W. **T. SHERMAN,**

Major-General.

The following was written in lead pencil on the same sheet: —

Dear Brother: Of course the telegraph has announced the evacuation of Corinth. I have sent to General Thomas commanding Eight Wing my report. You ask for a copy. This is wrong, as official reports are the property of the War Department. I have sent Ellen the rough draft to keep and I have instructed her to make and send you a copy. We have had no battle and I cannot imagine why Beauregard has declined battle. I was on the extreme right and yesterday pushed into the town and beyond it, but their army had gone off and I was ordered back to this camp.

Pope and Buell are in pursuit, I understand, around by the left, but you will have the result long before you can receive this letter.

I send you a copy of my Division Order which is public, inasmuch as it is issued to my own command. Its publication would interest no one, but lest you should print it on the supposition that it would interest people, I express the wish that it be not published until Halleck's announcement of the abandonment of Corinth be first made public.

I cannot imagine what turn things will now take, but I do not think Halleck will attempt to pursue far. I **think that Beauregard cannot now subsist his army or hold it together long.**

It must divide to live, and the greatest danger is that they will scatter and constitute guerilla bands. The people are as bitter against us as ever, but the leaders must admit now that they have been defeated. I hope all this army with some exceptions will be marched forthwith to Memphis. A part could be spared for Huntsville, Ala., and Nashville, but as to pursuing overland it would be absurd. We want the Mississippi now in its whole length and a moment should not be lost. I am glad the President has called for more men. He cannot have too many, and the more men the sooner the work will be done. All is not yet accomplished, although certainly great strides have been made. If McClellan succeeds at Richmond and we can take Memphis, we could afford to pause and let events work. Banks' repulse was certain. Three converging armies whose point was in possession of the enemy was worse generalship than they tried to force on me in Kentucky of diverging lines with a superior enemy between. Our people must respect the well-established principles of the art of war, else successful fighting will produce no results. I am glad you are pleased at my report at Shiloh. It possesses the merit of truth and you may safely rely on it, for I make no points but what I can sustain. Your speech was timely and proper for you. You could explain, whereas I had to report actual facts without fear or favor. I will write when more at leisure. The enemies' works are very extensive. They must have had 100,000 men.

Your brother,

W. T. SHERMAN.

Mansfield, Aug. 8, 1862.

Dear Brother:... The enlistment of recruits is now much more rapid than ever before. A regiment is organizing here and will be full in a few days. The new call for militia will also soon be filled up and I hope without a draft. Our people are beginning to feel a little more serious about the war, but the determination to wage it to a successful termination is stronger and firmer than ever. McClellan's misfortunes have allayed the political feeling that was gathering about him. His friends have much to say in his favor and his opponents are very moderate in condemning or criticising him. If you have time, write to me. For this month I will stay here as much as possible. In September I suppose I will be on the stump. After that I mean to remain as quiet as possible.

Yours affectionately,

JOHN SHERMAN.

MANSFIELD, OHIO, Aug. 24, 1862.

Dear Brother: Your letter of Aug. 13, with enclosures, was received. I have read carefully your general orders enclosed and also your order on the employment of negroes. I see no objection to the latter except the doubt and delay caused by postponing the pay of negroes until the courts determine their freedom. As the act securing their freedom is a military rule, you ought to presume their freedom until the contrary is known and pay them accordingly....

You can form no conception at the change of opinion here as to the Negro Question. Men of all parties who now appreciate the magnitude of the contest and who are determined to preserve the unity of the government at all hazards, agree that we must seek the aid and make it the interests of the negroes to help ns. Nothing but our party divisions and our natural prejudice of caste has kept us from using them as *allies* in the war, to be used for all purposes in which they can advance the cause of the country. Obedience and protection must go together. When rebels take up arms, not only refuse obedience but resist our force, they have no right to ask protection in any way. And especially that protection should not extend to a local right inconsistent with the general spirit of our laws and the existence of which has been from the beginning the chief element of discord in the country. I am prepared for one to meet the broad issue of universal emancipation.. .

By the way, the only criticism I notice of your management in Memphis is your leniency to the rebels. I enclose you an extract. I take it that most of these complaints are groundless, but you can see from it the point upon which public opinion rests. The energy and bitterness which they have infused into the contest must be met with energy and determination....

Such is not only the lesson of history, the dictate of policy, but it is the general popular sentiment. I know you care very little for the latter....

It is sometimes passionate, hasty and intemperate, but after a little fluctuation it settles very near the true line. You notice that Fremont, Butler, Mitchell, Turchin and Cochran are popular, while Buell, Thomas, McClellan and others are not. It is not for military merit, for most persons concede the inferiority in many respects of the officers first named, but it is because these officers agree with and act upon the popular idea....

I want to visit you in Memphis and if possible go see the 64th and 65th. If it is possible or advisable, let me know and give me directions how to get there. It is but right that I should see the regiments I organized, and besides I should like to see you if I should not incommode you and interfere with your public duties....

Since my return I have spent most of my time in my Library. I have always felt that my knowledge of American politics was rather the superficial view of the politician and not accurate enough for the position assigned me. I therefore read and study more and speak less than usual....

We all wait with intense anxiety the events impending in Virginia. We all fear results for a month to come. Now is the chance for the rebels.

Affectionately yours,

JOHN SHERMAN.

CHAPTER V

ON July 16th Halleck, who had just been ordered to the East to succeed McClellan, sent Sherman a dispatch telling him that Grant was to succeed to his (Halleck's) command, and ordering Sherman to Memphis. Sherman reached Memphis July 21st, and immediately took command, giving his time to the discipline and drill of his two divisions and to the administration of civil affairs.

Memphis, August 26th, 1862.

Dear Brother:... Gradually the practice has come into my original proposition that none but discharged soldiers should go home, or wounded men. All others should be in regimental hospitals, or hospitals established near at hand where as they convalesce they can join. Although from the President down to the lowest Brigadier orders to this effect have been issued, yet there are hundreds trying to get their brothers and sons home. I know full well the intense desire to get home, but any army would be ruined by this cause alone. McClellan has 70,000 absent from his army. Some were sick, but certainly not over 20,000; with the other 50,000 our country might have been saved the disgrace of a retreat from Richmond, for it has resolved itself into that. At last all have come to the conclusion that we are at war, and great as the draft has been on your population, don't suppose you outnumber the South yet. All their people are armed and at war. You hear of vast armies at Richmond, at Chattanooga and threatening New Orleans, whilst the whole country is full of guerilla bands numbering hundreds. All the people are armed. A year ago we could have taken them unprepared, but they have used the year to buy all kinds of arms and munitions of war and wherever we go we find them well prepared. They seem to have left this quarter. I am glad of the new levies and only regret the loss of the year. The present operations in Virginia and Kentucky are all important....

Affectionately,

W. **T. SHERMAN.**

Memphis, Sept. 3, 1862.

It is easy to say "thou shalt not steal," but to stop stealing puzzles the brains of hundreds of men and employs thousands of bailiffs, sheriffs, &c., &c. So you or Congress may command "slaves shall be free," but to make them free and see that they are not converted into thieves, idlers or worse is a difficult problem and will require much machinery to carry out. Our commissaries must be ordered to feed them and some provision must be made for the women and children. My order gives employment to say two thousand, all men. Now that is about £ of a command. Extend that population to the whole army of 80,000 gives 10,000 slaves, and if we pay 10 dollars a month the estimate can be made. If the women and children are to be provided for, we must allow for their support of, say, one million. Where are they to get work? Who is to feed them, clothe them, and house them?

We cannot now give tents to our soldiers and our wagon trains are a horrible impediment, and if we are to take along and feed the negroes who flee to us for refuge it will be an impossible task. You cannot solve this negro question in a day.

Your brigade is not here. I think it is with Buell near Chattanooga. The last I saw of them they were in Garfield's brigade at Shiloh, still I should be glad if you would come to Memphis on a visit. Provided the southern army do not reach Kentucky or get into Maryland. In either of those events the people of the North must rise en masse with such weapons as they can get and repair to the frontier....

The people are always right. Of course, in the long run, because this year they are one thing, next year another. Do you say the people were right last year in saying, acting and believing that 30,000 were enough to hold Kentucky and carry on an offensive war against the South? "The People" is a vague expression.

Here the people are not right because you are warring against them. People in the aggregate may be wrong. There is such a thing as absolute right and absolute wrong. And people may do wrong as well as right. *Our people* are always right, but another people may be and always are wrong.

Affectionately your brother,

W. T. Sherman.

Memphis, Sept. 22, 1862.

Dear Brother: Troops are moving up through Arkansas for Missouri. It looks as though they want to swap countries with us. It is about time the North understood the truth. That the entire South, man, woman and child are against us, armed and determined. It will call for a million men for several years to put them down. They are more confident than ever, none seem to doubt their independence, but some hope to conquer the northwest. My opinion is there never can be peace and we must fight it out. I guess you now see how, from the very first I argued, that you all underestimated the task. None of you would admit for a moment that after a year's fighting the enemy would still threaten Washington, Cincinnati and St. Louis. We ought to hold fast to the Mississippi as a great base of operation. I should regard the loss of St. Louis as more fatal to our future success than the capture by them of Harrisburg and Philadelphia. Your brigade is now with Buell. I don't understand his move, but now suppose he will cross Green River and fight north of it. Still I don't see exactly his strategy or tactics. The passage of the enemy north of us, leaving us among a hostile population, was a bold and successful movement and will give them great credit in Europe. You doubtless, like most Americans, attribute our want of success to bad generals. I do not. With us you insist the boys, the soldiers, govern. They must have this or that or will cry down their leaders in the newspapers, so no general can achieve much. They fight or run as they please and of course it is the general's fault. Until this is cured, we must not look for success. But on the whole, things look more favorable than at any former time, as the numbers engaged on both sides are approaching the occasion.

The war is, which race, that of the North or South, shall rule America. The greatest danger North is division and anarchy, but I hope the pressure from the South will keep all united until our armies begin to have some discipline and see how important it is to success.

Our fort here is nearly done, I have 20 heavy guns mounted and about 30 field pieces, 7000 Infantry and 600 Cavalry. Some of my regiments are now in fine drill and discipline and all are doing well. We are all, however, tied down till events elsewhere develop.

Affectionately yours,

W. T. SHERMAN.

Mansfield, Ohio, Sept. 23rd, 1862.

Dear Brother: The rapid change in our military condition in Kentucky drew to Cincinnati an immense body of irregular forces as well as a large number of the new regiments. I went there with the intention, if advisable, to go to Memphis, but all thought it wrong for me to venture....

Since the date of your letter the condition of affairs has changed very much for the worse. The sudden over running of Kentucky, the surrender of Murfreesville, the battle of Richmond, the long and unaccountable delay of Buell, have all combined to make a gloomy feeling here, but do not affect the resolution to fight this war to a successful conclusion. We are now anxiously awaiting further movements in Kentucky by Buell. If he fails it is manifest a year is lost and our new levies will have to commence the war in the West over again. The terrible battles in Maryland and the retreat of the rebels into Virginia give only a ray of comfort, for we lost more than we gained. The surrender at Harper's Berry loses us more material of war than the entire train of rebels is worth. And even now it is uncertain whether the retreat into Virginia is not a part of the plan of operations originally designed to carry the war into Western Virginia, Pennsylvania and Ohio. As one of the bad signs I regret to notice so many quarrels between officers....

The feeling among the people is general that the regular officers are indisposed to treat with decent civility those who, like most of the great military men of history, are educated in the field rather than in the school. And it is feared that habits of education and association make them feel indifferent of the success of the war — fighting rather from a pride of duty than from an earnest conviction that the rebellion must be put down with energy. Since Halleck went to Washington every movement is left to him absolutely. Ho interference or even advice is tendered. He has chosen his own officers, and if he fails I see nothing left but for the people to resort to such desperate means as the Prench and English did in their revolutions.

I am rejoiced that you have been able to keep out of the adversities that have befallen us. Your course in Memphis is judicious. Your speech I can heartily endorse. I hope you can maintain yourself at Memphis until relieved, and I have no doubt you will fill an honorable place in the history of our times. By the way, I received within a day or two a letter from a gentleman of the highest political status containing this passage: "Within the last few days I heard an officer say he heard your brother the General, abuse you roundly at Corinth as one of the *blank* abolitionists who had brought on the war, and that he was ashamed to own you as a brother." I have no doubt the officer said this but I knew you did not, and so contradicted it with decided emphasis. I only repeat it now to show you how persistently efforts are being made to separate the class of high regular officers to which you belong from civilians. Whenever that separation is effected all important commands will gradually be transferred to such officers as Banks, Sigel, Morgan, Nelson, and to such regular officers as show a sympathy with the Radical faction as Hunter, Premont and Doubleday. I earnestly deprecate all such tendencies. I want the war conducted regularly according to the tenets of civilized warfare. I prefer regular officers and scarcely ever criticise them and never in public, but if the time shall come when emancipation of blacks and civilization of whites is necessary in order to preserve the unity of this country, then I would prefer a fanatic like John Brown to lead our armies and an abolitionist like Chase with brains and energy to guide our counsels.

Affectionately yours,

JOHN SHERMAN.

Memphis, Oct. 1, 1862.

Dear Brother: I did not expect you would come if the confederates got possession of Kentucky. Even on the Mississippi the boats are fired on daily. I have been compelled to burn down one town and resort to retaliation. I understand Prentiss has ordered back from

Helena a part of the forces towards St. Louis, on the ground that the confederates are again advancing on Missouri. I rather think you now agree with me that this is no common war, that it was not going to end in a few months or a few years. For after eighteen months war the enemy is actually united, armed, and determined, with powerful forces well handled, disciplined and commanded on the Potomac, the Ohio, the Missouri. You must now see that I was right in not seeking prominence at the outstart. I knew and know yet that the northern people hare to unlearn all their experience of the past thirty years and be born again before they will see the truth....

The South has united people and as many men as she can arm, and though our armies pass across and through the land, the war closes in behind and leaves the same enemy behind. We attempt to occupy places, and the people rise up and make the detachments prisoners. I know you all recognize in these facts simply that Mason is a coward, Ford an ass, McClellan slow, Buell over-cautious, and Wright timid. This may all be so, but the causes lie deeper. Everybody thought I exaggerated the dangers, so I have no right to an opinion, but I rather think many now see the character of the war in which we are engaged. I don't see the end or the beginning of the end, but suppose we must prevail and persist or perish. I don't believe that two nations can exist within our old limits, and therefore that war is on us and we must fight it out....

When anybody tells you that I ever doubted your honesty and patriotism, tell him he says false. I may have said you were a politician and that we differed widely in the origin of this war, but that being in it, we fully agreed that it must be fought out. But you have more faith than I in the people. They are not infallible. People may err as much as men, as individuals and whole communities may err. Can the people of the North be right and the South too? One of the peoples must be wrong....

Your brother,

W. T. SHERMAN. The following letter from John Sherman was written just after the autumn elections, which resulted so disastrously to the Republican party: —

MANSFIELD, OHIO, Not. 16, 1862.

Dear Brother:

Two matters now excite attention among politicians. What is the cause and what will be the effect of the recent elections, and what are we to do about our depreciated paper money. No doubt many causes conspire to defeat the Union parties. The two I will name were the most influential, and yet the least will be said about them.

The first is, that the Republican organization was voluntarily abandoned by the President and his leading followers, and a no-party Union was formed to run against an old, well-drilled party organization. This was simply ridiculous. It was as if you should disband your army organization because it was tyrannical, and substitute the temporary enthusiasm of masses to fight regular armies. Political as well as military organization is necessary to success. Ward meetings, committees, conventions, party cries are just as necessary in politics, as drills, reviews, &c., are in war, so the Republicans have found out. If they have the wisdom to throw overboard the old debris that joined them in the Union movement, they will succeed. If not, they are doomed.

The other prominent reason for defeat is, the people were dissatisfied at the conduct and results of the war. The slow movements on the Potomac and worse still in Kentucky dissatisfied and discouraged people. It was a little singular that the Democrats, some of whom opposed the war, should reap the benefit of this feeling, but such is the fate of parties. Lincoln was a Republican. He put and kept in these slow generals and we shall be punished for it by having an organized opposition limiting appropriations. No doubt the wanton and unnecessary use of the power to arrest without trial and the ill-timed proclamation contributed to the general result. The other matter I allude to is demanding careful consideration. As it is my line of official duty, I have formed certain theories which may be all wrong; but as they are the result of reflection, I will act upon them. My remedy for paper money is, by taxation, to destroy the banks and confine the issue to Government paper. Let this only issue, as it is found to be difficult to negotiate the bonds of the government. As a matter of course there will a time come when this or any scheme of paper money will lead to bankruptcy, but that is the result of war and not of any particular plan of finance. I watch your course closely and take great interest and pride in your success.

Affectionately your brother,

JOHN SHERMAN.

Memphis, Nor. 24, 1862.

Dear Brother: I am just back from Columbus, Ky., where I went to meet Gen. Grant. I start on Wednesday, with all the troops that can be spared from Memphis, to co-operate with Grant against the enemy now enforced behind the Tallahatchie, about 60 miles S.E. of Memphis. Grant may have about 35,000 and I shall take 17,000. Our old regiments are very small, and I am sorry to learn that no recruits are ready to fill them up. So much clamor was raised about the draft that I really was led to believe there was something in it, but now I suppose it was one of those delusions of which the papers are so full. Your letter of the 16th is before me. I could write a good deal on the points that you make, but hardly have time to do them justice. The late election doesn't disturb me a particle. The people have so long been accustomed to think they could accomplish anything by a vote, that they still think so; but now a vote is nothing more than a change and will produce no effect. The war might have been staved off a few years, or the issue might have been made up more clearly, or the first enthusiasm of the country might have been better taken advantage of; but these are now all past, and fault-finding will do no good. We are involved in a war that will try the sincerity of all our professions of endurance, courage and patriotism. Leaders will of course be killed off by the score. Thousands will perish by the bullet or sickness; but war must go on—it can't be stopped. The North must rule or submit to degradation and insult forevermore. The war must now be fought out. The President, Congress, no earthly power can stop it without absolute submission....

Of course I foresaw all these complications at the outset, and was amused at the apathy of the country after the South had begun the war by the seizure of arsenals, forts, mints and public property, and still more at the call for 75,000 volunteers, when a million was the least that any man who had ever been South would have dreamed of. These half-way measures at the start only add labor in the end....

McClernand is announced as forming a grand army to sweep the Mississippi, when, the truth is, he is in Springfield, Ill., trying to be elected to the TJ. S. Senate. I believe at this moment we have more men under pay at home than in the field, and suppose there is no help for it If you want to make a good law, make a simple one, "No work, no pay." No pay unless on duty at the place where the army is. That would save tens of millions per annum.

I leave here the day after to-morrow for Tchullahoma, to communicate with Grant at Holly Springs. Our joint forces should reach near 50,000 men, but sickness and other causes will keep us down to about 40,000.

Yours affectionately,

W. T. SHERMAN.

COLLEGE HILL, MISS., NEAR OXFORD, Dec. 6, 1862.

Dear Brother: I left Memphis Wednesday, Nov. 26, with 26 regiments of Infantry, ten field batteries and one Cavalry regiment. In all about 18,000 men to cooperate with Grant in attacking the enemy, then lying on the south bank of the Tallahatchee, 18 miles south of Holly Springs and about 70 from Memphis. Their strength is estimated from about 40,000 to 50,000 men, under Pemberton, Price, Van Dorn and others. Grant allowed me 4 days to reach Tchullahoma. In 3 days I was near Tallahoosee, when I communicated with him, and next day reached Tchullahoma, he advancing to Waterford. Coincident with our movement, an expedition was planned to move from Helena under Gen. Harvey, to attack or threaten Grenada, about 60 miles to the rear of the position of the enemy. On approaching the Tallahatchee we found it abandoned, although its fords, ferries, and crossing places had been well fortified and obstructed. Grant moved on the main road south from Holly Springs, and I on his right about 10 miles, reaching the river at an old town called Wyatt. I had brought boats with me from Memphis, with which we soon crossed our infantry and cavalry regiments, swimming the horses, and found two long lines of intrenchments about 2 miles back from the river, where there is a kind of neck These were, however, completely abandoned. Sending the Cavalry ahead to co-operate with G-rant, then pressing the rear of the retreating forces, deliberately set to work, built a good bridge, and the day before yesterday I rode forward to Oxford, where I found Grant and received his further orders to cross and occupy College Hill, 4 miles to his right.

I have one division, Dunn's, here, and 2 on Hurricane Creek, to my rear. We have had two days' hard rain and snow, making the roads very bad. Indeed, since the building of the railroad, the mud roads, leading north and south are disused and are washed very badly, the country resembling that about Somerset, Ohio. We find plenty of corn, fodder, cattle, hogs, sheep, &c., so that our enemies have not been starving. Salt is scarce, but they are manufacturing it largely on the coast, and at well about Mobile. By our movement, we have for the time being cleared North Mississippi. I doubt if we shall proceed much further on this line, as operations should now proceed against Vicksburg and Yazoo. I hear nothing from Virginia or Kentucky. We are far ahead of them, and they should push up....

I suppose you hear little of me. I allow no reporters about. My official reports go to the proper office, and thus the enemy shall learn nothing of my forces, plans or purposes, through an egotistical and corrupt press....

Yours affectionately,

W. T. SHERMAN.

General Sherman sent to his brother copies of the orders he received from Grant before his [Sherman's] attack on Vicksburg. He also sent the following "Remarks/' which have never been published, and which were written by him in response to the severe criticisms of the press after the failure of his attempt: —

REMARKS

I put the division of M. L. Smith in motion the next day (9th Dec.) and in the three succeeding days we marched into Memphis arriving there the 12th. Forthwith sent special aids to Helena to which point Curtis' forces detached to Grenada had returned (to Columbus, Ky.), communicated daily to Gen. Grant progress made and fixed the 18th to embark. I got some boats in Memphis, loaded them with ammunition, provisions and forage in advance, calculating for 30,000 men for 40 days. I reported promptly the fact that by combining the Memphis and Helena forces and deducting the garrisons ordered, I could not make up more than 30,000 men. I reported the same fact to Halleck. I could not get the boats to embark at Memphis until the 20th and at Helena the 22nd, but I had appointed Christmas day to reach the mouth of the Yazoo and did it, detaching portions on my way down to break the very important railroad leading from Vicksburg to Texas finished out 100 miles to Monroe, La., and running three trains a day. Arrived at the mouth of the Yazoo I met all the Havy officers who had been running up and down for months. All agreed we could not land at Haines Bluff on account of the batteries and torpedoes. The only practicable landing place where we could emerge was at or near Johnson's plantation. All agreed on this, but no one knew 'of the road or roads leading back to Vicksburg save that there had been roads, and the distance was seven miles. I examined all the maps, questioned all the officers and negroes and then announced, in orders, the time, place and manner of landing, marching and fighting. G-rant had been advised of all my movements and his orders were "as soon as possible," naming to me the 18th. I had no reason to doubt that he would soon be heard of. I once did hear from a negro that the Yankees had got to Yazoo city. Had that been true we could have succeeded. Same of Banks coming up. My instructions never contemplated my taking Vicksburg alone. It was ridiculous, but I supposed every hour and minute I might hear Grant's guns to the north and Banks' south. Grant was, it appears, by rain and the acts of the enemy compelled to fall back of where I had left him and had no means of sending me word. I urged the attack because, from the masses of the enemy I saw and the sounds of cars coming 20 and 30 times a day, I felt the enemy was receiving large reinforcements. I know the attack was made on the best point and those who say otherwise don't know the ground. I do, having examined each spot in person by night and day. On the point of the real attack, the head of the Chickasaw Bayou, I had assembled all of Morgan's and Steele's divisions, more than half my whole force, and as many men as could be assembled on that ground. The other divisions at the same time also were actually engaged, though Morgan and Blair did not think so because they could not see and hear it, but I did....

It is not so that the troops were injured by my management. They were re-embarked as soon as such a thing could be done. We went by Millikin's bend to Arkansas Post, where as usual I had to lead and back again here before Banks can be heard of or Grant's troops have come up even by water. Grant is now here in command, well satisfied that I fulfilled his orders to the letter, only that he was unable to co-operate until too late.

Yours,

SHERMAN.

The city of Vicksburg occupied a well-nigh impregnable position on the east bank of the Mississippi, and its possession was considered absolutely essential to success by both armies. Early in December, 1862, General Sherman was ordered to Memphis to organize the forces there and to proceed down the river to Vicksburg. The plan was for Sherman, acting in conjunction with the naval force on the river, to attack and surprise Vicksburg, while Grant held in check the bulk of the rebel forces under General Pemberton, to the north of the city. General Banks, who had been sent to supersede General Butler at New Orleans, had meanwhile been ordered up the river. So Sherman made his attack on the city, expecting the co-operation of General Grant from the north and General Banks from the south. The attack was unsuccessful, as neither Grant nor Banks was able to co-operate with Sherman. The following letters refer to this attack: —

Memphis, Dec. 14, 1862.

Dear Brother: I am back in Memphis, having been charged by Gen. Grant to organize the forces here and such as may he assigned from Helena, and to proceed to Vicksburg and reduce that place and co-operate with Grant, whom I left at Oxford, Miss. He expected I would have 40,000 but I cannot count on more than 30,000, but expect if steamers arrive according to the design, by the 18th to embark for that destination. The move is one of vast importance and if successful will remove the obstacles to the navigation of the Mississippi, although it will as long as war lasts be a source of contention. I take it that now Vicksburg is fortified by land and water, and that it is a difficult task, but it must be undertaken. Things are not exactly right. Grant commands on this side, Curtis on the west and Admiral Porter on the River. All ought to be under one head, but thus far I meet the heartiest co-operation and I feel certain that we will all act in concert. Our move on the Tallahatchee was well planned and well executed. Though we had no battles yet the enemy had made every preparation for a determined resistance at the Tallahatchee, but were completely disconcerted by the move on their flank and rear from Helena, which was entirely unexpected. The country between the Yazoo and Mississippi is all alluvial and a few hours' rain renders the roads impassable to artillery, but fortunately the weather was good and all our forces reached their appointed places on time and the result accomplished the object without battle. The retreat of the Confederate army was rapid and confused and the effect was equal to a victory. Grant now has a well appointed army at Oxford, Miss., with which he will move south as soon as I am in position at Vicksburg. It is very difficult to keep up communications, as his railroad reaches the Mississippi at Columbus, Ky., and the river is lower than it was ever known at this season, so that navigation is very difficult. The country is full of guerilla bands so that couriers cannot be relied on across the country 75 miles. I will try and reach Vicksburg by a certain date, and will have Grant advised so that though far apart our movements will be in concert....

These surrenders of Harper's Perry, Mumfordsville, and Hartsville illustrate the danger of detachments. It is idle to talk about blaming the officers. These were the very loudest in boasting of their prowess, and their destruction don't cure the facts. All the orders won't stop it. Our people are taught insubordination and independence, and when confused and disordered their commanders are helpless....

I will only have one of my old Divisions, Morgan L. Smith's, but will rely much on the enthusiasm attached to this peculiar expedition....

W. T. S.

Memphis, Dec. 20th, 1862.

Dear Brother: I embarked to-day on the Forest Queen and will have 20,000 men in boats by noon and be off for the real South. At Helena I will get about 12,000 more. Like most of our boasts of the "Myriads of the northwest sweeping away to the G-ulf," "breaking the back bone," &c. &c., the great Mississippi expedition will be 32,000 men. Vicksburg is well fortified and is within telegraphic and railroad reach of Meridian, Mobile, Camp Moore and Grenada, where Pemberton has 30,000 to 35,000 men. Therefore don't expect me to achieve miracles. Vicksburg is not the only thing to be done. Grant is at Coffeeville! (?) with say 40,000 men. He expected me to have the same but they are not here. We can get the Yazoo, can front in any and every direction and can take Vicksburg, clean out the Yazoo, capture or destroy the fleet of enemy's gunboats and transports concealed up about Yazoo city — and do many other useful things. Blair is down at Helena and will doubtless form a part of the expedition. He will have a chance of catching the Elephant by the tail and get a good lift.

Of course the pressure of this force acting in concert with Grant must produce good results. Even if we don't open the Mississippi, by the way an event not so important as at first sight, until the great armies of the enemy are defeated — we are progressing. I wish Burnside and

Rosecrans were getting along faster, but I suppose they encounter the same troubles we all do....

The great evil is absenteeism, which is real desertion and should be punished with death. Of course I would have the wounded and sick well cared for, but the sick list real and feigned is fearful. More than one-half the paper army is not in the enemy's country and whilst the actual regiments present for duty are in arrears of pay and favor, sick and discharged men are carefully paid and provided for. Unite with others and discriminate in favor of the officers and soldiers who are with their companies. The "absent and sick" should receive half pay because of the advantages they receive of fine hospitals and quiet residence at home. The "absent without leave" should be treated as deserters and in no event receive a dollar's pay—clothing or anything else. In course of time we may get an army. Finance is very important but no use of discussing that now; we must fight it out if it devastates the land and costs every cent of the North....

I rise at 3 a m. to finish up necessary business and as usual write in haste.... I am very popular with the people here and officers and indeed with all my men. I don't seek popularity with the "sneaks and absentees" or the "Dear People."...

Affectionately,

W. **T. SHERMAN.**

WASHINGTON, January 2d, 1863.

My Dear Brother: We are watching with the most eager interest the progress of your expedition. We all hope its success wall brighten the gloom cast by operations here. If the Mississippi can only be opened and Texas and Arkansas detached it will be a gleam of hope by which I can see the end of the war. Without an outlet to the South and West and with such a blockade as we can easily keep up, the Southern Confederacy cannot exist. This will settle the cotton question, for Texas and Arkansas can with the free labor that can easily be thrown there grow enough cotton for the world — another ground of hope. Banks and yourself I regard as the best officers we have....

I have always believed in you even when you were under a cloud. If you and Banks can act harmoniously and actively together you are able to do more than any two men in the continent.

By the way, Banks is a reserved man, not from pride or over self-confidence, but from the defects of a limited education and from a sensitiveness this unnecessarily gives him. The more you know him the better you will like him. He and I are warm friends. We became early attached in his famous contest for speaker when I first entered Congress. Although new in political life, I *stuck* to him when his prospects were dark, and ever since then there has been a sincere friendship between us, although we have not often met. This feeling I know will *warm* him towards you, and his abilities will excite your respect. I write this in anticipation of your meeting and having to co-operate with him....

This Government has to be maintained and I now look to you and Banks as the "men of promise." I do not favor the Bankrupt Law as you suppose, and I can't conceive how you got that idea unless because I presented petitions. I am occasionally asked for letters to you. I generally decline, except where refusal would wound a valued friend.

Affectionately yours,

JOHN SHERMAN.

STEAMER FOREST QUEEN, Jan. 6, 1863.

Dear Brother: You will have heard of our attack on Vicksburg and failure to succeed. The place is too strong, and without the co-operation of a large army coming from the interior it is impracticable. Innumerable batteries prevent the approach of gun boats to the city or to the first bluff up the Yazoo, and the only landing between is on an insular space of low boggy ground, with innumerable bayous or deep sloughs. I did all that was possible to reach the main land, but was met at every point by batteries and rifle pits that we could not pass, and in the absence of Gen. Grant's co-operating force I was compelled to re-embark my command. My report to Gen. Grant, a copy of which I sent to Gen. Halleck, who will let you see it, is very full, and more than I could write to you with propriety. Whatever you or the absent may think, not a soldier or officer who was present but will admit I pushed the attack as far as prudence would justify, and that I re-embarked my command in the nick of time, for a heavy rain set in which would have swamped us and made it impossible to withdraw artillery and stores. Up to that time I was acting as the right wing of Gen. Grant's army; but Gen. McClernand has arrived, and we now have a new organization, — McClernand commanding the whole, and our present force divided into two commands, or *corps d'armée,* one of which. is commanded by me and one by Morgan of Cumberland Gap. We are now *en route* for the Arkansas. Up that river about 50 miles the enemy is entrenched and has sent down to the Mississippi and captured two steamboats, conveying to the fleets supplies. How it is unwise to leave such a force on our rear and flank, and inasmuch as General Grant is not prepared to march down to Vicksburg by land, we can attack this post of Arkansas and maybe reach Little Bock. Success in this quarter will have a good effect on the main river. But in the end Vicksburg must be reduced, and it is going to be a bard nut to crack. It is the strongest place I ever saw, both by nature and art; and so far as we could observe it is defended by a competent force of artillery, infantry and cavalry. Besides its railroad connections with the interior give them great advantages....

My orders from Grant were to leave Memphis by the 18th, and I got off the 20th and I was exactly on time to co-operate with Grant. I did not know that he was delayed by the breaking of his railroad communications to his rear. Indeed, I supposed him to be advancing south towards the Yazoo River. My entire force was and was every man I could raise at Memphis and Helena, and Grant and Halleck were fully advised of my strength and plans. I suppose you are now fully convinced of the stupendous energy of the South and their ability to prolong this war indefinitely, but I am further satisfied that if it lasts 30 years we must fight it out, for the moment the North relaxes its energies the South will assume the offensive and it is wonderful how well disciplined and provided they have their men. We found everywhere abundant supplies, even on the Yazoo, and all along the river we found cattle, and fat ones, feeding quietly. The country everywhere abounds with corn, and the soldiers, though coarsely, are well clad. We hear of the manufacture of all sorts of cloth and munitions of war. The river plantations are mostly abandoned, and all families, negroes, stock and cotton removed 25 miles back....

Affectionately,

W. T. Sherman.

Arkansas Post (Port Hindman) was captured January 11, 1863, and this ended the expedition up the Arkansas.

The letter of January 25th finds General Sherman back again near Vicksburg.

NAPOLEON, ARK., STEAMER FOREST QUEEN, Jan. 17, 1863.

Dear Brother:... The gun boats were handled beautifully, and without them we should have had hard work, with them it was easy. Our entire loss will be less than 1000. We took 5000 prisoners, killed and wounded some 500, took 16 guns, ammunition, com and wagons, mules and all sorts of traps of which you will hear enough. My official report is in, will go up to Grant at Memphis to-morrow and right on to Washington. Halleck will let you see it, and you can understand the whole thing by a glance at the maps I send along. But McClernand's reports will precede it and of course will be the accepted history....

On the supposition that Banks will have taken Port Hudson and reached Vicksburg, we start back for that place to-morrow. Of ourselves we cannot take Vicksburg. With Banks and a fleet below us and a fleet above, we may make a desperate attempt, but Vicksburg is as strong as Gibraltar, and is of vital importance to the cause of the South. Of course they will fight desperately for it. We must do the same, for all are conscious that the real danger of the war, anarchy among our people, begins to dawn. The people of the North mistake widely if they suppose they can have peace now by opposing this war....

Mr. Lincoln intended to insult me and the military profession by putting McClernand over me, and I would have quietly folded up my things and gone to St. Louis, only I know in times like these all must submit to insult and infamy if necessary. The very moment I think some other is at hand to take my corps Til slide out....

I hope the politicians will not interfere with Halleck. You have driven off McClellan, and is Burnside any better? Buell is displaced. Is Rosecrans any faster? His victory at Murfreesboro is dearly bought. Let Halleck alone, and if things don't go to your liking don't charge it to men but to the condition of things. Human power is limited, and you cannot appreciate the difficulty of moulding into an homogeneous machine the discordant elements which go to make up our armies. A thousand dollars a day would not pay me for the trouble of managing a volunteer army. I never dreamed of so severe a test of my patriotism as being superseded by McClernand, and if I can keep down my tamed (?) spirit and live I will claim a virtue higher than Brutus. I rarely see a newspaper and am far behind the times, indeed, am not conscious that a Congress sits, though I know it must. Do think of the army and try and give us the means to maintain discipline, prevent desertion, pillage and absenteeism. Under the present system of mere threats and no punishment, our armies melt away like snow before the sun. I doubt if Burnside, Rosecrans, Grant and Curtis now have, all combined, 300,000 in their front ranks. This army, 30,000 a month ago, though reinforced by 2400 men, is now down to 24,000, though we have lost only 2500 in battle — sickness and detachments make a perfect stream to the rear. Blair has a brigade in my corps and sees now the practices of war as contrasted with its theory, and could give some useful hints on these points.

Affectionately,

W. **T. SHERMAN.**

CAMP NEAR VICKSBURG, Jan. 25, 1863.

Dear Brother: I received yours of Jan. 2, to-day, and being in camp with some leisure hasten to answer. I shall be glad to meet Gen. Banks on many accounts, because of his known intelligence and high character and because we have been long expecting him. I was hurried down the river with positive orders to get away from

Memphis December 18, to co-operate with Grant to come down by land and Banks to ascend the river. I was on time and made every effort to carry Vicksburg, but unsuccessfully. Hearing nothing from Banks or Grant, and being superseded by McClernand, I proposed that we should go to the Arkansas and attack the Post from which the enemy threatened our rear and line of communications. We succeeded perfectly there, and General Grant came down and met us at Napoleon and hurried us back to Vicksburg, on the theory that Banks might be here, disappointed at our non-appearance.

So here we are again, but not a word of Banks. This time instead of landing up the Yazoo we have landed on the Louisiana side and I occupy a neck of low ground enclosed with a high levee directly in front of Vicksburg. Last summer when Vicksburg was invested by our troops from below a canal was dug across a narrow neck with the purpose of turning the river so as to leave Vicksburg out in the cold. The river is now rising rapidly and already fills the canal, which however is a narrow ditch — the water flows across it, but thus far it shows no symptoms of cutting a channel, but, on the contrary, threatens to overflow the low ground embraced in the levee. All my soldiers are busy day and night in throwing up a levee on the inside of this canal to prevent the water overflowing us. My right extends along the levee below Vicksburg, and I have some guns below, which will prevent the enemy's boats coming up to town. Since I broke the railroad leading west most of the necessary supplies to Vicksburg have come from Red River by water, and we now stop this; but as they hold Port Hudson, preventing Banks coming up, and Vicksburg prevents our boats going down, they hold substantially a long reach of the river embracing the mouth of Red River. Last night my extreme right brigade, Blair's, captured a ferry boat which came in for wood, not suspecting our presence. So we have also our boat below Vicksburg—I have not much faith in the canal. It starts after the current has been turned, and I doubt if the canal will draw in a volume and depth of water sufficient to cut a new channel, and if it do the enemy will simply shift his guns to Warrenton, a point on the same range of hills, below the mouth of our canal — at last we must attack the enemy in his strong position.

Outnumbering us in every sense in men, in guns, and holding a position stronger than Gibraltar....

We must get on land before we can fight. That was my attempt and the point I chose is the only one between Vicksburg and Haines Bluff—we may attempt the latter, and I think it is the safest place, but on this side of the river we do no good whatever, for the Mississippi is an ugly stream to ford at this season of the year.

Unless you enact a law denying to all citizens between the ages of 18 and 45 who do not enlist and serve 3 years faithfully, all right of suffrage, or to hold office after the war is over, you will have trouble. The Army growls a good deal at the apathy of the nation, at home quite comfortable and happy yet pushing them forward on all sorts of desperate expeditions. Newspapers can now turn armies against their leaders. Every officer and soldier knows I pushed the attack on Vicksburg as far as they wanted to venture, and if others think differently, they naturally say, Why not come down and try?...

Two years have passed and the rebel flag still haunts our nation's capital — our armies enter the best rebel territory and the wave closes in behind, scarcely leaving a furrow mark behind. The utmost we can claim is that our enemy respects our power to do them physical harm more than they did at first; but as to loving us any more, it were idle even to claim it. Our armies are devastating the land and it is sad to see the destruction that attends our progress — we cannot help it. Farms disappear, houses are burned and plundered, and every living animal killed and eaten. General officers make feeble efforts to stay the disorder, but it is idle....

The South abounds in corn, cattle and provisions and the progress in manufacturing shoes and cloth for the soldiers is wonderful. They are as well supplied as we and they have an abundance of the best cannon, arms and ammunition. In long range cannon they rather excel us and their regiments are armed with the very best Enfield rifles and cartridges, put up at Glasgow, Liverpool and their new Southern armories, and I still say they have now as large armies in the field as we. They give up cheerfully all they have. I still see no end or even the beginning of the end....

The early actors and heroes of the war will be swept away, and those who study its progress, its developments, and divine its course and destiny will be most appreciated. We are in for the war, and must fight it out, cost what it may. As to making popularity out of it, it is simply ridiculous and all who attempt it will be swept as chaff before the wind....

Tour affectionate brother,

W. T. SHERMAN.

WASHINGTON, D.C., Jan. 27, 1863.

Dear Brother: The pressure of official duties here prevented my writing sooner, but I have kept a watchful eye on all your movements recently.

I have not the slightest hesitation in justifying every movement you have made. The newspapers are generally down on you and will command the public attention to your prejudice, but intelligent persons do not fail to notice that not a specific allegation is made against you. The authorities sustain your actions throughout. This is especially so as to the Secretary of War. I read your official report, and was very anxious to have it published. It would correct many errors and would be a complete justification and explanation of many things not understood.

I asked Gen. Halleck to allow me to publish it. He declined, unless the Secretary of War consented, and said he would submit my application to the Secretary. Afterwards I saw the Secretary, and he told me he had directed a copy of the report to be furnished for publication. I again called at Halleck, and saw Gen. Cullum, who objected to the publication of the report on various grounds.

After a full conversation with Cullum, I supposed I had satisfied him that it ought to be published, and he agreed to submit my reasons to Halleck and ask a reconsideration. This morning I received a note from Halleck stating that, as further operations would occur before Vicksburg, he did not deem it advisable to publish the report at present. Thus the matter ends. Cullum stated to me that there was no officer of the army who did not entirely justify your attack on

Vicksburg under the circumstances as you supposed them to be. In the end you will be justified in public opinion.

Military affairs look dark here in the army of the Potomac. Burnside is relieved and Hooker is in command. The entire army seems demoralized. Perhaps when it is ready to move it may be all right. A certain amount of dissatisfaction always will exist in an army. I was very glad to notice that you were popular with and had the confidence of your men. This is the case with but few officers. I deeply pity Porter....

If we recover from the folly of legislators and the quarrels of our generals, it will be evidence of vitality, remarkable in the history of any nation. I believe we shall survive all these dangers, and I agree with you that no course is left for us but to fight it out. I cannot respect some of the constituted authorities, yet I will cordially support and aid them while they are authorized to administer the government. Pray write me as often as you can.

Affectionately yours,

John SHERMAN.

HEADQUARTERS, 15th ARMY CORPS, CAMP BEFORE VICKSBURG, Feb. , 1863.

Dear Brother:

Continental, the headquarters of Generals Steele and Blair, gives to these general officers and their division undue praise, and libels and abuses all others. This not only plays into the hands of our enemies by sowing dissensions among us, but it encourages discontent among the officers who find themselves abused by men seemingly under the influence of officers high in command. I caused Knox's communication to be read to him, paragraph by paragraph, and then showed him my instructions, by my orders made at the time, and the official reports of others, and how wide he was of the truth. And now I have asked his arrest and trial by General Grant, on charges as a spy and informer. The 57th Article of war, which is a Law of Congress, is as follows: Who shall be convicted of holding correspondence with, or giving intelligence to the enemy, either directly or indirectly, shall suffer death, &c." I will endeavor to bring in all the facts, by means of the evidence of officers who took part in all these events. My purpose is not to bring Knox to death or other severe punishment, but I do want to establish the principle that citizens shall not, against the orders of the competent military superior, attend a military expedition, report its proceedings, and comment on its officers....

Affectionately your Brother,

W. **T. SHERMAN.**

In the above letter to John Sherman, General Sherman enclosed the following copy of General Orders No. 67, in regard to the giving of intelligence to the enemy, together with his own comments upon them.

GENERAL ORDERS NO. 67.

By the 57th Article of the Act of Congress entitled an Act for establishing Buies and Articles for the Government of the Armies of the United States approved April 10, 1806, "Holding correspondence with or giving intelligence to the enemy either directly or indirectly is made punishable by death or such other punishment as shall be ordered by the sentence of a Court Martial. Public safety requires strict enforcement of this article. It is therefore ordered that all correspondence and communication, verbally or by writing, printing, or telegraphing, respecting operations of the Army, or military movements on land or water, or respecting the troops, camps, arsenals, intrenchments, or military affairs within the several military districts by which intelligence shall be directly or indirectly given to the enemy, without the authority and sanction of the General in command, be and the same are absolutely prohibited, and from and after the date of this order, persons violating the same will be proceeded against under the 57th Article of War." By order L. Thomas, Adjt.-General.

... Now, to every army and almost every general a newspaper reporter goes along, filling up our transports, swelling our trains, reporting our progress, guessing at places, picking up dropped expressions, inciting jealousy and discontent, and doing infinite mischief. We are commanded absolutely to proceed against them under the 57th article of war. Shall the laws of Congress be obeyed? Shall the orders of the War Department be respected? Or shall the press go on sweeping everything before it....

The press has now killed McClellan, Buell, Fitz-John Porter, Sumner, Franklin, and Burnside. Add my name and I am not ashamed of the association. If the press can govern the country, let them fight the battles.

CAMP BEFORE VICKSBURG, Feb. 12, 1863.

Dear Brother: I have hitherto sent you original papers or copies to satisfy any one of the falsehood of the attacks against me in the late Vicksburg matter. I had a newspaper reporter arrested and tried by a court-martial, but by the rulings of the court I infer they are of opinion that to make the accused come within the order of the War Department the fact should be proven that the very substance of the objectionable matter went to the enemy. I have been unable to find the identical matter, but in every Southern paper I get I find abundance of evidence to show that Northern papers furnish the Southern leaders abundant and timely notice of every movement. I send you two to show this fact. In the Vicksburg "Whig" (?), at the bottom of the last column of the first page you will see that it states positively that a correspondent of one of the Northern journals wrote *in advance of* the federal plans in the late move on Vicksburg. Had they received three days notice of our coming to the Post of Arkansas, they could have so reinforced that it would have cost us a siege. But then we were beyond the power of the press and succeeded. And so it must ever be. These newspaper correspondents hanging about the skirts of our army reveal all plans, and are worth a hundred thousand men to the enemy....

I have no faith in the canal here, save we may enlarge it to pass supplies for gunboats below, which will enable the latter to keep supplies from Vicksburg, via the river, but we in no wise threatened Vicksburg, for the bluffs extended many miles below the outlet of the canal. The river is bank full and threatens to overflow our camps — but I have more faith in the efforts above at Yazoo Pass and Lake Providence. The former may admit us to the Yazoo from above and the latter may open a channel down the Tensas to Red, or by Atchafalaya below Port Hudson. If Banks had orders to meet me at Vicksburg on Christmas he has been slow of execution, for I cannot hear that he has even felt of Port Hudson. At all events we have not heard from him save via New York. Grant is now up at Lake Providence, McClernand and my corps are here in sight of Vicksburg, but the great Mississippi flows between us.

Affectionately your brother,

W. T. SHERMAN.

CAMP *before* **VICKSBURG,** Ten. 18, 1863.

My Dear Brother: We have reproached the South for arbitrary conduct in coercing their people — at last we find we must imitate their example. We have denounced their tyranny in filling their armies with conscripts, and now we must follow her example. We have denounced their tyranny in suppressing freedom of speech and the press, and here too in time we must follow their example. The longer it is deferred the worse it becomes. Who gave notice of McDowell's movement on Manassas, and enabled Johnston so to reinforce Beauregard that our army was defeated? The press. Who gave notice of the movement on Vicksburg? The press. Who has prevented all secret combinations and movements against our enemy? The press....

In the South this powerful machine was at once scotched and used by the rebel government, but at the North was allowed to go free. What are the results? After arousing the passions of the people till the two great sections hate each other with a hate hardly paralleled in history, it now begins to stir up sedition at home, and even to encourage mutiny in our armies. What has paralyzed the Army of the Potomac? Mutual jealousies kept alive by the press. What has enabled the enemy to combine so as to hold Tennessee after we have twice crossed it with victorious armies? What defeats and will continue to defeat our best plans here and elsewhere? The press. I cannot pick up a paper but tells of our situation here, in the mud, sickness, and digging a canal in which we have little faith. But our officers attempt secretly to cut two other channels — one into Yazoo

153

by an old pass and one through Lake Providence into Tensas, Black, Bed, &e., whereby we could turn not only Vicksburg, Port Hudson, but also Grand (Gulf), Natchez, Ellis Cliff, Fort Adams and all the strategic points on the main river, and the busy agents of the press follow up and proclaim to the world the whole thing, and instead of surprising our enemy we find him felling trees and blocking passages that would without this have been in our possession, and all the real effects of surprise are lost. I say with the press unfettered as now we are defeated to the end of time. Tis folly to say the people must have news. Every soldier can and does write to his family and friends, and all have ample opportunities for so doing, and this pretext forms no good reason why agents of the press should reveal prematurely all our plans and designs. We cannot prevent it. Clerks of steamboats, correspondents in disguise or openly attend each army and detachment, and presto! appear in Memphis and St. Louis minute accounts of our plans and designs. These reach Vicksburg by telegraph from Hernando and Holly Springs before we know of it. The only two really successful military strokes out here have succeeded because of the absence of newspapers, or by throwing them off the trail. Halleck had to make a simulated attack on Columbus to prevent the press giving notice of Jus intended move against Forts Henry and Donelson. We succeeded in reaching the Post of Arkansas before the correspondents could reach the papers.

Affectionately,

SHERMAN.

During this time John Sherman writes to his brother, urging him to be more moderate in his dealings with the newspaper men, and protesting against his threats of retiring, which have given him grave concern.

CAMP BEFORE VICKSBURG, March 14, '63.

Dear Brother:

The Conscript Bill is all even I could ask, it is the first real step toward war. And if Mr. Lincoln will now use the power thus conferred, ignore popular clamor and do as near right as he can, we may at last have an army somewhat approximating the vast undertaking which was begun in utter, blind, wilful ignorance of the difficulties and dangers that we were forced to encounter....

I have been much pleased with your course in Congress, and regret that anything I have done or may do has given you trouble or concern. I could easily have been popular, as I believe I am with my own command, by courting the newspaper men; but it does go hard to know that our camps are full of spies revealing our most secret steps, conveying regularly to the enemy our every act, when a thousand dollars won't procure us a word of information from Vicksburg. I know the press has defeated us, and will continue to do it, and as an honest man I cannot flatter them. I know they will ruin me, but they will ruin the country too....

Napoleon himself would have been defeated with a free press. But I will honestly try to be patient, though I know in this, as in other matters, time *must* bring about its true result, just as the summer ripens the fruits of the season....

My corps is alone here at the neck opposite Vicksburg, fighting off the water of the Mississippi which threatens to drown us. Grant is here on board a boat and Admiral Porter at the mouth of Yazoo.

Affectionately,

W. T. SHERMAN.

And on March 20, 1863, John Sherman writes from his home in Mansfield, Ohio: —

Dear Brother: I am at length at home with sufficient leisure to think, but still somewhat jaded from a very laborious session. When I went into the Senate I anticipated quiet and dignified leisure with ample time to read, reflect and study such grave questions of politics as I chose to turn my attention to. Such thus far has not been my experience. The vast and complicated legislature required by war, demands of Senators an amount of labor in committees never before given. The Senate has become a laborious committee where bills are drawn as well as discussed. It has so happened that although a junior yet I have had to carry the most important financial bills, such as the Bank Loan and Tax Bills, subjects full of difficulty and detail....

The laws passed at the last session will be a monument of evil or of good. They cover such vast sums, delegate and regulate such vast powers, and are so far-reaching in their effects, that generations will be affected well or ill by them. These measures are distinguished as much by what were omitted as by what were adopted. The negro was not legislated upon. The laws of confiscation, emancipation, &c., were left precisely upon the basis of previous laws, the proclamations of the President and ultimate decisions of the courts. The arming and employment of negroes is left upon the old law and mainly to the discretion of the President. There was but little speech-making and that mainly to the matter in hand. The Union or rather Republican members made scarcely a political speech in either house. They felt too constantly the pressure of practical measures demanding action. On the whole, the recent Congress may fairly appeal to their constituents for a favorable judgment upon the general aggregate of their acts. For myself, I do not reproach myself with any glaring fault.

I opposed arbitrary arrests, general confiscation, the destruction of State lines and other extreme measures, and thereby have lost the confidence of some of my old friends. On the other hand, I have taken my full share in framing and supporting other great measures that have proved a success, and think I may fairly claim credit for many of the most valuable features of our financial system, which has been wonderfully sustained under enormous expenditure. I can also claim the paternity of the Bank Law yet to be tested by experience, and for the main features of the Conscription Law. This latter law is vital to our success, and although it was adopted with fear and trembling and only after all other expedients failed, yet I am confident it will be enforced with the general acquiescence of the people and that through it we see the road to peace. But after all, Congress cannot help us out of our difficulties. It may by its acts and omissions prolong the war, but there is no solution to it except through the military forces. The people have got beyond the first danger of the war. They no longer underrate the power of the

Confederates and no longer expect a short or holiday war. When coming home at Philadelphia, and in the cars, and here among plain people I find a healthy feeling. They want peace. But very few would accept it on any other terms than the preservation of the Union. They know very well that the South will only yield to this after being thoroughly whipped, and this has not been done.

I am very much rejoiced that you did not act upon your hasty impressions about resigning. The history of your Vicksburg expedition is now well understood and you stand well with all classes.

Most of the papers who joined in the clamor against you have corrected their statements. You never lost the confidence of the department and especially of Stanton and Halleck....

Affectionately yours,

JOHN SHERMAN.

CAMP BEFORE VICKSBURG, April 3, '63.

My Dear Brother: I received your long letter from Mansfield, for which I am much obliged. You certainly have achieved an envious name in the Senate, and I confess I am astonished at your industry and acquirements. I readily understand how, in a revolution of the magnitude that now involves us all, older men should devolve on you and the younger school of men the legislation and experiments necessary to meet a state of facts so different from the common run of events. The Finance Bill and Conscription Acts of the late Congress in my judgment may keep the management of the affairs of the nation in the hands of the Constitutional Government. Anything short of them, the war would have drifted out of the control of President and Congress. Now if Mr. Lincoln will assume the same position that Davis did at the outset he can unite the fighting [North against the fighting South, and numerical force systematized will settle the war. I know the impatience of the people, but this is one of the lessons of war. People must learn that war is a question of physical force and courage. A million of men engaged in peaceful pursuits will be vanquished by a few thousand determined armed men. The justice of the cause has nothing to do

157

with it. It is a question of force. Again we are the assailants, and have to overcome not only an equal number of determined men, however wrongfully engaged, but the natural obstacles of a most difficult country....

They [i e. newspaper correspondents] are unknown to me, appear in disguise of sutlers clerks, cotton thieves and that class of vultures that hang around every army. I never saw or heard of Knox till he had published his falsehoods; and when I did send for him, and he admitted how false he had been, he enunciated the sentiment that his trade was to collect news — he must furnish reading matter for sale, true, if possible; otherwise, false....

It is absurd to say these correspondents relieve the anxiety of parents, friends, &e. My soldiers write constantly and receive immense numbers of letters. This is right, and if newspapers will report only local matters and discuss matters within their knowledge, parents and families would not be kept half frantic with the accounts of sickness, death, massacres, &c., of their children and relatives. We have hundreds of visitors from every quarter to examine our camps, because correspondents represented us as all dying, when the truth is no army was ever better provided for and supplied. We are camped on narrow slips of levee and ground, because all else is under water. To get on dry ground we must go back to Memphis or Helena....

McPherson is a splendid officer. Grant is honest and does his best. I will do as ordered. I will suggest little, as others talk of my failing to take Vicksburg and I want them to try a hand....

Affectionately,

W. T. SHERMAN.

CAMP BEFORE VICKSBURG, April 10, 1863.

Dear Brother:

Mr. Dana is here. He spent a few hours with me yesterday, and I went over with him many of the events of the past year, with the maps and records with which I am well supplied. Indeed, all look to me for maps and facts. Dana remarked to one of Grant's staff incidentally, that he was better pleased with me than he could possibly have expected. In the two days he has been here he has seen an illustration of the truth of my proposition, which has drawn on me such volumes of abuse. We have had thousands of men working by night, putting batteries as close up to Vicksburg as possible, *secretly*, and in opening a channel by which we may in high water reach the river twenty-five miles below Vicksburg. Secrecy *was* essential, but the papers of Memphis announce the whole fact. I know the Memphis dailies go before daylight each day to Hernando, 25 miles, and are telegraphed to Vicksburg by noon of the same day. Indeed, the day before yesterday we met some Vicksburg officers, who asked that I should come with a flag of truce to discuss a point as to exchange of prisoners, and as we parted, one, a Major Watts, asked me not to open our batteries (the secret) last night, as he was going to have a party and did not want to be disturbed....

Nothing can prevent the fatal practice, but excluding all men from our camp but men who *must* fight. They at least have a personal interest in what should be revealed and what concealed....

Affectionately,

W. **T. SHERMAN.**

CAMP BEFORE VICKSBURG, April 23, 1863.

Dear Brother: I have noticed in the Conscript Act the clauses which empowered the President to consolidate the ten companies of a regiment into five, when the aggregate was below one-half the maximum standard, and to reduce the officers accordingly. Had I dreamed that this was going to be made universal, I should have written you and begged you for the love of our ruined country to implore Lincoln to spare us this last and fatal blow. Two years of costly war have enabled the North to realize the fact that by organized and disciplined armies alone can she hope to restore the old and found a new empire. We had succeeded in making the skeletons of armies, eliminating out of the crude materials that first came forth the worthless material, and had just begun to have some good young colonels, captains, sergeants and corporals. And Congress had passed the Conscript Bill, which would have enabled the President to fill up these skeleton regiments full of privates who soon, from their fellows, and with experienced officers, would make an army capable of marching and being handled and directed. But to my amazement comes this order.... This is a far worse defeat than Manassas. Mr. Wade, in his report to condemn McClellan, gave a positive assurance to the army that henceforth, instead of fighting with diminishing ranks, we should feel assured that the gaps made by the bullet, by disease, desertion, &c., would be promptly filled, whereas only such parts of the Conscript Law as tend to weaken us are enforced, viz.: 5 per cent for furlough and 50 per cent of officers and non-commissioned officers discharged to consolidate regiments. Even Blair is amazed at this. He protests the order cannot be executed, and we should appeal to Mr. Lincoln, whom he still insists has no desire to destroy the army. But the order is positive and I don't see how we can hesitate. G-rant started to-day down to Carthage, and I have written to him, which may stave it off for a few days, but I tremble at the loss of so many young and good officers, who have been hard at work for two years, and now that they begin to see how to take care of soldiers, must be turned out....

If not too late, do, for mercy's sake, exhaust your influence to stop this consolidation of regiments. Fill all the regiments with conscripts, and if the army is then too large disband the regiments that prefer to serve north of the Potomac and the Ohio. Keep the war South at all hazards. If this Consolidation Law is literally enforced, and no new draft is made, this campaign is over. And the outside world will have a perfect right to say our Government is afraid of its own people....

Affectionately yours,

W. T. SHERMAN.

CHAPTER VI

Up to this time General Sherman had passed through various stages of popular misunderstanding and criticism, but the movements about Vicksburg referred to in the following letters seem to have resulted in the very general appreciation throughout the country, of his abilities. At this time John Sherman was in Ohio, much concerned at the turn political affairs were taking, and eager for military success because of the influence it would have upon the people.

CAMP BEFORE VICKSBURG, April 26, 1863.

My Dear Brother: To-morrow I start with my corps to bring up the rear of the movement against Grand Gulf, and, maybe, Jackson, Miss. I feel in its success less confidence than in any similar undertaking of the war, but it is my duty to co-operate with zeal, and I shall endeavor to do it....

Grant came down by river, and his entire army, about seventy thousand, is now near here, hut the whole country is under water, save little ribands of alluvial ground along the main Mississippi and all parallel bayous. One month ago my proposition was to fall back upon our original plan, modified by the fact that Yazoo River could be entered by its head and could be used as far down as Greenwood, which is the mouth of Yolobusha. If our gunboats could have passed that point, a real substantial advantage would have been gained, for it would have enabled the army to pass the Yolobusha, whereas now it is a serious obstacle like the Rappahannock, and will have to be fought for....

McClernand's corps marched from Milliken's Bend along a narrow road to Carthage. McPherson has followed, and I start to-morrow. Sixty thousand men will thus be on a single road, narrow, crooked, and liable to become a quagmire on the occurrence of a single rain. We hope to carry ten days rations with us. Seven iron-clad gunboats and seven transports have run the Vicksburg batteries; with these we can reach Grand Gulf below the mouth of Black River, whence there is a road to Raymond sixty-five miles, and Jackson. The destruction of this road isolates Vicksburg. Now if we can sustain the army it may do, but I know the materials or food, forage or ammunition, cannot be conveyed on that single precarious road. Grant has been opening a canal from the Mississippi to Willow Bayou, three miles, and Willow Bayou roundaway and Bayou Vidal form a connected channel for forty-seven miles, terminating at Carthage, but it is crooked, narrow, and full of trees. Large working parties are employed in removing trees, but at best it is only calculated that it can be used by scows drawn by small steam tugs. It is not even contemplated that the smallest transports can navigate it. The canal itself is far from being done. I went through it yesterday in a small boat, and estimate it will take one month to give it eight feet of water with the present stage, but the water in the river is now falling rapidly. We count on another rise in June from the Missouri, but these rises are accidental and may or not come. The great difficulty will be to support an army operating from Grand Gulf....

Between the two choices open to him I far prefer Grenada. One is sure and natural, the other is difficult and hazardous in the extreme. There is no national or political reason why this army should be forced to undertake unnecessary hazard. It is far in advance of Hooker, Rosecrans, or Curtis. We have done far more than either of these armies, but have encountered more calumny and abuse than all....

Banks is afraid even to attempt Port Hudson, and from all I can hear is more likely to be caged up in Hew Orleans than to assist us against Vicksburg....

Affectionately your brother,

W. T. SHERMAN.

MANSFIELD, OHIO, May 7, 1863.

My Dear Brother: We have been eagerly watching the course of military events. Here nothing occurs worth noting. If there is any change, it is for the better. The tone of popular opinion is more patriotic. There are fewer noisy Butternuts, and most of these think their bad talk is only fair opposition to the administration. The only danger is that this will become downright opposition, resistance to

162

the war and the laws where mobs and civil war will be the inevitable result. A good many scary people are afraid of this, but I am too well accustomed to violent political quarrels to look for danger from them. There may be occasional mobs, as there were the other day at Port Wayne, where I made a speech, but both parties pledged themselves to the war and only differed about the "nigger" and administration measures. The difference may widen, and unless we have decided military success, will widen until we have open and hostile war and peace parties. Then God knows what will be the result. One tendency I noticed. Nearly every man in debt is paying off his debts. The inflation of the currency and the rise of property make this easy. Unluckily for me, most of my means is or was "in bills receivable." These are paid, or will be, and so I find myself with plenty of money, but can't buy anything at reasonable prices. This is the general rule of creditors, and perhaps it is better so for the community, as the creditor class can more easily bear the loss of inflation. There is nothing in the condition at all discouraging except our military condition. This I confess looks discouraging. The defeat of Hooker, of which as yet we have not full particulars, is a terrible event. Experience should have taught us not to hope much from his army, and yet the impression was so strong after his confident assertions and his promising commencement that we all feel the disappointment. It is gloomy. Still what can we do, but fight on....

I regret to notice from your letter that Grant's recent movements do not meet your approval. It was regarded as a bold and successful plan to turn the flank of the enemy, but if he is weaker from the south side of Vicksburg than from above, I do not see what we have gained. We have a telegraphic account of your recent attack on Haines Bluff, but do not understand its purpose.

As for the consolidation of regiments, it is idle for me to interpose. Halleck regulates all these matters. He is king in all questions regulating the detail affecting the army. Stanton has far less power than Halleck, and, indeed, holds office by a frail tenure and with limited influence. It is no use for a civilian to talk to Halleck. He would regard your opinion, but certainly not mine, though we are good friends. You have been sagacious in your anticipation of military events. Charleston is not taken, the war is prolonged, and but little chance of its ending until we have a new deal.

If only the people will be patient so long, all will be well. The best of it is, they can't help themselves. The rebels won't let us have peace even if we wanted it. It may be better that the Democrats be allowed to take the helm, as they could not make peace, and then war would be more vigorous and united....

This war has always seemed to me a tragic necessity. I have watched its progress, and hope to see its termination. It may, like the French Revolution, travel in a large circle, destroying all that have taken part in it; still there is no way but to go ahead. We may slowly learn wisdom in its prosecution, for we certainly have not shown it thus far....

Affectionately your brother,

JOHN SHERMAN.

Late in May, 1863, it became evident that the Confederate works were too strong to be taken by assault, and on May 25th, the orders for besieging Vicksburg were given out.

WALNUT HILLS, VICKSBURG, May 29, 1863.

My Dear Brother: I received a few days since your most acceptable letter of May 7th, which met me here. You will now have a fine understanding of the whole move thus far. The move by way of Grand Gulf to secure a foothold on the hills wherefrom to assail Vicksburg, appeared to me too risky at the time, and General

Grant is entitled to all the merit of its conception and execution.

In our route we consumed the fruits of the country, broke up the important railroad communications, whipped the enemy wherever encountered, and secured the Yazoo as a base, the object for which we have contended so long and so patiently....

We have Vicksburg closely invested, and its fate is sealed unless the enemy raises a large force from Carolina and Tennessee and assails us from without. In that event we must catch them at the crossing of Black, and fight them desperately.

The place is very well fortified, and is defended by twenty thousand brave troops. We have assaulted at five distinct points at two distinct times, and failed to cross the parapet. Our loss was heavy and we are now approaching with pick and shovel. If we did not apprehend an attempt on our rear, we could wait patiently the slow process of besiegers; but as this danger is great, we may try and assault again. In the mean time we are daily pouring into the city a perfect storm of shot and shells, and our sharp-shooters are close up and fire at any head that is rash enough to show itself above ground.

[Not signed.]

MANSFIELD, OHIO, July 18, 1863.

My Dear Brother: I supposed when Vicksburg fell that you would have a period of rest, and perhaps might return to Ohio to find yourself popular and famous. But the fortune of war carries you into new dangers and I hope new successes. We have been very anxious for news from your movements, but as yet we have only had uncertain reports, and can only live in the hope that you will whip Johnston and win new laurels. I have just returned from Cincinnati, where I was during the whole of Morgan's raid. How completely the tone of the press has changed in regard to you. Even the "Gazette," which has been malignant to the last degree, published quite a number of letters in which your share of the movements about Vicksburg was highly praised. I notice, however, that the editor has said nothing. All other papers, and indeed all officers and citizens with whom I converse, gave you great credit. So that now in the Northern States, and especially here in Ohio, your popularity is second only to that of Grant. You need care but little for this, as you passed through a storm of obloquy which would have submerged many an officer. Popular opinion is so changeable that it is worthless. It is founded upon rumor, and is as explosive as gas. Meade has had a foretaste of this. His drawn battle at Gettysburg relieved the country from a great danger, and he was at once a hero; he was the coming man. He has allowed Lee to escape him, and all his popular honors are lt. McClellan has succeeded in establishing the position of a party leader, and now enjoys the bad honor of being cheered by a New York mob of thieves and scoundrels, while poor

Hooker is dropped by all just when he thought he had Lee in his power.

While the war goes on there is a danger looming up that seems to me more ominous than any other. It is the Presidential election next summer. We shall have a fierce canvass.... If the election cannot be held in the Southern States, no one is likely to get a majority of the electoral college. This must be, to secure an election by the people. All the States must be counted, and under the Constitution the successful candidate must have a majority of all the electoral votes. Can this be secured by any one man? If not, the election then goes into the House, and who can tell the result. The war has done a great deal to shake that implicit obedience to law which has been the great conservative element, but in the struggle for so vast a prize will it not be easy to clog the machinery for a legal election? — and then civil war or anarchy is the certain result. These are only possible dangers, but it is well to look them in the face.

At present I do not stand very well with my political associates, because I have openly differed with them on important questions. But I am too well grounded in the principles of the [Republican party to be shaken in my faith. Indeed, nearly all the errors into which the administration has fallen, have arisen from the advice of an old school of politicians who never belonged to the [Republican party.

Affectionately your brother,

JOHN SHERMAN.

JACKSON, MISS., July 19, 1863.

My Dear Brother: The fall of Vicksburg and consequent capitulation of Port Hudson, the opening the navigation of the Mississippi, and now the driving out of this great valley the only strong army that threatened us, complete as pretty a page in the history of war and of our country as ever you could ask my name to be identified with. The share I have personally borne in all these events is one in which you may take pride for me. You know I have avoided notoriety; and the press, my standard enemy, may strip me of all popular applause, but not a soldier of the Army of the Tennessee but knows the part I

166

have borne in this great drama, and the day will come when that army will speak in a voice that cannot be drowned....

In the events resulting thus, the guiding minds and hands were Grant's, Sherman's, and McPherson's, all natives of Ohio....

Jackson will never again he a point where an enemy can assemble and threaten ns.... As soon as my detachments are in, I will return to Black River. Our men and officers must have rest. For months in trenches, working day and night in the heat and dust of the roads, all are exhausted and need rest. I hope the Army of the Potomac will finish Lee. Morgan should not escape from Indiana. Love to all.

Your brother,

W. T. SHERMAN.

CAMP 18 M. E. OF VICKSBURG, July 28, 1863.

Dear Brother: Since my return from Jackson, I have been very busy — every general officer but two has gone on furlough, and everybody wants to go....

The railroad comes within four miles of my tent, and I have its exclusive use and a telegraph at my elbow. If you come down you will find your name a passport, but should that fail you, see General Grant or McPherson in Vicksburg, and they will put you through. I don't think there is any danger on the river now unless it be on the Ohio, which you can avoid by taking cars to Cairo. Vicksburg is worth seeing, and a glance will tell you more than reams of paper why it took us six months to take the place. I am camped near Big Black, four and one-half miles northeast of where the railroad crosses it. My depot of supplies is at the crossing. Col. J. Condit Smith is my quartermaster, and should you reach that point before I am advised by telegraph, apply to him and he will send you to my camp. I have four divisions here much reduced, but still a good stock. In the riots of New York I recognize the second stage of this war, but I trust our Government will deal with them summarily. The war has progressed as fast and as successfully as should be.

Your brother,

My Dear Brother: Your letter dated July 19, at Jackson, is received. What you say about the injustice of the press was undoubtedly true a month ago, but it is true no longer. Since the fall of Vicksburg each of the officers named by you has been very highly lauded, and that by all parties and papers. With you it has been especially laudatory. Even your old enemy, the Cincinnati "Gazette," has in several recent numbers spoken of you in very complimentary terms, and without any apparent recollection that it has libelled you for months. With the officers of the army you stand very high. Indeed it is now unnecessary for you to care for defenders.

I will think of your proposition to visit Vicksburg, and will probably do so this fall. At present I am involved in the political canvass now going on in Ohio, but shall not be long. My position does not require me to take a very active part....

Affectionately yours,

JOHN SHERMAN.

General Sherman did not visit Ohio until the following Christmas.

Camp on Big Black, 18 miles from Vicksburg, Aug. 3, 1863.

You and I may differ in our premises, but will agree in our conclusions. A government resting immediately on the caprice of a people is too unstable to last. The will of the people is the ultimate appeal, but the Constitution, laws of Congress, and regulations of the executive departments subject to the decisions of the Supreme Court are the laws which all must obey without stopping to inquire why. All *must* obey. Government, that is, the executive, having no discretion but to execute the law, must be to that extent despotic. If this be our Government, it is the "best on earth —but if the people of localities can bias and twist the law or execution of it to suit their local prejudices, then our Government is the worst on earth. If you look back only two years, you will see the application. There are about six millions of men in this country all thinking themselves sovereign and qualified to govern. Some thirty-four governors of

States who feel like petty kings, and about ten thousand editors who presume to dictate to generals, presidents, and cabinets. I treat all these as nothing, but when a case arises I simply ask: Where is the law? Supposing the pilot of a ship should steer his vessel according to the opinion of every fellow who watched the clouds above or the currents below, where would his ship land? Ho, the pilot has before him a little needle; he watches that, and he never errs. So if we make that our simple code, the law of the land must and shall be executed; no matter what the consequences, we cannot err. Hundreds and thousands may honestly differ as to what the law should be, but it is rarely the case; but all men of ordinary understanding can tell what the law is. We have for years been drifting towards an unadulterated democracy or demagogism, and its signs were manifest in Mob Laws and Vigilance Committees all over our country. And States and towns and mere squads of men took upon themselves to set aside the Constitution and laws of Congress and substitute therefor their own opinions. I saw it, and tried to resist it in California, but always the General Government yielded to the pressure. I say that our Government, judged by its conduct as a whole, paved the way for rebellion. The South that lived on slavery saw the United States yield to abolition pressure at the North, to pro-slavery pressure at the South, to the miners of California, the rowdies of Baltimore, and to the people everywhere. They paved the way to this rebellion. The people of the South were assured that, so far from resisting an attempt to set up an independent Government of homogeneous interests, the United States would give in and yield. They appealed to precedents, and proved it, and I confess I had seen so much of it that I doubted whether our Government would not yield to the pressure, and die a natural death. But I confess my agreeable surprise. Though full of corruption and base materials, our country is a majestic one, full of natural wealth and good people. They have risen not in full majesty, but enough to give all hopes of vitality. Our progress has been as rapid as any philosopher could ask. The resources of the land in money, in men, in provisions, in forage, and in intelligence, has surprised us all, and we have had as much success as could be hoped for. The Mississippi is now ours, not by commission but by right, by the right of manly power.... No great interest in our land has risen superior to Government, and I deem it fortunate that no man has risen to dictate terms to all. Better as it is. Lincoln is but the last of the old school Presidents, the index (mathematically) of one stage of our national existence.... Our Government should become a machine, self-regulating, independent of the man....

As to the press of America, it is a shame and a reproach to a civilized people.... I begin to feel a high opinion of myself that I am their butt; I shall begin to suspect myself of being in a decline when a compliment appears in type. I know in what estimation I am held by my press,— those who have been with me all the time,— and they are capable to judge, from private to major-generals. I saw a move to bring Grant and myself East. No they don't....

We will be in Mobile in October and Georgia by Christmas if required....

I see much of the people here — men of heretofore high repute. The fall of Vicksburg has had a powerful effect. They are subjugated. I even am amazed at the effect; we are actually feeding the people....

Grant and wife visited me in camp yesterday. I have the handsomest camp I ever saw, and should really be glad to have visitors come down. I don't think a shot will be fired at a boat till Jeff Davis can call his friends about him and agree upon the next campaign. I want recruits and conscripts, and shall be all ready in October.

As ever, your brother,

W. T. SHERMAN.

MANSFIELD, OHIO, Aug. 29, 1863.

Dear Brother: I am very desirous to accept your invitation. The trip would be an instructive and pleasant one, and if I were not restrained by the interests of others I would surely go at once. But we are now involved in an exciting and important political contest. The canvass in Ohio is substantially between the Government and the Rebellion, and is assuming all the bitterness of such a step. If I should leave now, it would be like a General leaving before the day of battle. I have been speaking very often, and must keep it up. I propose, however, to arrange all my business so that I may leave soon after the election, say about the 20th of October, and will then go down the river and spend all the time until the meeting of Congress. I hope to be able to go via Vicksburg, Hew Orleans, Charleston, to Washington. If a favorable opportunity offers at Vicksburg and Hew Orleans, I wish to develop my ideas as to a reconstruction of the Union. I know these will suit you a good deal better than they will the administration, but I feel quite independent of the latter and am disposed to follow my own course....

General Ord stopped with me last Sunday on his way East. We were all glad to see him, as he gave us many interesting details of your situation and operations. Your promotion as Brigadier in the Regular Army gave unusual satisfaction. I was in Dayton, Springfield, Marysville, and Stanton's neighborhood and conversed with many about his attacks on you. I find he is terribly unpopular. Your recent success and his libels on you are the subject of general remarks. At one place I mentioned your name in connection with other Ohio Generals who have distinguished themselves, and the crowd stopped me and gave you three as hearty cheers as ever man got....

Affectionately yours,

JOHN SHERMAN.

After the fall of Vicksburg and Port Hudson, the Western armies lay comparatively idle for a time; and early in the autumn General Sherman was engaged in rebuilding the Memphis & Charleston R. R. to the east so that the armies might draw supplies by that route. While engaged on this work, he was ordered to cross the Tennessee and march eastward. The battle of Chattanooga followed, and then Sherman was sent to Burnside's relief, the latter being besieged in Knoxville in November. The siege of Knoxville was raised December 5, 1863, and Sherman went slowly back to Chattanooga, and then was ordered to northern Alabama to put his army into winter quarters.

General Sherman spent Christmas of 1863 with his family, in Lancaster, Ohio, but missed seeing John, who had already gone to Washington.

MANSFIELD, OHIO, Nov. 14, 1868.

My Dear Brother:

On Tuesday next I start for Gettysburg, to take part in the pageant of a dedication of the battle-field as a national cemetery. Prom thence I shall probably go to Washington, two weeks in advance of the session. The very first thing I mean to do is to press the enforcement of the draft. The long delay and the various shifts and subterfuges by which the execution of the law has thus far been defeated, is disgraceful, and very injurious to the cause.... I notice in some of the Southern papers that a hope is entertained that the draft cannot be enforced. This is idle. The war was never more popular than at this moment. The new call will fall lightly. Ohio must send thirty-five thousand, or one to fifteen of her voters. The apportionment has been made even to townships and wards, and in very many places the quota will be made by voluntary enlistments, aided by large gratuitous bounties from citizens. There is no lack of men or of a determination to send them. The wonderful prosperity of all classes, especially of laborers, has a tendency to secure acquiescence in all measures demanded to carry on the war. We are only another example of a people growing rich in a great war. And this is not shown simply by inflated prices, but by increased production, new manufacturing establishments, new railroads, houses, etc.... Indeed, every branch of business is active and hopeful. This is not a mere temporary inflation caused by paper money, but is a steady progress, and almost entirely upon actual capital. The people are prospering and show their readiness to push on the war. Taxes are paid cheerfully, and the voluntary donations for our soldiers and their families are counted by thousands.... I confide in your success.

Affectionately,

JOHN SHERMAN.

LANCASTER, OHIO, Dec. 29, 1863.

My Dear Brother:... I hear you have gone on to New York, and therefore I must go off without seeing you. I have been off the line of communication since leaving Memphis, save a few hours at Bridgeport, during which I had hardly time to put my official signature to papers demanding my hand. I have made a report of our movements up to the return to Bridgeport and enclose it with this, a copy which I brought here, and which you may keep, only, of course, under the confidence of absolute secrecy until the War Department thinks proper to make the original public....

I suppose you will read this report, and I invite attention to the part referring to the assault on Tunnel Hill. I know that Grant in his report will dwell on this same part. I was provoked that Meigs, looking at us from Chattanooga, should report me repulsed, and that Mr. Stanton should publish his letter as semi-official. Meigs apologized to me for using Thomas's name instead of mine throughout, which he charged to a copyist, but made no amends for the repulse. The whole philosophy of the battle was that I should get, by a dash, a position on the extremity of the Missionary Ridge, from which the enemy would be forced to drive me, or allow his depot at Chickamauga station to be in danger. I expected Bragg to attack me at daylight, but he did not, and to bring matters to a crisis quickly, as time was precious, for the sake of Burnside in East Tennessee, Grant ordered me to assume the offensive. My report contains the rest. Again, after the battle, Granger was ordered to push for Knoxville, but his movements were so slow that Grant, impatient, called on me, and my move was the most rapid of the war and perfectly successful. I could have gone on after Longstreet, but Burnside ranked me, and it was his business, not mine. So I reinforced him all he asked, and returned.

The Fifteenth Corps, now Logan's, and Dodge's division of the Sixteenth Corps are now at work on the railroad from Nashville to Decatur, and from Decatur to Stevenson, thus making a triangle of railroad which it is estimated will relieve the great difficulty of supplies which has paralyzed the Army of the Cumberland. This will take five weeks. I leave my headquarters at Huntsville, and go in person down the Mississippi to strike some lateral blows, to punish the country for allowing guerillas to attack the boats. I go on Friday to Cincinnati, and thence to Cairo, where with Admiral Porter I will concert measures to produce the result. I expect to send one expedition up the Yazoo, and go myself with another up Red River, levying contributions to make good losses to boats, and punish for deaths and wounds inflicted. I think we can make people feel that they must actually prevent guerillas from carrying out their threats that though we have the river, it will do us no good. My address will be Memphis, for a month, and Huntsville after. We can hardly fashion out the next campaign, but it looks as though we should have to move from the Tennessee River. I should prefer to take Mobile and the Alabama as well as the Chattahoochee, and move east from Montgomery and Columbus, Miss.

I wish you would introduce a bill in Congress increasing the number of cadets on this basis — one from each congressional district per annum. In districts not represented, vest the appointments in the Secretary of War out of boys not over eighteen in the armies in the field, to be selected in any manner that may be prescribed by law, or by the regulation of the President. This would hold out to young fellows the prospect of getting a cadetship. Last summer we were called on to recommend candidates, and I was amazed to find so many worthy applicants. All who came forward for examination preferred West Point to a commission. The great want of the army is good subordinate officers. The army is a good school, but West Point is better. It is useless to deny that a special preliminary education is necessary to the military officers, and the cheapest school is now at West Point and is susceptible of infinite increase....

I think the President's proclamation unwise. Knowing the temper of the South, I know that it but protracts the war by seeming to court peace. It to them looks like weakness. I tell them that as they cool off, we warm to the work. That we are just getting ready for the war, and I know the effect is better than to coax them to come back into the Union. The organization of a Civil Government but complicates the game. All the Southern States will need a pure military Government for years after resistance has ceased. You have noticed the debate in Richmond, on the President's proclamation. That is a true exhibit of the feeling South. Don't fall into the error that the masses think differently. Of course property-holding classes South deplore the devastation that marks the progress of their own and our armies, but the South is no longer consulted. The Army of the Confederacy is the South, and they still hope to worry us out. The moment we relax, they gain strength and confidence. We must hammer away and show such resistance, such bottom that even that slender hope will fail them.

I still am opposed to all bounties. The draft pure and simple, annual, to fill vacancies in the ranks. Pay of men in the front increased to even forty dollars a month, and that of men at depots and to the rear diminished to a bare maintenance if not less. Pour hundred dollars bounty is an absurd commentary where two-thirds draw bounty and remain absent from their rank and are discharged for disability without hearing a shot. Deal with the army as you would if you were hiring men for special work. Pay those who do the work high; those who are sick, unfortunate, or shirking, pay little or nothing. The same of officers from the major-general to lieutenant. The President must make vacancies for the rising officers, the "creations" of the war. I am willing to quit if a younger and better man can be found for my place....

Your affectionate brother,

W. T. SHERMAN.

LANCASTER, Dec. 30, 1863.

Dear Brother: I have been importuned from many quarters for my likeness, autographs, and biography. I have managed to fend off all parties and hope to do so till the end of the war. I don't want to rise or be notorious, for the reason that a mere slip or accident may let me fall, and I don't care about falling so far as most of the temporary heroes of the war. The real men of the war will be determined by the closing scenes, and then the army will determine the questions. Newspaper puffs and self-written biographies will then be ridiculous caricatures. Already has time marked this progress and indicated this conclusion.

If parties apply to you for materials in my behalf, give the most brief and general items, and leave the results to the close of the war or of my career. As well might a judge or senator seek for fame outside their spheres of action as an officer of the army. We must all be judged by our own peers, stand or fall by their verdict. I know I stand very high with the army, and feel no concern on that score. To-day I can do more with Admiral Porter or the Generals than any general officer out West except Grant, and with him I am as a second self. We are personal and official friends.

Affectionately yours,

W. T. SHERMAN.

The following letters were written in the winter and spring of 1864, while General Sherman commanded the troops along the Mississippi, and John Sherman was in the Senate at Washington. General Sherman's letters contain expressions of confidence in General Grant, who had just been ordered to command the Armies of the United States.

ON BOARD JOLIET, Bound for Vicksburg in a fog,

Dear Brother: -

I have organized a cavalry force to sweep down from Memphis towards Mobile, and have gathered together out of my garrisons a very pretty force of twenty thousand men which I shall command in person, and move from Vicksburg down east in connection with the cavalry named, to reach Meridian and break up the railroad connections there. This will have the effect to disconnect Mississippi from the eastern Southern States, and without this single remaining link they cannot keep any army of importance west of the Alabama River. Our armies are now at the lowest point, and so many are going home as re-enlisted veterans that I shall have a less force than should attempt it; but this is the time and I shall attempt it. It seems my luck to have to take the initiative and to come in at desperate times, but thus far having done a full share of the real achievements of this war, I need not fear accidents....

You who attach more importance to popular fame would be delighted to see in what estimation I am held by the people of Memphis, Tenn., and all along this mighty river. I could not well decline an offer of a public dinner in Memphis, but I dreaded it more than I did the assault on Vicksburg. I had to speak, and sent you the report that best suited me, viz., that in the "Argus." The report of the bulletin which may reach the Northern press is disjointed and not so correct. Indeed, I cannot speak from notes or keep myself strictly to the point, but tis said that the effect of my crude speeches is good....

I know that for us to assume that slavery is killed, not by a predetermined act of ours, but as the natural, logical, and legal consequence of the acts of its self constituted admirers, we gain strength and the enemy loses it. I think it is the true doctoring for the time being. The South has made the interests of slavery the issue of the war. If they lose the war, they lose slavery. Instead of our being abolitionists, it is thereby proven that they are the abolitionists....

The Mississippi is a substantial conquest; we should next get the Red River, then the Alabama, and last push into Georgia....

Your affectionate brother,

W. T. SHERMAN.

UNITED STATES SENATE, Jan. 29, 1864.

My Dear Brother: I received your letter from Lancaster, and also one from Cairo. If I had known when I left Washington that you were to be at Lancaster, I would have met you there. But on leaving Washington I engaged to meet certain gentlemen at New York, on New Year's Lay, and this left me no time. I have met several from Cincinnati who saw you there, and all concur in saying you bear the storms of life well, and appear in better health and spirits than before the war. Your official report is very interesting, and I wish to see it published. I inquired of Cullen if it has yet come by military channels to the adjutant-general, and he says not. When it does come, he will have it published. As to your proposition to increase the cadets at West Point, I find some difference of opinion among regular officers. Cullen says that to graduate the number would require new buildings, professors, etc.; that the utmost capacity of the school is four hundred and fifty. Both he and Hardie seem backward about drawing the bill without the assent of Stanton, but promised to send me a bill doubling the cadets if Stanton would consent. This delicacy seems to me absurd, for I will assume it, introduce it, and may be able to pass it.... We are all looking to the operation on the Mississippi and at Knoxville. The latter seems to me the point of danger. If Longstreet should be reinforced, why could he not pounce upon Foster, or his successor, and make another march necessary for his relief. The movement of recruiting is going on well enough. The draft will then be thoroughly enforced. So Stanton says, and I believe him. The general prosperity of the country is so marked that I am afraid of a reaction or a collapse. The currency is awfully inflated, and our ability to borrow and to pay interest has a limit. If the war continues two years longer, we shall be terribly embarrassed. Still we have the sure foundation of public credit, a great country, and a large and active population. Let me hear from you as often as possible.

Affectionately yours,

JOHN SHERMAN.

On March 24, 1864, General Sherman writes from his headquarters, then at Nashville, Tenn.

Potomac will have all the fighting they want. He will expect your friendship — we are close friends. His simplicity and modesty are natural and not affected. Whatever part is assigned me I will attempt, cost what it may in life and treasure....

And again he writes: —

Grant encourages his juniors and takes pleasure in supporting them.... Newspaper men are afraid of me, and I hope before the war is much older we shall be allowed to conscript every citizen of good physique found about our camps, on the ground that he has fled to escape the draft. Such an order would have an admirable effect.

Washington, D. C., March 26, 1864.

178

My Dear Brother: Your movements have been so rapid of late that I scarcely knew where to address you. I have recently met with several officers who have been with you, among others General Grant and General Butterfield. General Grant is all the rage; he is subjected to the disgusting but dangerous process of being lionized. He is followed by crowds and is cheered everywhere. While he must despise the fickle fools who run after him, he, like most others, may be spoiled by this excess of flattery. He may be so elated as to forget the uncertain tenure upon which he holds and stakes his really well-earned laurels. I conversed with him but little, as I did not wish either to occupy his time or to be considered his flatterer. The opinion I form of him from his appearance is this,— his will and common-sense are the strongest features of his character. He is plain and modest, and so far bears himself well. All here give him hearty co-operation, but an officer who does not like Halleck tells me that Halleck will ruin Grant with, the President in sixty days, or on failure to do so will resign....

We all here are disposed to take a hopeful view of the *status in quo*. The enormous Government bounties have been effective, but they are terribly severe on our finances. We can't forever endure such expenditures. Warning and caution to this danger are unheeded. Our people are so hopeful and energetic that they will bear more than any other....

You are now in a position where any act of yours will command public attention. You will be unduly lauded and sharply abused. I hope you have seen enough of the base motives that dictate praise and blame to disregard both, but preserve the best of your judgment in utter disregard of flattery or clamor.

When any of your friends come to Washington, give them notes to me. I may be of service to them. At all events I like to see them.

Affectionately yours,

JOHN SHERMAN.

HEADQUARTERS MILITARY DIVISION or THE MISSISSIPPI, NASHVILLE, TENN., April 5, 1864.

Dear Brother:

Grant is as good a leader as we can find. He has honesty, simplicity of character, singleness of purpose, and no hope or claim to usurp civil power. His character, more than his genius, will reconcile armies and attach the people. Let him alone. Don't disgust him by flattery or importunity. Let him alone.... If bothered, hampered, or embarrassed, he would drop you all in disgust, and let you slide into anarchy.... Let us manage the whites and "niggers" and all the physical resources of the country, and apply them where most needed. Let us accomplish great results, leaving small ones to conform in due season....

I have in hand three armies here, and one in Arkansas. All are in harmony, and all are willing to go and come at my bidding. I am also in perfect harmony with the civil authorities. I know their province and my own. I believe also our enemies have more respect for me than they have for Congress, so that I shall be ready with the spring. But I see with regret causes still at work North which should not be. States quarrelling about quotas, when we see their regiments here dwindling to mere squads. Absentees by the hundreds of thousands; and all efforts to get men, who have drawn large bounties and are drawing large pay still lingering at a safe distance, are vain, yet I hope that by the voluntary consent of the men themselves we shall have enough.

As our enemy fills his ranks by conscription, ours dwindle by sickness and furloughs. I am laboring hard to put all on the rolls into position, and still harder to put forward the stores on which they must feed as we advance. The country through which we have marched is cleared of all subsistence and forage, and everything must be sent forward by cars and wagons. It is estimated that there are now the carcasses of thirty thousand animals in the valley of the Tennessee. Not one cavalry soldier in ten has a horse, and on a recent visit to Schofield, out of forty-one thousand men who should have, I find but seven thousand in line of battle, but the furloughed men are returning, and I will see that by May 1st I have on the Tennessee one of the best armies in the world. You may look for the causes of these apparent incongruities not in the army, but among our people.

I shall be here about two weeks, and then to the front. Let me hear from you. I care no more for the squabbles about the Presidency than I do for the causes of the Schleswig-Holstein difficulty, and Grant cares still less....

Your brother,

W. T. SHERMAN.

On April 11th, General Sherman writes again from Nashville, enclosing an interesting letter of his own, written to Major Sawyer in the previous January.

Of course I have enough to do, but more to think about. We have now been two years and more at war, and have reached a period when we should consider the war as fairly begun. Don't you delude yourself that it is even approaching an end. Por a shrewd people we have less sense even than the Mexicans, paying fabulous bounties for a parcel of boys and old men, and swelling our muster-rolls, but adding nothing to our real fighting strength. Instead of enlarging, we are all cutting down our organizations. I shall have the fragments of seven corps on the Tennessee, but over thirty thousand animals have died, and it is going to be a terrible job to replace them, and to accumulate to the front the necessary food for mules and men in time; but though assured that the country for a long distance into Georgia and Alabama is stripped as it is on this side, yet at the right time I shall go ahead, and, if necessary, feed on anything. I shall not be behindhand when the grand beginning is announced. I can tell you nothing more.

... I expect soon to have a new howl against me. The pressure to go in our cars to the front was so great and the difficulty of getting to Chattanooga so momentous, that I ordered absolutely no citizen, private freight, or anything but freight purely military to be taken till the wants of the troops were supplied....

It will require the conjoined energies of the whole nation to meet the shock this spring, and it may be the end will be made certain, but still the long, persistent struggle with half a million of men far more desperate than our old Indians is yet to come....

I enclose you a letter of instructions I made to my adjutant Sawyer, who remained at my headquarters, Huntsville, when I went to Meridian. I should not object to have this letter printed, as it is something new and is true. Sawyer tells me it had a powerful effect on the people of Huntsville. As the letter is equally applicable to large districts still to be gone over, its publication would do no harm except to turn the Richmond press against me, as the prince of barbarians.

Yours in haste,

W. **T. SHERMAN.**

HEADQUARTERS DEPT, OF THE TENN., VICKSBURG,
Jan. 31, 1864.

MAJOR R. M. SAWYER,

A. A. C. Army of the Tenn.,

Huntsville, Alabama.

Dear Sawyer: In my former letters I have answered all your questions save one, and that relates to the treatment of inhabitants known or suspected to be hostile or "Secesh." This is in truth the most difficult business of our army as it advances and occupies the Southern country. It is almost impossible to lay down rules, and I invariably leave the whole subject to the local commanders, but am willing to give them the benefit of my acquired knowledge and experience. In Europe, whence we derive our principles of war, wars are between kings or rulers through hired armies, and not between peoples. These remain, as it were, neutral, and sell their produce to whatever army is in possession.

Napoleon when at war with Prussia, Austria, and Russia bought forage and provisions of the inhabitants, and consequently had an interest to protect the farms and factories which ministered to his wants. In like manner the Allied Armies in Prance could buy of the French habitants whatever they needed, the produce of the soil or manufactures of the country. Therefore, the general rule was and is that war is confined to the armies engaged, and should not visit the houses of families or private interests. But in other examples a different rule obtained the sanction of historical authority. I will only instance one, where in the siege of William and Mary the English army occupied Ireland, then in a state of revolt. The inhabitants were actually driven into foreign lands, and were dispossessed of their property and a new population introduced.

To this day a large part of the north of Ireland is held by the descendants of the Scotch emigrants sent there by William's order and an act of Parliament. The war which now prevails in our land is essentially a war of races. The Southern people entered into a clear compact of government with us of the North, but still maintained through state organizations a species of separate existence, with separate interests, history, and prejudices. These latter became stronger and stronger, till at last they have led to war and have developed fruits of the bitterest kind. We of the North are beyond all question right in our cause, but we are not bound to ignore the fact that the people of the South have prejudices which form a part of their nature, and which they cannot throw off without an effort of reason or the slower process of natural change. The question then arises, Should we treat as absolute enemies all in the South who differ from us in opinion or prejudice, kill or banish them, or should we give them time to think and gradually change their conduct so as to conform to the new order of things which is slowly and gradually creeping into their country?

When men take up arms to resist a rightful authority, we are compelled to use like force, because all reason and argument cease when arms are resorted to. When the provisions, forage, horses, mules, wagons, etc., are used by our enemy, it is clearly our duty and right to take them also, because otherwise they might be used against us. In like manner all houses left vacant by an inimical people are clearly our right, and as such are needed as storehouses, hospitals, and quarters. But the question arises as to dwellings used by women, children, and non-combatants. So long as non-combatants remain in their houses and keep to their accustomed

183

peaceful business, their opinions and prejudices can in no wise influence the war, and therefore should not be noticed; but if any one conies out into the public streets and creates disorder, he or she should be punished, restrained, or banished to the rear or front, as the officer in command adjudges. If the people, or any of them, keep up a correspondence with parties in hostility, they are spies, and can be punished according to law with death or minor punishment. These are well-established principles of war, and the people of the South having appealed to *war*, are barred from appealing for protection to our constitution, which they have practically and publicly defied. They have appealed to war, and must abide *its* rules and laws....

It is all idle nonsense for these Southern planters to say that they made the South, that they own it, and can do as they please to break up our Government and shut up the natural avenues of trade, intercourse, and commerce. We know, and they know, if they are intelligent beings, that as compared with the whole world they are but as five millions to one thousand millions, that they did not create the land, that the only title to use and usufruct is the deed of the United States, and that if they appeal to war they hold their all by a very insecure tenure. For my part, I believe that this war is the result of false political doctrine, for which we are all as a people more or less responsible, and I would give all a chance to reflect, and, when in error, to recant. I know the slave-owners, finding themselves in possession of a species of property in opposition to the growing sentiment of the whole civilized world, conceived their property to be in danger and foolishly appealed to war, and that by skilful political handling they involved with themselves the whole South on this result of error and prejudice. I believe that some of the rich and slave-holding are prejudiced to an extent that nothing but death and ruin will ever extinguish, but I hope that as the poorer and industrious classes of the South realize their relative weakness and their dependence upon the fruits of the earth and good-will of their fellow-men they will not only discover the error of their ways and repent of their hasty action, but bless those who persistently have maintained a constitutional government strong enough to sustain itself, protect its citizens, and promise peaceful homes to millions yet unborn.

If the people of Huntsville think differently, let them persist in this war three years longer, and then they will not be consulted.

Three years ago, by a little reflection and patience, they could have had a hundred years of peace and prosperity, but they *preferred* war. Last year they could have saved their slaves, but now it is too late, — all the powers of earth cannot restore to them their slaves any more than their dead grandfathers....

A people who will persevere in war beyond a certain limit ought to know the consequences. Many, many people, with less pertinacity than the South has already shown, have been wiped out of national existence.

My own belief is that even now the non-slave-holding classes of the South are alienating from their associates in war. Already I hear crimination and recrimination. Those who have property left should take warning in time.

Since I have come down here I have seen many Southern planters, who now hire their own negroes and acknowledge that they were mistaken and knew not the earthquake they were to make by appealing to secession. They thought that the politicians had prepared the way, and that they could part the States of this Union in peace. They now see that we are bound together as one nation by indissoluble ties, and that any interest, or any fraction of the people that set themselves up in antagonism to the nation, must perish.

Whilst I would not remit one jot or tittle of our nation's rights in peace or war, I do make allowances for past political errors and prejudices.

Our national Congress and the Supreme Court are the proper arenas on which to discuss conflicting opinions, and not the battle-field.

You may not hear from me again for some time, and if you think it will do any good, call some of the better people of Huntsville together and explain to them my views. Yon may even read to them

185

this letter and let them use it, so as to prepare them for my coming....

We are progressing well in this quarter, but I have not changed my opinion that although we may soon make certain the existence of the power of our national government, yet years must pass before ruffianism, murder, and robbery will cease to afflict this region of our country.

Your friend,

WM. T. SHERMAN,

Major Gen. Comd.

WASHINGTON, D.C., April 17, 1864.

My Dear Brother:... Our finances are bubbling up and down in that feverish state where a panic might easily come. Chase is a man of ability, but in recent measures he has failed. I have been generally the laboring one in the Senate, on these measures, though very often my judgment has been against them. I have felt like a subordinate officer, who, while he does not approve the plan of operations, yet deems it his duty fairly to execute his part of it rather than by fault-finding to impair it. The war is daily driving us to extraordinary measures, and our form of Government is not *unit* enough to carry them out. We are embarrassed by state banks, state laws, and local issues and interests. The other day a determined effort was made in New York to run gold up to 200, but was promptly met by a free sale by the Government of gold and exchange, and the movement failed. It was aided by this very bad news from Fort Pillow, not so bad from the loss of men, but from the question of retaliation raised by the massacre of negro troops. We all feel that we must either disband negro troops or protect them. It is fearful to think about the measures that may be necessary, but what else can we do? An investigation will be made by the Secretary of Wax and by Congress, and if the rebels are determined to massacre prisoners, then a new and terrible stage of this war will be commenced....

Affectionately yours,

JOHN SHERMAN.

On March 18th, 1864, General Sherman relieved General Grant of the command of the Military Division of the Mississippi. During the spring and summer of that year he was busily engaged provisioning and moving his great army into Georgia, following General Joseph E. Johnston according to orders from General Grant. On May 20th and June 9th, he writes from the heart of Georgia.

HEADQUARTERS MILITARY DIVISION OF THE MISSISSIPPI,

KINGSTON, GA., May 20, 1864.

Dear Brother: I have daily telegraphed to General Halleck our progress, and have no doubt you have kept pace with our movement. Johnston had chosen Dalton as his place of battle, but he had made all the roads to it so difficult that I resolved to turn it, so I passed my army through a pass twenty miles south of Dalton and forced him to battle at Resaca. That, too, was very strong, but we beat him at all points, and as I had got a bridge across the Oostenaula below him and was gradually getting to his rear, he again abandoned his position in the night and I have been pushing my force after him as fast as possible; yet his knowledge of the country and the advantage of a good railroad to his rear enabled him to escape me, but I now have full possession of all the rich country of the Etowah. We occupy Rome, Kingston, and Cassville. I have repaired {he railroad to these points and now have ordered the essential supplies forward to replenish our wagons, when I will make for Atlanta, fifty-nine miles from here and about fifty from the advance. Johnston has halted across the Etowah at a place called Allatoona, where the railroad and common road passes through a spur of the mountain, making one of those formidable passes which gives an army on the defensive so much advantage, but I propose to cross the Etowah here and to go for Marietta via Dallas. Look at your map and you will see the move. We expect to cross the Etowah on the 23d, when we will move straight on fighting when opposed. Of course our laboring and difficulties increase as we progress, whereas our enemy gains strength by picking up his rear guard and detachments.

Put forth the whole strength of the nation now, and if we cant whip the Sduth we must bow our necks in patient submission. A division

187

of our territory by the old lines is impossible. Grant surely is fighting hard enough, and I think this army will make its mark.

Your brother,

W. T. SHERMAN.

HEADQUARTERS MILITARY DIVISION OF THE MISSISSIPPI,
ACWORTH, GA., 9 June, 1864.

Dear Brother: It is out of all reason to expect me to write much, and I know you do not expect it. Were I to attempt narration, it would swell to unreasonable lengths, and even in my communication to the War Department I must confine myself almost to generalities. Suffice it to say that General Grant and I had a perfect understanding, and all things are now as near our calculations as possible, save and except that the Red River failure has clipped from the general plan our main feature, a simultaneous attack on Mobile from New Orleans. But the Red River expedition is out, and I have substituted a smaller force subject to my own orders, in lieu of the larger one contemplated made up by General Banks.

My long and single line of railroad to my rear, of limited capacity, is the delicate point of my game, as also the fact that all of Georgia, except the cleared bottoms, is densely wooded, with few roads, and at any point an enterprising enemy can, in a few hours with axes and spades, make across our path formidable works, whilst his sharp-shooters, spies, and scouts, in the guise of peaceable farmers, can hang around us and kill our wagonmen, messengers, and couriers. It is a big Indian war; still thus far I have won four strong positions, advanced a hundred miles, and am in possession of a large wheat growing region and all the iron mines and works of Georgia. Johnston's army is still at my front and can fight or fall back, as he pleases. The future is uncertain, but I will do all that is possible.

As ever,

Your brother,

W. T. SHERMAN.

After the adjournment of the Senate in the spring of 1864, John Sherman returned to Ohio, where he spent the spring and summer.

MANSFIELD, OHIO, July 24, 1864.

My Dear Brother: I have not written you for some time as I knew you were so well occupied and hoped by this time you have attained the goal of your present movements, Atlanta. We all feel that upon Grant and you, and the armies under your command, the fate of this country depends. If you are successful, it is ardently hoped that peace may soon follow with a restored union. If you fail, the wisest can hope for nothing but a long train of disasters and the strife of factions. All our people cling to the hope of success, and seem perfectly willing to submit to taxation, bad administration, and every ill short of disunion. Whether it is the result of education, the constant warnings of the early Southern statesman, or the reason of the thing, everybody here dreads the breaking up of the union as the beginning of anarchy. The very thing they fight for in the South is for them, and for us, the worst calamity. What can be more terrible than the fate of Kentucky and Missouri. A man cannot go to bed at night, except in fear of the knife and torch. This lawlessness will extend all over the country if we do not have military success. All the clamor the Copperheads can make about personal liberty doesn't affect the people, if they can only see security and success. Bad precedents in time of war will easily be corrected by peace. But the anarchy of unsuccessful war will reduce us to a pitiable state, in which we shall easily fall victims to demagogism or tyranny. Every one feels that you have done your part nobly. G-rant has not had such success. No doubt he has done as well as any one could with his resources and such adversaries. Still he has not taken Richmond, and I fear will not this campaign....

I congratulate you on the ability and success of your campaign. I see many officers, and they all speak of it, not only as a success but as a scientific success, evincing abilities of a high order. I found on a short visit to Cincinnati that you were very popular there. I saw Anderson, Swords, Dunn, and a host of others, all of whom entertained great kindness for you....

Affectionately yours,

189

JOHN SHERMAN.

The following letter of Ang. 12, 1864, written from Atlanta, Ga., to Hon. Schuyler Colfax, in answer to a request from him to allow soldiers to return to their homes to vote, shows the intense feeling General Sherman had regarding the political use of the soldiers during the war. This letter was sent through John Sherman, and is in his letter-book.

HEADQUARTERS MILITARY DIVISION OF THE MISSISSIPPI.

IN THE FIELD, ATLANTA, Aug. 12, 1864.

SCHUYLER COLFAX, Esq.,

South Bend, Ind.

My Dear Sir: John Sherman has sent me your letter of Aug. 2d, in which you intimate a wish that certain nine regiments of Indiana troops should be ordered where they can be furloughed so as to vote in the fall elections.

Of course it is impossible. I have not now troops enough to do what the case admits of without extra hazard, and to send away a single man would be an act of injustice to the remainder. I think you need not be concerned about the soldiers' vote. They will vote, — it may not be in the coming election, — but you may rest assured the day will come when the soldiers will vote, and the only doubt is if they will permit the stay-at homes to vote at all.

I hope you will be elected; but I do think the conscript-law is the only one that is wanted for the next few years, and if the President uses it freely he can checkmate the Copperheads, who are not in favor of being governed by Jeff Davis, but are afraid to go to the war. Their motives are transparent. Jeff Davis despises them more than you do, and if he prevails in this war he will deal with Copperheads with infinitely more severity than lie will with men who fight for their country and for principle.

I am, etc.,

W. T. SHERMAN,

On Sept. 4th John Sherman writes from Mansfield, Ohio: —

We have just heard of the occupation of Atlanta by your forces, and that a battle had occurred at West Point, in which Harvie was killed and our side victorious. This is glorious news, and I sincerely congratulate you on your part of a campaign remarkable for the difficulties overcome, and for your skill and energy. As the possession of Atlanta was the ostensible point of your whole campaign, its possession is a complete triumph, though I suppose it the beginning of new movements. You will be assisted by the capture of Mobile, and I hope by the gunboat occupation of the river to Montgomery. From the map I judge that Atlanta is about equally distant from Augusta and Montgomery, the occupation of either of which would cut in two the Confederacy. We are looking for details of your recent movements with anxiety....

The nomination of McClellan makes a closer fight in the political arena than I hoped....

I believe Lincoln's election necessary to prevent disunion, and support him with all my might.

General Sherman's letters during the summer and autumn of 1864 were very hurried and infrequent, and he seems to have received few from his brother. On Sept. 17th he writes from Atlanta, Ga., in a letter otherwise devoted to family affairs: —

We are all in good condition here, and await the next great combination which will carry me deeper and deeper into the heart of Georgia.

And on Oct. 11th from Kingston, Ga.: —

Hood swung over against my road and broke it this side of Marietta, and forced me to come out of Atlanta to drive him off. He sheered off to the west, and is now below Borne. I have taken position here where I can watch him. I still hold Atlanta in strength, and have so many detachments guarding the railroad that Hood thinks he may venture to fight me. He certainly surpasses me in the quantity and quality of cavalry, which hangs all around and breaks the railroad and telegraph wires every night. You can imagine what a task I have, 138 miles of railroad, and my forces falling off very fast. I hear some new regiments are now arriving at Nashville, and they may strengthen my line so that I may go ahead, but Mobile or Savannah should be taken before I venture further. I am far beyond all other columns.

On Dec. 18th John Sherman writes from the Senate in Washington, after hearing news of the march through Georgia: —

I need hardly congratulate you on your magnificent campaign through Georgia. This has been and will be done so often that you will not need anything from me on the subject. We have watched with the deepest interest every step of your march that we could trace through the rebel papers. A very excellent map from the Coast

Survey is posted in my room, marked with your stopping places, and has daily been changed, as you progressed to the coast. No such anxiety has been evinced in any campaign by all classes, as in yours. We now hear rumors of the capture of Savannah. I hope we shall get official advices to-day. I live next door to Stanton, and he favors me with the despatches when they come. By the way, he is your fast friend, and was when you had fewer.

The election of Lincoln scarcely raised a ripple on the surface. It was anticipated. Even the Democratic congressmen seem willing to acquiesce cheerfully, and silently submit to all measures deemed necessary. In Congress we have but little to do. New taxes and loans are the principal point of legislation. We will impose taxes enough. Hitherto New England influence has prevented suitable taxation, but now its necessity is imperative. I am assigned Fessenden's place in the Senate as Chairman of Finance, and have enough to do. Chase is Chief Justice....

I could send you letters from very distinguished persons, very complimentary to you, but you will have enough of that incense.

The march to Atlanta and its capture consumes the spring and summer months, the Union armies entering Atlanta in the first days of September, 1864. The fall months were occupied by the march to Savannah, and that city was evacuated by the Southern armies Dec.

21, 1864. No letters appear to have been written by General Sherman during the march from Atlanta to Savannah. In the next letter, written Dec. 31st, from Savannah, he says: — value their lives as much as my own. I do not feel any older, and have no gray hairs yet. My health is good, and, save a little rheumatism in my right arm during the last march, I have not been indisposed a day, and even then I rode daily my march.... I do not fear want of appreciation, but, on the contrary, that an exaggerated faith will be generated in my ability, that no man can fulfil.... I cannot do anything looking to permanency till the war is ended. Thomas' success in Tennessee, which was part of my plan, will go far to assure the safety of the Ohio Valley.

The following order, issued to his army after the capture of Savannah and the news of the victory at Nashville, General Sherman forwarded to John Sherman, and it is in his letter-book.

HEADQUARTERS MILITARY DIVISION OF THE MISSISSIPPI.

IN THE FIELD, SAVANNAH, GA. , Jan. 8, 1865.

Special Field Orders |

No. 6.}

The General commanding announces to the troops composing the Military Division of the Mississippi, that he has received from the President of the United States and from Lieutenant General Grant, letters conveying their high sense and appreciation of the campaign just closed resulting in the capture of Savannah and the defeat of Hood's army in Tennessee.

In order that all may understand the importance of events it is proper to revert to the situation of affairs in September last. We held Atlanta, a city of little value to us, but so important to the enemy that Mr. Davis, the head of the rebellious faction in the South, visited his army near Palmetto, and commanded it to regain it, as well as to ruin and destroy us by a series of measures which lie thought would be effectual. That army, by a rapid march, gained our railroad near Big Shanty, and afterwards about Dalton. We pursued it, but it moved so rapidly that we could not overtake it, and General Hood led his army successfully far over towards Mississippi in hopes to decoy us out of Georgia. But we were not thus to be led away by him, and preferred to lead and control events ourselves. Generals Thomas and Schofield, commanding departments to our rear, returned to their posts and prepared to decoy General Hood into their meshes, whilst we came on to complete the original journey. We quietly and deliberately destroyed Atlanta and all the railroads which the enemy had used to carry on war against us, occupied the state capitol and then captured his commercial capital, which had been so strongly fortified from the sea as to defy approach from that quarter.

Almost at the moment of our victorious entry into Savannah, came the welcome and expected news that our comrades in Tennessee had also fulfilled nobly and well their part, had decoyed General Hood to Nashville, and then turned on him, defeating his army thoroughly, capturing nearly all his artillery, great numbers of prisoners, and were still pursuing the fugitives down into Alabama. So complete a success in military operations extending over a half a continent is an achievement that entitles it to a place in the military history of the world. The armies serving in Georgia and Tennessee, as well as the local garrisons of Decatur, Bridgeport, Chattanooga, and Murfreesboro, are alike entitled to the common honors, and each regiment may inscribe on its colors at pleasure the words "Savannah" or "Nashville."

The General-in-Chief embraces in the same general success the operations of the cavalry column under Generals Stoneman, Burbridge, and Gillem, that penetrated into southwest Virginia and paralyzed the efforts of the enemy to disturb the peace and safety of east Tennessee. Instead of being put on the defensive, we have at all points assumed the bold offensive, and completely thwarted the designs of the enemies of our country.

By Order of Major General,

W. T. SHERMAN-.

CHAPTER VII

The enthusiasm created in the North by the capture of Savannah and the victory at Nashville occasioned much talk of General S her man s promotion, and even some political rumors concerning the use of his name in future elections. On Jan. 22, 1865, he writes from Savannah, touching upon these rumors. to assure them that I would be offended by such association. I would rather be an engineer of a railroad, than President of the United States, or any political officer. Of military titles I have now the maximum, and it makes no difference whether that be Major-General or Marshal. It means the same thing. I haye commanded one hundred thousand men in battle, and on the march, successfully and without confusion, and that is enough for reputation. Next, I want rest and peace, and they can only be had through war. You will hear of me, but not from me for some time.

Affectionately your brother,

W. T. SHERMAN.

The next letter from General Sherman is a short and hurried one of April 6th from Goldsboro after he had completed the last and most difficult part of his march; *i e.* 425 miles from Savannah to Goldsboro, through marshy land, during much rainy weather, following Johnston's retreating army, and with five large navigable rivers, with their bridges burned, to cross. He says:—

Railroads work well, our supplies are well up, and we shall march next Monday, April 10. The next two months will demonstrate whether we can manoeuvre Lee out of Richmond and whip him in open battle.

In a note of April 11th, John Sherman, writing from Ohio, says of Lee's surrender: "The news from Grant is so glorious that the whole country is wild with joy."

The terms of General Johnston's surrender, in which General Sherman believed he was fulfilling Mr. Lincoln's instructions, were disapproved at Washington, General Grant was sent to supersede him in command, and General Halleck issued orders to Sherman's generals "to pay no regard to any truce or order of General Sherman's." These harsh measures, which General Sherman believed to be quite unnecessary, inasmuch as the terms of surrender awaited the approval of authority at Washington before they could be acted upon, deeply wounded him, as the following letters show.

HEADQUARTERS MILITARY Division OF THE MISSISSIPPI, AT SEA, April 8, 1865. Steamer *Russia.*

Dear Brother: We are now running in from Cape Henry Light and expect to reach Old Point by ten o'clock to-night. The ship vibrates so I can hardly write, but I must give you a few items. I have been to Savannah, Charleston, Wilmington, and Morehead City, closing up certain matters, whilst my army is marching up from Raleigh to Richmond. I will look for the advance at City Point by the 11th, and hope we will be ordered on to Washington to be mustered out. The South is whipped and submissive, and if any statesmanship is displayed will be the last part of our country to rebel again. Thirty thousand surrendered at Goldsboro, and other scattered bands are surrendering at Tallahassee, Macon, Augusta, and different posts, that will swell the number to 50,000. We might as well have had Taylor's army in Alabama, and Smith's in Texas, but of that hereafter. On my way up the coast I met the New York papers of the 24th and 28th, which were dead against me. Of course I expected that, but I did not expect Halleck and Stanton. They *suppressed* everything, save parts that by context with matters I never saw made a plausible case, but when I make my official report of the whole you will appreciate the game they have attempted. I met Mr. Chase at Morehead City, and even he was surprised to learn what I knew and told him, and I have from him the clue to the whole, which I must suppress for the time being.

Grant at Raleigh got his eyes opened also. I expect to spend the summer in Ohio, and we can discuss everything with my books and records before you; but in the meantime do not commit yourself to any plan of reconstruction, but let Stanton try his hand and watch the consequences. My belief is that to force the enfranchised negroes, as "loyal" voters at the South, will produce new riot and war, and I fear Sumner, Wilson, and men of that school will force it on the Government or prolong the war *ad infinitum.* My army won't fight in that war. The slaves are free, but are not yet voters. The time has not yet come. Such a course will alienate a strength your party cannot spare. Don't fear me turning politician. Nothing changes my unalterable resolution, and you may so announce it....

Yours,

W. T. SHERMAN.

John Sherman spent the spring of 1865 in Ohio, and was there when he heard of his brother's arrangement with General Johnston. He writes of this in the two following letters.

MANSFIELD, OHIO, May 2, 1865,

My Dear Brother: Since my return home I have been constantly and often painfully engaged. I spoke at a general jubilee at Columbus on the day of Mr. Lincoln's assassination. This tragic event suspended business, and cast a general gloom over all things....

The universal topic of conversation and of discussion in the newspapers was your arrangement with Johnston, and it is fair to say it was generally disapproved. The stipulation, to secure to the rebels their property was construed to mean slaves, — an impossible condition after we had induced them to enter our service by promise of freedom. It was felt also that to give them the benefit of their state organizations with all their political power would be unjust to those who have been friendly to us, especially in the border States, and would inevitably lead to a renewal of the war. But while the arrangement was disapproved, the manner in which Stanton and Halleck treated it, and especially the gross and damnable perversions of many of the papers and their arraignment of your motives, was more severely condemned than your arrangement. The conduct of Grant is deserving of the highest praise. I shall always feel grateful to him. What you were reported to have said about the effect of a single mistake proved literally true. For a time, you lost all the popularity gained by your achievements. But now the reaction has commenced, and you find some defenders, but many more to denounce the base and malicious conduct of a gang of envious scamps, who seized upon this matter as a pretext for calumny. What to make of Stanton, I don't know. I was beyond measure surprised at his conduct. He telegraphs me that he has written me in full I still think he only gave away to passion, and not to envy or malice. If you. have time, I hope to have some explanation from you. I suppose the war is about over, and you will, I trust, come to Ohio.

Affectionately,

JOHN SHERMAN.

MANSFIELD, OHIO, May 16, 1865.

Dear Brother: Your letter of the 8th is received this morning, and at the same moment I hear through K. W. that you will be in Lancaster to-day. I wrote you some days ago about public opinion as to your arrangement with Johnston, but presume you did not get it. It is now manifest that many high officials seized upon that arrangement to ruin you, and you will not be wise if you allow them to do it. Especially don't ever think of resigning. Your position is too high and valuable to be drawn from it by temporary hostile political power. Remember the case of Scott after the Mexican War. The mystery to me is that Stanton acted as he did. If his motive was malicious, he is certainly the worst devil I ever read of. He manifested and assumed the intensest kindness for you, and certainly showed it to me. I still think that with him it was mere anger, — the explosion of a very bad temper,— and if so, I sincerely trust no breach will be made. With Halleck I was not disappointed. Has Johnson any enmity to you? I have not seen him since his elevation, and have feared he was at the bottom of the business. It is also manifest to me, that the bitter hostility shown you springs partly from political jealousy,—a fear of the future. Much of this is aimed at me. I have observed that every man who is opposed to me is eager to assail you, while my personal friends, even among the Radicals, have defended you.... Chase, you know, is in favor of negro suffrage, and Jay and Henry Cooke are old Republicans, yet they have uniformly, in public and in social circles, sustained you. So with the newspapers. The feeling has so subsided and reacted that you can afford to be calm and cautious. Grant is a jewel. I hope two things,— that you will have no controversy with him, and never resign.

It was my purpose to go to-morrow to Washington, but I will now delay it until Friday or Saturday. I suppose you will soon return to Washington. I may be there some days, and hope to meet you there....

Now as to your arrangement with Johnston. I think the judgment of unprejudiced men has settled upon the conviction that your terms were too liberal. The recognition of the rebel state organizations, now completely in the hands of the worst men of the South, will not answer. They could perpetuate their sway, and we should inevitably have new difficulties. Lincoln first recognized the Legislature of Virginia, but after full reflection abandoned it. Why did not Stanton and Halleck denounce Lincoln? And why suppress the fact that you were acting in accordance with that precedent? Still I think it was not advisable to recognize the state officials. In my opinion, it would have been wise for you to have insisted upon the recognition of the emancipation proclamation, at least until the courts passed upon it. It would be very wrong to let these rebels enjoy again the unpaid labor of their slaves. Both these questions are past.

As to negro suffrage, I admit the negroes are not intelligent enough to vote, but some one must vote their political representation in the States where they live, and their representation is increased by their being free. Who shall exercise this political power? Shall the rebels do so? If yes, will they not now in effect restore slavery?

Will they not oppress the negroes? Is it not hard to turn these negroes over to the laws made by the very men who endeavored to overthrow the Government? After all, how much more ignorant are these slaves than the uneducated white people down South? I assure you, that while I will not commit myself on these matters, I feel sorely troubled about them, and would be glad to talk with you in respect to them....

Affectionately yours,

JOHN SHERMAN.

The letters of the years following the war treat entirely of the difficulties of reconstruction. John Sherman, while firmly attached to the Republican party, endeavored through all these troubles to be moderate and conciliatory. But he believed it necessary to extend suffrage to the negroes, and was intensely opposed to Mr. Johnson and his policies. General Sherman, on the other hand, never acknowledged allegiance to any party, and resented all appearance of such allegiance. He opposed universal suffrage, and believed that extending it to negroes was but adding to an existing evil.

After the Grand Review at Washington, May 24, 1865, General Sherman was ordered to St. Louis to command the Military Division of the Mississippi, and writes from there on Aug. 3, 1865.

Cox's letter on the subject of negro suffrage is a new bombshell in your camp. He has thought for himself, and come to a conclusion different from the new creed of the East, and will in my judgment be sat upon and badgered, but he is as near right as he can get. Negro equality will lead to endless strife, and to remove and separate the races will be a big job; so any way we approach the subject it is full of difficulty. But it is better to study the case and adapt measures to it, than to lay down the theory or force facts to meet it....

I think I will make that trip, and that is all this year. I did think of coming to Detroit to see Ord, but am bothered by people in travelling so much that I prefer to be quiet till the people run after new gods. In a short time new issues will drop us out of memory.

Affectionately,

W. T. SHERMAN.

And again, after a few days, from Ohio, where he passed part of that summer, he writes: —

LANCASTER, OHIO, Aug. 9, 1865.

Dear Brother: After I get fixed in St. Louis, I will cast about for some chance to be independent of our Government, for I feel there is a desire to be rid of me. Stanton, in Grant's absence, has ordered one of my chief staff-officers away from me, Beckwith, without as much as "by your leave." Now this was never done save by Jeff Davis

200

when he was Secretary of War, for orders to the army officers always should go by command of the commander-in-chief, but Stanton orders about as though it was his lawful prerogative. I would resist publicly, but don't want to bring on another controversy. Of course, if my staff-officers are taken away without my being consulted, they will feel little dependence on me, and my influence will subside. But that is a small matter compared with turning the army into a machine auxiliary to politics. If the War Department is to give orders direct to the army below us and not through us, you can see that we are dissolved from all control, responsibility, or interest. The true way is for the War Department to indicate to us what the Administration wants done, and then hold us responsible for the means used. But if the Secretary handles the army behind us, how can we take an interest? My own opinion is the Administration will either break itself down or drive us out. Grant is so anxious for harmony that he will not interfere until it is too late, when he will find somebody else commands instead of him.

I think the agitation of the suffrage question now before the people has got far enough advanced to show how they (the negroes) can make a living, and will give trouble, but we hope still that even that question will be allowed to rest until the forms and shapes of the States South are adjusted.... I fear you will all have a burden to carry in the form of Military Governments South, which are awkward and expensive. My command only embraces Arkansas, and there things seem quiet, though I know but little of the actual state of affairs. In no other point of my command do these questions arise.

Yours affectionately,

W. T. SHERMAN.

And a few days later he writes from St. Louis: —

We cannot keep the South out long, and it is a physical impossibility for us to guard the entire South by armies; nor can we change opinions by force; nor can the President pass on the merits of all pardons, but must delegate it, when the power will be corrupted or gradually embrace all exempts, for the class exempted is the vital part of the South. I would have used it and had it subservient to the uses of Government. The poor whites and negroes of the South have not the intelligence to fill the offices of governors, clerks, judges, etc., etc., and for some time the marching of state Governments must be controlled by the same class of whites as went into the Rebellion against us....

John Sherman passed the summer of 1865 in Mansfield, Ohio, from where he writes on August 29th, in answer to an invitation from General Sherman to go on a Western trip during that autumn.

I am very desirous to accept your invitation. The trip would be an instructive and pleasant one, and if I was not restrained by the interests of others I would surely go at once. But we are now involved in an exciting and important political contest. The canvass in Ohio is substantially between the Government and the Rebellion, and is assuming all the bitterness of such a strife. If I should leave now, it would be like a general leaving before the day of battle. I have been speaking very often, and must keep it up. I propose, however, to arrange all my business so that I may leave soon after the election, say about the 20th of October, and will then go down the river and spend all the time until the meeting of Congress. I hope to be able to go via Vicksburg, Kew Orleans, Charleston, to Washington. If a favorable opportunity offers at Vicksburg or *New* Orleans, I wish to develop my ideas as to a reconstruction of the Union. I know these will suit you a good deal better than they will the Administration, but I feel quite independent of the latter, and am disposed to follow my own course....

HEADQUARTERS MILITARY DIVISION OF THE MISSISSIPPI,

ST. LOUIS, MO., Sept. 21, 1865.

Dear Brother: I got your letters by Mr. Kinneard, and spent a whole day with him and his party, first in a steamboat going up and down the river, then in carriages, and finally at a banquet. The whole party seemed much pleased with the courtesies shown them, and to me were sufficiently complimentary. General Grant was here also, and they expressed themselves more than usually pleased at the opportunity to see us together. In Europe they are settling down to the conviction that Grant and I accomplished the military problem, and now they look to yon to bring order, system, and prosperity out of the wreck. I am well satisfied at the course things are taking. Ho matter what change we may desire in the feelings and thoughts of people South, we cannot accomplish it by force. Nor can we afford to maintain there an army large enough to hold them in subjugation. All we can, or should, attempt is to give them rope, to develop in an honest way if possible, preserving in reserve enough military power to check any excesses if they attempt any. But I know they will not attempt any, and you may look for outbreaks in Ohio quicker than in Georgia or Mississippi. You hardly yet realize how completely this country has been devastated, and how completely humbled the man of the South is. Of course editors and talkers may express opinions we don't like, but they will take good care not to reduce those opinions to acts.

Affectionately,

W. T. SHERMAN.

HEADQUARTERS MILITARY DIVISION OF THE MISSISSIPPI,

St. LOUIS, Nov. 4, 1865.

Dear Brother: Ever since my return from my trip in Iowa, Nebraska, and Kansas, I have been so busy that I have neglected to write to you. We are now most comfortable in our new house, and I am settling down into a kind of routine that looks like old banking times.

I see a great many people, and get any quantity of letters with all sorts of invitations, but I decline all save a few here in the city. I think I will go to see Henry Sherman at his commencement at Dartmouth next spring, and that will carry me to Boston, where I expect to he besieged. Strange to say, I receive more strong feeling of favor from that quarter than any other, spite the attempt made to put me in antagonism to their special hobbies. I shall not go near Washington this year, nor take part in the reorganization of the new army until ordered to do so officially. I have the report for the

Committee on the conduct of the war nearly done, and will send it by a staff-officer to Mr. Wade before the meeting of Congress.

It will contain much detailed and original matter which has never seen the light, and will make the great campaigns as clear as possible, being composed wholly of letters which passed at the time between me and all the officers above and below me. It is more voluminous than I intended, and I will curtail it all I can, but as it is now it is very interesting. I will also accompany it with a map which is very valuable, and I want it engraved on metal. I know Congress will appropriate for proper maps, and not insult us with such lithographs as have heretofore been customary. I may have to get you to help me in this, as I have expended vast labor on this map and want it done *right,*

I notice that foreigners are very anxious to see me, and all who come here come to call. I shall be here all winter, and if you want anything I can do it. I hope you are sure of your re-election. I have many inquiries as to your prospects, and cannot answer them. I think you have more influence and reputation out of Ohio than any man of the State.... You observe that Mr. Johnson is drifting toward my terms to Johnston. He cannot help it, for there is no other solution. Any plan will have objections, but that least of all.

Affectionately,

W. T. SHERMAN.

John Sherman, having returned to Washington for the winter, writes from there: —

UNITED STATES SENATE CHAMBER, WASHINGTON, NOV. 10, 1865.

Dear Brother: Your note of the 4th is received. I am glad to hear you are settled, and from all accounts delightfully. You deserve quiet and repose after five years of change and labor. When in New York the other day, I found that party of English capitalists were delighted with their visit with you, and seemed especially polite to me on that account. I got for two of them Bowman and Nichols' works, which they wanted to take home. But for my political employment I could have received from them very lucrative employment in the prosecution of their vast railroad schemes. Even as it is, if they, within six months, show their ability to execute their plans, I will identify myself much more with them. The truth is, the close of the war with our resources unimpaired gives an elevation, a scope to the ideas of leading capitalists, far higher than anything ever undertaken in this country before. They talk of millions as confidently as formerly of thousands. No doubt the contraction that must soon come will explode merely visionary schemes, but many vast undertakings will be executed. Among them will be the Pacific B. B. and extensive iron works, like some in England. Our manufactures are yet in their infancy, but soon I expect to see, under the stimulus of a great demand and the protection of our tariff, locomotive and machine shops worthy of the name. I do not fear, whatever may be the result of the senatorial election, but I can find enough to do, and without lowering the position I have occupied. As for the chances, from all the information I can gather, there is but little doubt a majority of the Legislature is for me. Still I know enough of the shifts and dangers in a new body of men like a Legislature not to be over sanguine. Since I am in the contest I will do all I can for success, and hope my friends will do likewise, but if defeated will bear it patiently. In a short time I will send you a list of the members who are from the military service, in the hope that you may know some of them well enough to influence them. You can feel perfectly easy in doing this, as my opponents use to the uttermost against me any prejudice or feeling against you. This election over, I think I shall be very willing to say good by to politics, and will then seek to settle myself comfortably in some part of Ohio where I can engage in railroads, banking, or manufacturing. The law in this country is now only useful as the pathway to other pursuits.

I have seen Johnson several times. He seems kind and patient with all his terrible responsibility. I think he feels what every one must have observed, that the people will not trust the party or men who, during the war, sided with the rebels. The Democratic party is doomed forever as a disloyal organization, and no promises, or pledges, or platform they can make will redeem them from the odium they justly gained.

Yours affectionately,

John **SHERMAN.**

On Nov. 29, 1865, General Sherman writes from St. Louis: — be on the question of the admission of the Southern members. I have never committed myself on that point, and though everybody supposes that my terms with Johnston looked to that result, you will remember that those terms specially provided that the laws of Congress were to control all questions. Now the new oath is and was a law of Congress, and the members elect must take the new oath, and if they cannot it is their fault or misfortune, not ours. If they take the prescribed oath, I think they should be admitted, simply because you cannot expect to hold a people always without representation, and it will give them additional weight, if they be denied now and afterward received. It is always better when concessions are to be made to make them at once, and not seem to be forced to do it after contest. You can now simply say, "Certainly, come in by subscribing to the conditions and oaths already prescribed by law, the same oaths we take."

Affectionately,

W. T. SHERMAN.

ST. LOUIS, Dec. 22, 1865.

And on January 17th he writes again from St. Louis: —

I get a great many commentaries on the past, and hare no reason to object to the exalted examples with which my name is connected. According to some enthusiasts, Hannibal, Alexander, and Napoleon fall below my standard. Of course I always laugh at these, and prefer to stand by the record, being perfectly satisfied with Grant's *résumé* of the campaigns of 1864-5.

Affectionately,

W. T. SHERMAN.

HEADQUARTERS MILITARY DIVISION OF THE MISSISSIPPI,

St. Louis, Jan. 19, 1866.

Dear Brother: The papers this morning announce your election by a strong vote, and settle that question. I am of course very glad, for it demonstrates not only your strength but that the people of Ohio approve your past. As to the future, of course in all things political you have far more knowledge than I, but I do believe that the extension of the election franchise is being pushed beyond the Rule of Right. All beings are entitled to the protection of the law, even "infants not born," but because of such natural right it is not to be inferred they must vote. To vote implies an understanding almost equivalent to the ability to make laws. It is legislative—not natural Right. Instead of enlarging the privilege, we must gradually curtail it, in order to have stability and security. It was this popular clamor for supposed rights that carried the South into rebellion. Ho people were ever more unanimous than they, and > though now they concede themselves vanquished, yet on this and kindred subjects they are as unanimous as ever.

To place or attempt to place the negro on a par with the whites will produce new convulsions. The country is in no condition to go on with such contests. Better pacify or acknowledge conditions than attempt new ones dangerous to the peace of the whole country. It will take ten years for the South to regain full prosperity with the negro free, and that should precede any new complication.

Affectionately, etc.,

W. T. SHERMAN-.

HEADQUARTERS MILITARY DIVISION OF THE MISSISSIPPI,

ST. LOUIS, Feb. 11, 1866.

Dear Brother: I had a pleasant trip to Detroit, reaching there in a snowstorm on Wednesday morning. I got a couple hours of quiet, and then for two days was kept on the jump, visited and dined, when I got away. I think I must have touched the hands of 10,000 people. At the dinner we had the best people of the city, who were even more eulogistic than usual. I saw Mr. Cass, who sat in a chair and was seemingly much flattered by my visit. He simply said that he hoped the present peace would not be disturbed by experiments. We cannot shove the South back as Territories, and all steps to that end must fail for many reasons, if no other than that it compels the people already there to assume a hostile attitude. The well disposed of the South must again be trusted — we cannot help it.

You are classed universally as one of the rising statesmen, above mere party rules. And whilst you should not separate from your party, you can moderate the severity of their counsels....

Affectionately,

W. T. SHERMAN.

HEADQUARTERS MILITARY DIVISION OF THE MISSISSIPPI,

ST. LOUIS, Feb. 23, 1866.

Dear Brother: The political aspect now is interesting to a looker-on. Sumner and Stevens would have made another civil war inevitably — the President's antagonistic position saves us war save of words, and as I am a peace man I go for Johnson and the Veto.

I recollect that Congress is but one of three co-ordinate branches of the Government. I want to hear the Supreme Court manifest itself, and then can guess at the conclusion.... Let Johnson fight it out with Sumner, who, though sincere, represents an antagonism as ultra as of Davis himself. Both are representative men, and it will be a pity if the great mass of our people have to go on fighting forever to demonstrate the fallacy of extreme opinions.

The Republican party has lost forever the best chance they can ever expect of gaining recruits from the great middle class who want peace and industry. The white men of this country will control it, and the negro, in mass, will occupy a subordinate place as a race. We can secure them the liberty now gained, but we cannot raise them to a full equality in our day, even if at all. Had the Republicans graciously admitted the great principle of representation, leaving members to take the Ironclad Oath, you would have secured the active cooperation of such men as Sharkey, Parsons, Wm. A. Graham, Johnson, and others of the South, and it would not be many years before some of these States would have grown as rabid as Missouri, Maryland, and Arkansas are now disposed to be. The foolish querulousness of the Secessionists untamed would soon make a snarlish minority in their own States. Now, however, by the extreme measures begun and urged with so much vindictiveness, Sumner has turned all the Union people South as well as of the West against the party.... It is surely unfortunate that the President is thus thrown seemingly on the old mischievous anti-war Democrats, but from his standpoint he had no alternative. To outsiders it looks as though he was purposely forced into that category.

I know that the Freedmen Bureau Bill, and that for universal suffrage in the District, are impracticable and impolitic. Better let them slide, and devote time to putting the actual Government into the best shape the country admits of, letting other natural causes produce the results you aim at. Whenever State Legislatures and people oppress the negro they cut their own throats, for the negro cannot again be enslaved. Their mistakes will work to the interests of the great Union party.

I can readily understand what the effect must be in your circle. How difficult it is to do anything, but if Congress does nothing it will be the greatest wisdom; for the business relations opening throughout the South will do more to restore peace and prosperity than all the laws that could be published in six months.

I think Mr. Johnson would consent to a modification of the Constitution to change the basis of representation to suit the changed condition of the population South, but that is all he can or should do....

We need the Army Bills to get to work. I will have to abandon all the remote settlements to the chances of the Indians, for even after the bill passes, it will take months to enlist the men, and in the meantime all volunteers are clamorous for discharge, and must be discharged as soon as winter lets them come in.

Affectionately,

W. T. SHERMAN.

And on February 28th, he writes again: —

Dear Brother: Of course I agree substantially with the President. If we do not design to make a complete revolution in our form of Government, but rather to preserve it, you must, sooner or later, allow representation from the South, and the longer it is deferred the worse will be its effect.

Any seeming purpose to restrict them from retaining political power with your party will react against you.

The case is very different when a native conquers an adversary, but even in that case we have always incorporated new conquests as a part of the whole, as in Louisiana, Texas, and California. If the people of the South are to be punished, It must be done by trials and convictions of individuals.

Affectionately,

W. T. SHERMAN.

On March 24th, General Sherman writes from St. Louis: —

I am sorry to hear that the President is likely to break with the party. It should not be, but Congress should defer much to him, as an executive feels how much more difficult to execute plans than a Congress dealing with abstract ideas. I still hope that mutual concessions will result in a practical solution.

The question as to the burning of Columbia, S.C., having been raised by Wade Hampton, General Sherman writes the two following letters on the subject and encloses an old order given at the time.

I have no doubt myself, and Howard, Logan, Woods, and all who were in Columbia that night concur with me. The fire which burned up the city, began about dawn, after I had been in six hours, and I know that great exertions were made to stop it, but there had been all day and continued till late at night, a perfect tempest of wind, and I saw hundreds of bales of cotton on fire flying hundreds of yards. It is barely possible some malicious soldier started the fire, but I rather think this devilish spirit grew as the fire progressed. I know that the general judgment of the country is that no matter how it began it was all right, still I know that the cotton was the cause of the rapid spread of the fire, and this resulted from the fact that the bales had been ripped open with knives, so that long before the fire began the houses and trees were white with it, and it was plain a spark would spread like gunpowder. It was not specially my business, for Howard was in actual command of the troops in Columbia, but being present in person the world holds me responsible. I should like you to introduce the petition, and to say that I have no doubt as to the parties responsible for all the consequences.

It was not until the day after the conflagration that I destroyed the Arsenal and other public factories which were in the suburbs and had escaped the fire that burned the town.

Affectionately,

W. **T. SHERMAN.**

HEADQUARTERS MILITARY DIVISION OF THE MISSISSIPPI,

ST. LOUIS, MO., April 2, 1866.

Dear Brother:

I know the railroad depot and three large bridges were burned *before* a soldier of ours had entered Columbia, and I know that six hours before the real conflagration began I saw half-a-dozen piles of cotton *on fire* in the streets — one large pile near the market house where the great conflagration began, which fire our soldiers were putting out as I rode by it.... Wade Hampton defended Columbia as long as he dared, and then ran away, leaving the city full of cotton blowing about like flakes of snow. So that trees and frame houses and garden fences were literally white. Of course a mayor could expect no terms. Being helpless, he took what he could get. I told him, of course, I had no intention to bum or destroy anything except what my previous orders defined. I saw Wade Hampton's cotton order printed in a Columbia paper, but kept no copy, as it was notorious; for he openly declared that Yankee footsteps should not pollute his threshold, and he commanded everything like com fodder, etc., to be burnt, lest we should get it....

They boasted that we would find a Moscow and its consequences.

The treatment of our officers, prisoners at Columbia, was enough to have warranted its utter annihilation, and after the fire began it required all our efforts to prevent its extending to the suburbs, including the Old Hampton house, — now owned by Preston, brother-in-law of Wade Hampton, — which was saved by John Logan.

Affectionately yours,

W. T. SHERMAN-.

HEADQUARTERS MILITARY DIVISION OF THE MISSISSIPPI,

IN THE FIELD NEAR COLUMBIA, S.C., Feb. 16, 1865.

Special Field Orders,)

No. 26. J

EXTRACT.

The next series of movements will be at Fayetteville, N.C., and thence to Wilmington or Goldsboro, according to events. Great care must be taken to collect forage and food, and at the same time in covering the wagon trains from cavalry dashes.

General Howard will cross the Saluda and Broad rivers as near their mouths as possible, occupy Columbia, destroy the public buildings, railroad property, manufacturing and machine shops, but will spare libraries, and asylums, and private dwellings. He will then move to Winnsboro, destroying en route utterly that section of the railroad....

By order of Major-General

W. T. SHERMAN-.

L. M. Dayton, Assistant Adjutant-General.

[Probably April 6-7, 1866.]

This order was made the day before we entered Columbia, about the time the rebels were cannonading our camps on the west side of the Congaree, and burning their three splendid bridges (Saluda and Broad unite at Columbia and make the Congaree). During the 16th Howard crossed the Saluda at the factory above Columbia, and that night crossed Stone's brigade to the east side of the Broad River, and under its cover laid the pontoon bridge, completing it about noon of the 17th. Stone's brigade went into Columbia about 11 a m., the mayor having come out three miles and notified him that Beauregard and Hampton had evacuated. They evacuated because they knew that Slocum and Kilpatrick were moving straight for Winnsboro, 26 miles in their rear, and I wanted them to stay in Columbia another day. Their hasty evacuation was not to spare Columbia, but to save being caught in the forks of the Congaree and Catawba, which would have resulted, had they given time for Slocum to reach Winnsboro. Mayor Goodwin complained to me of the cotton-burning order of Wade Hampton, and especially that Hampton and Beauregard would not consent to his request that the liquor (which had run the blockade and been transferred from the coast to Columbia for safety) was not removed or destroyed. This liquor, which our men got in bucketfuls, was an aggravation, and occasioned much of the disorder at night after the fires had got headway. We all know how the soldiers and junior officers hated South Carolina, and I can hardly say what excesses would have resulted had the general officers allowed them free scope....

W. T. SHERMAN.

The latter part of March, 1866, John Sherman says in a long letter on family matters: —

You may have noticed that I have been in Connecticut making two speeches. That at Bridgeport is reported in full in "The New York Times" of yesterday. Our difficulties here are not over; Johnson is suspicious of every one, and I fear will drift into his old party relations. If so, he will carry with him but little peace and prestige, and will soon be in deserved disgrace. It is also evident that Grant has some political aspirations and can, if he wishes it, easily attain the Presidency....

Affectionately yours,

JOHST SHERMAN.

And on April 23d he writes: —

Dear Brother: So little attention is paid to Wade Hampton's gasconade, that I do not think it worth while to give it importance by an answer. Indeed, I do not find it printed in any Northern paper, and having sent you the only copy I have seen, I find it impossible to get another. The materials of a reply are on hand, and are entirely satisfactory, but I will let it rest until the charge is taken up by some one else.

As for the Civil Eights Bill, I felt it so clearly right that I was prepared for the very general acquiescence in its provisions both North and South.

To have refused the negroes the simplest right granted to every other inhabitant, native or foreigner, would be outrageous *j* and to confess that our Government is strong enough to compel their military services, and yet not strong enough to secure them the right to acquire and hold property would involve a gross inconsistency. I hope this bill will be made the basis of a compromise. If fairly enforced in the South, the public mind will be satisfied for the negro to take his chances for political privileges....

Affectionately,

John SHERMAN.

On May 12th, John Sherman writes of a contemplated Western trip.

The chief motive I have in the trip this fall is to notice the country through which the Pacific E. E. runs. The mistake made by Congress was in not concentrating its aid on *one* road commencing far enough west to be the common meeting point of all the Eastern roads, and then push it through with all the means of the Government. As it is too late to alter the law, it is probable *one* of the roads now building will be selected, and gratuities will not be given to the other further than the one hundredth meridian, I am a member of the Railroad Committee, and therefore take an active interest in the question.

UNITED STATES SENATE, WASHINGTON, July 2, 1866.

Dear Brother: I have read the enclosed letter with a good deal of interest. The feeling of the writer is manly and proper. A man may lose his cause both in law or in war without yielding his sense of right or his pride or honor. If he will only submit to the decision of the tribunal to which he appeals, it is all that can be asked of him. I meet a great many from the South whom I knew before the war, and I confess I am gratified with their sentiments and conduct. If they could now see their manifest interests to accept the recent adjustment or amendments to the Constitution as a reasonable and fair settlement, the South would soon be resurrected into greater wealth and power. I only fear their political alliance with the pestilent Copperheads of the North, and thus perpetuation of sectional enmity. I really fear that Johnson, who is an honest man, will from sheer stubbornness and bitter dislike to Stevens and a few others, lend himself to this faction. The very moment the South will agree to a firm basis of representation, I am for general amnesty and a repeal of the test oaths. But the signs of the times indicate another stirring political contest. I see no way to avoid it. I will have to take part in it, but you can, and I hope will, stand aloof. Don't commit yourself to any political faction, and don't fail to remember that the Republican, or anti-slavery and now anti-rebel feeling, is deeper and stronger than any other in the Northern States. We could surely contend with a manly, fighting rebel like your friend, but never will with those who raised the white flag in the rear....

Affectionately,

JOHN SHERMAN.

The letter referred to by Senator Sherman is one written by Mr. Boyd to General Sherman. Mr. Boyd was, at the time he writes, the Superintendent of the Louisiana State Military Academy, a position which General Sherman held just before the war. The letter follows this one of Senator Sherman's.

LOUISIANA STATE SEMINARY, May 1, 1866. General W. T. Sherman,

United States America.

Dear General: Your most welcome favor of 12 ult. is at hand.

I am glad to know that you still feel so much interest in the seminary as to use your valuable time in writing me such wholesome advice regarding its management. None can appreciate your suggestions more than I do; for them I thank you, both in my official capacity and personally; and for the personal interest which I know you have always taken m my welfare I tender you my most sincere thanks. In the *late* war through which the country has passed, I was opposed to you; and in my own feeble and humble way did my best to help secure the secession of the Southern States.

For you, the great Federal Commander, I feel as do all good Southerners, not *amiably,* nor yet unkindly; for the noble and brilliant manner in which you did your duty commands our admiration, and now the struggle is over and I am one of the poor, subjugated band, I can truly say that I have not a particle of ill feeling towards any man in the Federal Army. On the contrary, I have a few friends whom I value none the less for whipping me. Understand me rightly. I speak with no cringing spirit. Though beaten and so poor that none do me reverence, I am *patient* and *proud.* The end of matters has decided that the rights I battled for were in vain. I have no other, and none will I ask. I have taken the oath of allegiance in good faith, hoping to be allowed to remain in the country, and if not a useful citizen to be a harmless one.

Certainly I have no intention of ever again attempting to say who shall *not* be President of the United States. I am cured of that. That question must hereafter be decided by the *faithful* and not the *rebellious.*

For a similar reason I am addressing these lines not to the *General,* but to *W. T.* Sherman, and I congratulate myself that no one knows the difference between the two characters better than my friend, the report of whose death at Shiloh gave me great grief, when I was a poor *rebel* soldier lying in the Rappahannock mud, and whose "Union Scouts" {alias Confederate jayhawkers and deserters) two years after kidnapped me and took me a prisoner to him at Natchez, where he treated me both like a prisoner of war and his personal friend! And the friendship of such a man I value, and hope ever to have his confidence and esteem....

Your chair is filled by Venable, Kirby Smith's topographical engineer. He has extraordinary capacity and fine character....

216

In one way you can be of great use to the seminary, and I claim the right to call your attention to the matter. Although I have bought some few books for the boys to read we are still in great need of a library, and as I have no doubt that you are showered with patent office reports, military books, maps, etc., much, of which, you do not want. Please have your orderly to pack up the rubbish and send them to us by Adams' express, *I* to pay all charges. If not in all, at least in the more important books, put *your name* as *donor*. I would like, also, to have a large picture of you in *citizen's* dress (unless you prefer your *uniform,)*, to be put in our library as our first superintendent. By sending us the books as asked for, you can really do us great good. You must know that we outsiders (not being represented at Washington) can't even get a patent office report....

I must beg pardon for asking you to read so long a letter, but really, when I sit down to write to you, the past, so pleasant to recollect, and the present, so changed from then, make me feel like telling you all I know, and think, and feel. To a Southern man — a conscientious Calhounite as I was and am — the present is dark and sad, and the future gives but little hope. It is all not your fault nor mine. Present me most kindly to Mrs. Sherman and your children.

Your friend,

D. **F. BOYD.**

CHAPTER VIII

During the unfortunate struggle between the President and Congress with reference to the Secretary of War, it became almost impossible for General Sherman to keep out of the trouble. The President, finding himself at variance with Mr. Stanton, his Secretary of War, attempted to remove him without the sanction of Congress. Mr. Stanton declined to leave his office, and General Grant refused to comply with the President's request and assume the position of Secretary of War. The President, believing that General Sherman was more friendly to him than General Grant, made several attempts to bring him to Washington and to send General Grant away on the Mexican mission. General Grant refused to be disposed of in any such manner and General Sherman declined to be made Secretary of War. But he offered to go to Mexico in General Grant's place, and this plan was finally decided upon.

UNITED STATES SENATE CHAMBER, WASHINGTON, July 8, 1866.

Dear Brother: It is now wise for you to avoid all expressions of political opinion. Congress and the President are drifting from each other into open warfare. Congress is not weak in what it has done, but in *what it has failed to do.* It has adopted no unwise or extreme measures. The Civil Rights Bill and constitutional amendments can be defended as reasonable, moderate, and in harmony with Johnson's old position and yours. As Congress has thus far failed to provide measures to allow legal senators and representatives to take their seats, it has failed in a plain duty. This is its weakness; but even in this it will have the sympathy of the most of the soldiers, and the people who are not too eager to secure rebel political power. As to the President, he is becoming Tylerized. He was elected by the Union party for his openly expressed radical sentiments, and now he seeks to rend to pieces this party. There is a sentiment among the people that this is dishonor. It looks so to me. What Johnson is, is from and by the Union party. He now deserts it and betrays it. He may varnish it up, but, after all, he must admit that he disappoints the reasonable expectations of those who entrusted him with power.

He may, by a coalition with Copperheads and rebels, succeed, but the simple fact that nine tenths of them who voted for him do not agree with him, and that he only controls the other tenth by power entrusted to him by the Union party will damn him forever. Besides, he is insincere; he has deceived and misled his best friends. I know he led many to believe he would agree to the Civil Eights Bill, and nearly all who conversed with him until within a few days believed he would acquiesce in the amendments, and even aid in securing their adoption. I almost fear he contemplates civil war. Under these circumstances you, Grant, and Thomas ought to be clear of political complications. As for myself, I intend to stick to finance, but wherever I can will moderate the actions of the Union party, and favor conciliation and restoration.

Affectionately yours,

JOHN SHERMAN.

During August and September, 1866, Senator Sherman accompanied General Sherman on a trip to the western posts including Denver, but returned through Kansas, leaving General Sherman to complete his tour.

HEADQUARTERS MILITARY DIVISION OF THE MISSOURI, ST. LOUIS, MO., Oct. 20, 1866.

Dear Brother:

I got back all safe and well the day before yesterday, having met no trouble whatever, notwithstanding the many rumors of Indian troubles. These are all mysterious, and only accountable on the supposition that our people out West are resolved on trouble for the sake of the profit resulting from military occupation. I kept the same ambulances, and made the very route I had prescribed to myself by Garland, Lyon, etc., to Ellsworth, Riley, etc. The railroad is finished to Riley, so that I came all the way thence in cars....

I see rumors of my being called to Washington. Of this I know nothing, and if offered I shall decline. I must keep clear of politics in all its phases, for I must serve any administration that arises. I am not aware that I have ever on paper expressed any opinion of this seeming conflict between Congress and the President. I deplore it as much as you do, and still hope that some solution will be found...

Affectionately,

W. T. SHERMAN.

Mansfield, Oct. 26, 1866.

..Dear Brother: Your letter of the 20th has been received. I thought, and was glad to hear, that you had a charming trip. I saw enough of the mountain region to give me a new estimate of its great value. In some respects I regret that I did not go with you, but situated as I am, it was extremely fortunate that I returned as I did. My political position ought not to be misunderstood, but unfriendly critics took occasion of my absence in the canvass to attribute it to duplicity or cowardice. The President's course on the Civil Eights Bill and constitutional amendment was so unwise that I could not for a moment allow any one to suppose that I meant with him to join a coalition with rebels and Copperheads. Besides, Johnson was elected by a party upon professions before and after his election and inauguration so pointedly different from his recent course that it appeared to me a betrayal of those who trusted his professions, and therefore in the highest sense dishonorable. But worse than all, his turning out good men — sometimes wounded soldiers — merely because they adhered to their party convictions, and putting in men who opposed the war throughout, is simply an unmitigated outrage that will stain the name of any man connected with such conduct. This was the deliberate judgment of *nearly every man in the Union party,* and the feeling was intensified by the President's conduct in his recent tour, when he sunk the Presidential office to the level of a grog-house.

I do trust you will not connect your name with this administration. You lose in every way by it. Grant ought not to ask it, for in the common judgment it places you in equivocal relations with him. You will have all the odium caused by disappointment in the reorganization of the Army, and will have a most difficult, delicate, and responsible duty to discharge, in which you can gain no credit and may lose much. Besides, it connects you as a partisan with

Johnson — just what he wants, but what you ought to dread. What can you think of the recent telegrams about your private letter? If you wrote a private letter, what business had they to make it public in the most offensive way by innuendo? Grant and you are above the ephemera of party politics, and for the sake of the country I hope will keep so. Let Johnson take Cowan, or some one that left the Union party with him, but my convictions are so strong that you ought not to play "Administrator de bonis non" of Stanton, that I write thus freely. If you conclude otherwise, I can only say I shall deeply regret it....

Affectionately,

JOHN SHERMAN.

After returning from his Western trip, General Sherman was summoned to Washington in October by the President, who wished to make him Secretary of War.

Washington, Oct. 31, 1866.

Dear Brother: I got your letter, and have this morning answered by telegraph, but wish to write more fully. When here last winter, I did not call to say good-by to the President, and wrote him a good letter of apology, enclosing my good wishes for his success in his professed desire to accomplish in his term of office the restoration of Civil Government all over our land. When I got in to Riley I received a despatch from the President, asking leave to publish it. I answered that he could publish anything I ever wrote if it would do any good,— if Mr. Stanbury would advise it,— but desiring, if possible, to avoid any controversy. On this he did not publish, and I have not made any request in the premises. I don't believe lie will publish it, and I don't care much, for it contains nothing more than I thought then; *viz.,* in February last, when I got here, there was a move to send Grant to Mexico with Campbell in an advisory capacity. Grant could not then be put to one side in that way, and on my arrival I found out that the President was aiming to get Grant out of the way, and me in, not only as Secretary of War but to command the army, on the supposition that I would be more friendly to him than Grant. Grant was willing that I should be Secretary of War, but I was not. I would not be put in such a category, and after much pro and con we have settled down that I shall go with Campbell. The Secretary of the Navy is preparing a steamer for us, and it will be ready next week at New York, when we will go forth to search for the Governor of Mexico; not a task at all to my liking, but I cheerfully consented because it removes at once a crisis. Both Grant and I desire to keep plainly and strictly to our duty in the Army, and not to be construed as partisans. We must be prepared to serve every administration as it arises. We recognize Mr. Johnson as the lawful President, without commit-. ting ourselves in the remotest degree to an approval or disapproval of his specific acts. We recognize the present Congress as the lawful Congress of the United States, and its laws binding on us and all alike, and we are most anxious to see, somehow or other, the Supreme Court brought in to pass on the legal and constitutional differences between the President and Congress.

We see nothing objectionable in the proposed amendments to the Constitution, only there ought to have been some further action on the part of Congress committing it ,to the admission of members when the amendments are adopted; also the minor exceptions to hold office, etc., should be relaxed as the people show an adherence to the national cause.... I feel sure the President is so in the habit of being controlled by popular majorities that he will yield — save he may argue against Congress and in favor of his own past-expressed opinions. Congress should not attempt an impeachment or interference with the current acts of the executive unless some overt act clearly within the definition of the Constitution be attempted, of which I see no signs whatever. Some very bad appointments have been made, but I find here that he was backed by long lists of names that were Union men in the war. Of course our army cannot be in force everywhere: to suppress riots in the South, Indians in that vast region, only a part of which we saw, where whites and Indians both require watching, and the thousand and one duties that devolve on us. This army can never be used in the political complications, nothing more than to hold arsenals, depots, etc., against riots, or to form the nucleus of an army of which Congress must provide the laws for government and the means of support. Neither the President nor Congress ought to ask us of the army to manifest any favor or disfavor to any political measures. We are naturally desirous for harmonious action — for peace and civility. We naturally resist the clamor of temporary popular changes, but as each administration comes in we must serve its executive and the War Department with seeming friendship.

I have called on Mr. Stanton, who received me with all cordiality, and placed at my disposal ample means to execute my present task with ease and comfort.

I start from here to-night, and shall reach St. Louis on Friday night, ready to start for New York as soon as the vessel is ready and as soon as Campbell is ready, say all next week.... I don't know that I can come byway of Mansfield, as, you see, I must move fast, staying every spare minute I can at home. Write me fully, and let us all pull together and get past this present difficulty; then all will he well....

Yours affectionately,

W. T. SHERMAN.

In the fall of 1866, the Hon. Lewis D. Campbell, of Ohio, was appointed Minister to Juarez in Mexico, which country was still in possession of the Emperor Maximilian, supported by French troops under Marshal Bazaine, although Juarez was the President-elect of the country.

General Grant was ordered to escort Mr. Campbell to Mexico, but did not wish to go, as related by General Sherman, and the latter was ordered to go in his stead. On November 11th, General Sherman sailed on his mission on the United States ship *Susquehanna*.

United States Ship Susquehanna (off Sandy Hook),Nov. 11, 1866.

Dear Brother: we have no right to go to Mexico to offer ourselves as their example and special friends. You can write me through the Navy Department, as I may run to New Orleans where Sheridan could hold a letter for me, hut I expect little the next two months....

Affectionately,

W. T. SHERMAN.

Dear Brother:... I was heartily glad you got out of the War Department. The mission to Mexico is a very honorable one, and with your views on "annexation is a very safe one for the country. We all hope that the Drench will go out, and that you will keep the United States out. We want as little to do with Mexico politically as possible, and as much trade with her as is profitable. She is terribly in need of a strong government, and if her mixed population would elect you or some other firm military ruler as emperor or king, it would be lucky for her, but a bad business for the elected one. I have never seen the elements of a stable government in Mexico, but she has physical resources that might, under a firm ruler, make her the second power in America. Self-government is out of the question. The worst enemies of Mexico are her own mixed, ignorant population. If Maximilian could have held on, he would have secured them physical prosperity; but sooner or later the pride of our people aroused against European intervention would have got us into a quarrel with him. It is therefore best that he leave. What you can do for or with Mexico we will see. Your military reputation and aptitude with all classes may help to bring order out of chaos....

Your reception at Havana must have been grateful, and the whole Mexican trip will no doubt close agreeably for yon a year of trials and orations. If they don't make you emperor down there, we will welcome you back as the "republicanizer" of the worst anarchy on the globe. If you establish Juarez, come away by all means in hot haste before the next pronunciamiento.

As for domestic matters, Congress meets to-morrow, very much irritated at the President. As for Butler or impeachment, you need not fear we shall follow the one or attempt the other. Johnson ought to acquiesce in the public judgment, agree to the amendment, and we shall have peace. The personal feeling grows out of the wholesale removal of good Union men from office. Campbell is as responsible for this as any man in Ohio while I was under a cloud for being friendly to Johnson and absent from the State, they turned out all my special friends and put in Copperheads....

Affectionately,

JOHN SHERMAN.

SANTIAGO, NOV. 7, 1866.

Dear Brother: We have nearly completed the circle without finding Juarez, who is about as far as ever, away up in Chihuahua for no other possible purpose than to be where the devil himself cannot get at him.

I have not the remotest idea of riding on mule back a thousand miles in Mexico to find its chief magistrate, and although the French go away and Maximilian follow, I doubt if Juarez can be made to trust his life and safety to his own countrymen. We found Vera Cruz in possession of the Prench and Maximilian, and we found Tucapiso in possession of local troops in the interest of Maximilian, but they had not the remotest idea where we should look for Juarez. We have just reached here, and shall to-morrow go up to Matamoras to meet General Escobedo, who can possibly fix some date when Juarez will come within reach of civilization.

The truth is these Mexicans were and are still as unable as children to appreciate the value of time. They shrug their shoulders and exclaim "Quien sabe*!* (who knows) and "Poco tiempo" (in a short time), utterly regardless of combinations with others.

Mr. Campbell can deal with none but Juarez and the Republican Government he represents, and that government partakes of the characteristics of Mexicans; *viz.,* indecision and utter want of combination.

I believe the French want to leave, but would like to bring us into the scrape. Their scheme of giving Mexico a stable government has cost them $ 200,000,000 of gold, and the whole conception was in hostility to us, to be ready to reabsolve the old Louisiana purchase, where, as • Napoleon calculated, our Union had failed. But our Union has not failed, and the French are willing to go, but they are scattered and must collect before they can march for the seacoast to embark. By reason of the everlasting contest between the rival factions of Mexico, the property-holders desire some sort of stable government, and these favor Maximilian. He may attempt to remain after the French go, but I think would soon be forced to go. Then

Mexico must of necessity settle her own difficulties. Some think she can, some that she cannot without our aid. This cannot be done without Congress, and on that point I am no advocate. All I can say is that Mexico does not belong to our system. All its northern part is very barren and costly. Its southern part is very good tropical country, but not suited to our people or pursuits. Its inhabitants are a mixture of Indians, negroes, and Spanish, that can never be tortured into good citizens, and would have to be exterminated before the country could be made available to us.

I am obeying orders and not carrying out a project of my own, and it is well you should understand it, though I cannot impart it to others.

I don't know what policy the Administration has adopted, but I should deplore anything that would make us assume Mexico in any shape — its territory, its government, or its people. Still the French occupation designed in hostility to us should be made to terminate.

Affectionately,

W. T. SHERMAN.

UNITED STATES SENATE CHAMBER, WASHINGTON, Dec. 27, 1866.

Dear Brother:

On the whole I am not sorry that your mission failed, since the French are leaving; my sympathies are rather with Maximilian. The usual factions of Ortega and Juarez will divide the native population, while Maximilian can have the support of the clergy and property. They are a miserable set, and we ought to keep away from them. Here political strife is hushed, and the South have two months more in which to accept the constitutional amendment. What folly they exhibit! To me Johnson and the old encrusted politicians who view everything in the light of thirty years ago seem like blind guides. After the 4th of March they will rally to the amendment, and it will then be too late....

Very truly yours,

JOHN SHERMAN.

The 14th amendment, then pending before the State Legislatures.

General Sherman returned to St. Louis from Mexico by way of New Orleans.

ST. Louis, Sunday, Dec. 30, 1866.

Dear Brother: I came up from New Orleans right through the country that I had been the means of raiding so thoroughly, and did not know but I should hear some things that would not be pleasant, but, on the contrary, many people met me all along the road in the most friendly spirit. I spent a whole day at Jackson, where chimney stacks and broken railroads marked the presence of Shermans army. But all sorts of people pressed to see me, and evinced their natural curiosity, nothing more....

I expect to have two Indian wars on my hands, and have no time for other things. The Sioux and Cheyennes are now so circumscribed that I suppose they must be exterminated, for they cannot and will not settle down, and our people will force us to it. It will also call for all possible prudence to keep us from war with the Mormons, for there are people that yearn for the farms and property the Mormons have created in the wilderness.

I have a despatch from Mr. Stanton, saying that my action in the delicate mission to Mexico meets the approval of the President, the Cabinet, and himself, so I got out of that scrape easily. I do not want to come to Washington, but to stay here quietly as long as possible. When Grant goes to Europe, then I shall be forced to come. The longer that is deferred the better for me.

Affectionately,

W. T. SHERMAN.

General Sherman, having been summoned to Washington, writes from St. Louis on January 8, 1867.

Dear Brother:

I need not say I don't want to come. There can be no satisfaction to me in being drawn into the Yortex of confusion in which public affairs seem to be. I cannot do or say anything that will influence

227

either the President or Congress. If the President be impeached and the South reduced to Territories, the country will, of course, relapse to a state of war or quasi war, and what good it is to do passes my comprehension. Our debt is already as much as the country can stand, and we shall, with Indians and local troubles, have full employment for all the regular army. I suppose the Southern States will then require a standing army of an hundred thousand men, and it would be prudent to provide them before the emergency is created.

Affectionately,

W. **T. SHERMAN.**

About this time General Sherman writes: —

I see occasionally that a move in Congress is made about the Mormons. We shall this year and next have our hands full with the Indians, and the conflict of races in the South, without begging any new cause of trouble. As I am interested, I want you to know that my opinion is emphatic that we should attempt nothing with the Mormons until the railroad is finished as far as Port Bridges. That cannot be until about the year 1869. As long as cases have to be tried by juries, all laws counter to the prejudice of the whole people are waste paper.

I got your letter a few days ago, and am glad you feel so confident of the political situation. I am not alarmed at the fact that universal suffrage—blacks, whites, Chinese, and Indians—is to be the basis, but the devil comes in when we shall be forced to contract the right of suffrage. It is easy enough to roll down hill, but the trouble is in getting back again; but I am out and shall keep out....G.W. [sic] Custer, Lieutenant-Colonel Seventh Cavalry [George Armstrong Custer], is young, *very* brave, even to rashness, a good trait for a cavalry officer. He came to duty immediately on being appointed, and is ready and willing now to fight the Indians. He is in my command, and I am bound to befriend him. I think he merits confirmation for military service already rendered, and military qualities still needed—youth, health, energy, and extreme willingness to act and fight....

Dear Brother:... You will have noticed that my name is connected with the Reconstruction Law. I did nothing but reduce and group the ideas of others, carefully leaving open to the South the whole machinery of reconstruction. The bill was much injured by the additions in the House, but, after all, there is nothing obnoxious to the South in it but general suffrage. This they must take, and the only question is whether they will take it in their own way by their own popular movements, or whether we shall be compelled at the next session to organize provisional governments. I hope and trust they will learn wisdom from the past. Can't you in some way give them that advice? Three years ago they hated you and Johnson most of all men; now, your advice goes farther than any two men of the nation. We will adjourn soon until November next. The impeachment movement has, so far, been a complete failure. Butler and Logan are reinforcements, but will effect nothing.

The President has only to forward and inforce the law as they stand, and he is safe. He ought not to, and must not stand in the way of the determined movement to recognize the rebel States. He has had his way and it failed; he ought now fairly to try the Congressional way. I think some of going to Paris in April. I am tendered an honorary membership of the commission, and a free passage. The occasion is tempting; if I go, it will be about the middle of April.

Affectionately,

JOHN SHERMAN.

After a short and hurried trip abroad, John Sherman writes: —

UNITED STATES SENATE, July 15, 1867.

Dear Brother:... I have no time to write you more as to my trip, except to convey the earnest personal message sent by Emperor Louis Napoleon to you. He asked me to say to you, in his name, that he considered you the genius of our war, and that he had for you as a military man the highest regard. He and his Court treated me with unusual attention, no doubt partly on your account. You would have been received with much heartiness. While I am glad you abandoned that excursion, yet I hope you will arrange to go this winter to Paris and London.

The Indian War is an inglorious one. We shall probably pass a bill to authorize you and others to make a treaty with the Indians, with a view to gather them into reservations. I have many things to write about, but must defer them for the present.

On July 16, 1867, General Sherman writes to his brother of the Indian troubles in the West. foresee where they will turn up. *Not* only real depredations are committed, but every fear, or apprehension, on whatever it may be founded, is published, and protection claimed and demanded....

You have doubtless heard much of the war. The fact is, this contact of the two races has caused universal hostility, and the Indians operate in small, scattered bands, avoiding the posts and well-guarded trains, and hitting little parties who are off their guard. I have a much heavier force on the plains, but they are so large that it is impossible to guard at all points, and the clamor for protection everywhere has prevented our being able to collect a large force to go into the country where we believe the Indians have hid their families; viz., up on the Yellowstone, and down on the Eed River. I see it stated the Indian War is costing a million a week. This cannot be; for I have not employed anything but the regular troops or the regular appropriations, except from companies of Kansas volunteers, who know they can't get any pay at all till Congress appropriates.

I have sent full reports to Washington, and hope Congress now will act in one way or the other. A commission going out can meet only little squads of Indians. They are scattered from Minnesota to Texas, and if they make treaties they won't last twenty-four hours.

We must fight the Indians, and force them to collect in agreed-on limits far away from the continental roads.

I do think this subject as important as Reconstruction.

Affectionately yours,

W. T. SHERMAN-.

About this time Congress appointed General Sherman a member of a Commission to investigate the Indian troubles, and to make treaties with the Indians. This

Commission was rendered necessary on account of the discontent of the Indians with regard to their reservations.

HEADQUARTERS MILITARY DIVISION OF THE MISSOURI,

MADISON, WIS., Aug. 3, 1867.

Dear Brother:

As I expected, I am on the detail, and have official notice that I shall be required in St. Louis, Tuesday, August 6th....

I got your message from Napoleon. He sent me a similar message by Schofield, but I would hardly venture to France as the representative of our military system, as it would subject me to heavy expense and much trouble.

Grant told me he would not accept a nomination for President, and if he departs from this, his natural conclusion, it will be by side influence, and because no good candidate has thus far been brought forward by the ruling party. I don't think he has clearly defined political opinions, but would let Congress and the departments work out the problem of the future, which is probably better than to form a theory and force matters to conform to it....

Yours affectionately,

W. **T. SHERMAN.**

MANSFIELD, OHIO, Aug. 9, 1867.

Dear Brother:... It is now becoming extremely important to know precisely what Grant wants in connection with the Presidency. If he has really made up his mind that he would like to hold that office, he can have it. Popular opinion is all in his favor. His position is the The Indian Commission. rare one of having that office within his easy reach, and yet it is clear that his interest is against his acceptance. The moment he is nominated, he at once becomes the victim of abuse; and even his great services will not shield him. Our politics for years will be a maelstrom, destroying and building up

231

reputations with rapidity. My conviction is clear that G-rant ought not to change his present position to that of President; and if he declines, then by all odds Chase is the safest man for the country. He is wise, politic, and safe. Our finances, the public credit, and the general interests of all parts of the country will be safe with him. His opinions are advanced on the suffrage question, but this waived, he would be a most conservative President. He is not a partisan, scarcely enough so for his own interests; still, if Grant wishes to be President, all other candidates will have to stand aside. I see nothing in his way unless he is foolish enough to connect his future with the Democratic party. This party cannot dictate the next President. They would deaden any man they praise. Even Grant could not overcome any fellowship with them. If they should take a wise course on future political questions, their course during the war will bar their way. You may not think so, but I know it. The strength is with the Republicans. Hot of the Butler stripe, but with just that kind of men who would be satisfied with the position of Grant. The suffrage and reconstruction questions will be settled before the election, and in such a way as to secure the Republican party an even chance in every Southern State except Kentucky....

I agree with you that Indian wars will not cease until all the Indian tribes are absorbed in our population, and can be controlled by constables instead of soldiers.

I mean to remain as quiet as possible this fall. I am not now in high favor with the Radicals, and can afford to wait awhile. The election in Ohio will go as usual. The suffrage amendment will be adopted by a close vote, and that will settle forever the negro question in Ohio. A reaction and struggle may occur in the South, but no change will occur in the loyal States until they decide on financial questions. This is inevitable after the next election....

Affectionately yours,

JOHN SHERMAN.

HEADQUARTERS, OMAHA, NEB., Sept. 12, 1867.

Dear Brother:

As to politics, I hardly know if I should approach Grant, as I can hardly judge of the influences that have operated on him since we were together last November. In accepting the acting office of Secretary of War, I doubt not he realized the delicacy of his position, and was willing to risk the chances. It is not for the interest of the United States that in a temporary political office he should sink his character as a military officer. In the former he should be in harmony with the executive, but in the latter he should be simply a high sheriff to execute the process of the court. My belief is that Congress cannot qualify the President's right to command the army and navy. He is the Constitutional Commander-in-Chief. But Congress can make rules and laws for the government of the army and thereby control the President as such Commander-in-Chief. In trying to array the President and General Grant in antagonism, Congress did wrong, and reaction is sure to result. It damages all parties, because few people take the trouble to study out the right, yet time moves along so rapidly and the election of a new President will soon settle these and all kindred questions. Your course has been fair, and you cannot wish to alter or amend it. Our country ought not to be ruled by the extreme views of Sumner or Stevens any more than by the extreme views of Calhoun, Yancey, etc., that have produced our Civil War. There is some just middle course, and events will flow into it whether any one man or set of men is wise enough to foresee it and lay down its maxims. I think Chase is the ablest man of his school, and I would personally prefer him to Wade, Colfax, or any of the men whose names I notice in this connection. Whether the precedent of a Chief Justice being a political aspirant may not be bad, I don't know. This is the Mexican rule, and has resulted in anarchy.

I don't think Grant, Sheridan, Thomas, or any real military man wants to be President. All see that, however pure or exalted their past reputations may have been, it don't shield them from the lies and aspersions of a besotted press.... Grant writes me in the most unreserved confidence, and never has said a word that looks like wanting the office of President. His whole nature is to smooth over troubles, and he waits with the most seeming

indifference, under false and unjust assertions, till the right time, when the truth peeps out, so as to defy contradiction....

Affectionately,

W. T. SHERMAN. HEADQUARTERS MILITARY DIVISION of THE MISSOURI,

St. Louis, Sept. 28, 1867.

Dear Brother;

We have now been near two months on the Indian Commission, and I can pretty closely judge of the result. It cannot be complete or final, because it will take years to do all the law requires, and I suppose the pressure will force Congress to do something conclusive this winter. According to existing treaties with Indians, they have a right to wander and hunt across all the railroads toward the West, and Henderson thinks we had no right to locate roads through without a prior assent, and by the payment of damages. Whether right or wrong, those roads will be built, and everybody knows that Congress, after granting the charts and fixing the routes, cannot now back out and surrender the country to a few bands of roving Indians. Henderson says, also, that the demand of these railroads, stage, telegraph, and other lines on me for military aid or protection were not contemplated, but that these companies took their franchises and contracts with a full knowledge of the difficulties. Now I and all who have gone before me have acted on the general theory that when Congress located a road, that it amounted to an implied promise to give reasonable military protection. However, by the time Congress meets, we can, I think, submit to you some general plan that is practicable, and will in time — not at once — attain a result....

Yours,

W. T. SHERMAN.

Early in October, 1867, General Sherman was again summoned to Washington by the President.

Dear Brother: I have no doubt you have been duly concerned about my being summoned to Washington.

It was imprudently done by the President without going through G-rant. But I think I have smoothed it over so that Grant does not feel hurt. I cannot place myself in a situation even partially antagonistic with Grant. We must work together. Mr. Johnson has not offered me anything, only has talked over every subject, and because I listen to him patiently, and make short and decisive answers, he says he would like to have me here. Still he does not oppose my going back home....

On Monday I will start for St. Louis by the Atlantic and G. W. Road, and pass Mansfield Tuesday. Can't you meet me and ride some miles? I have been away from home so much, and must go right along to Fort Laramie, that I cannot well stop at Cleveland or Mansfield, and would like to see you for an hour or so to hear your views of the coming events....

Yours affectionately,

W. T. SHERMAN.

And on his return to St. Louis he continues: — made to displease the President by a simple Law of Congress. This is as much as I have ever said to anybody. I have never by word or inference given anybody the right to class me in opposition to or in support of Congress. On the contrary, I told Mr. Johnson that from the nature of things he could not dispense with a Congress to mate laws and appropriate money, and suggested to him to receive and make overtures to such men as Pessenden, Trumbull, Sherman, Morgan, and Morton, who, though differing with him in abstract views of Constitutional Law and Practice, were not destructive. That if the Congressional plan of reconstruction succeeded, he could do nothing, and if it failed or led to confusion, the future developed results in his favor, etc.; and that is pretty much all I have ever said or done. At the meeting of the Society of the Army of the Tennessee on the 13th inst., I will be forced to speak, if here, and though I can confine myself purely to the military events of the past, I can make the opportunity of stating that in no event will I be drawn into the complications of the civil politics of this country.

If Congress could meet and confine itself to current and committee business, I feel certain that everything will work along quietly till the nominations are made, and a new Presidential election will likely settle the principle if negroes are to be voters in the States without the consent of the whites. This is more a question of prejudice than principle, but a voter has as much right to his prejudices as to his vote.

Tours affectionately,

W. T. SHERMAN.

MANSFIELD, OHIO, NOV. 1, 1867.

Dear Brother:

I see no real occasion for trouble with Johnson. The great error of his life was in not acquiescing in and supporting the 14th Amendment of the Constitution in the Thirty-ninth Congress. This he could easily have carried. It referred the suffrage question to each State, and if adopted long ago the whole controversy would have culminated; or if further opposed by the extreme Radicals, they would have been easily beaten. Now I see nothing short of universal suffrage and universal amnesty as the basis. When you come on, I suggest that you give out that you go on to make your annual report and settle Indian affairs. Give us notice when you will be on, and come directly to my house, where we will make you one of the family.

Grant, I think, is inevitably a candidate. He allows himself to drift into a position where he can't decline if he would, and I feel sure he don't want to decline. My judgment is that Chase is better for the country and for Grant himself, but I will not quarrel with what I cannot control.

JOHN SHERMAN.

And later he writes: —

If you can keep free from committals to Johnson, you will surely as you live be called upon to act as President. The danger now is that the mistakes of the Republicans may drift the Democratic party into power. If so, the rebellion is triumphant, and no man active in suppressing it will be trusted or honored. Grant is not injured by his correspondence with Johnson, but no doubt feels annoyed....

At this time President Johnson had come to open disagreement with Mr. Stanton, his Secretary of War, and wished to force him from the Cabinet. Mr. Stanton had refused to resign and had been upheld by Congress. The President then turned for help in his difficulties to General Grant, commanding the army; but the latter found that any interference on his part would be illegal and impossible.

Mr. Johnson then planned to create a new office for General Sherman, that of Brevet General of the army, in order to bring him to Washington.

The following letters and telegrams refer to this difficulty.

CONFIDENTIAL.

LIBRARY ROOM, WAR DEPARTMENT, WASHINGTON, D.C., Jan. 31, 1868.

To THE PRESIDENT:

Since our interview of yesterday I have given the subject of our conversation all my thoughts, and I beg you will pardon my reducing the result to writing.

My personal preferences, if expressed, were to be allowed to return to St. Louis to resume my present command; because my command was important, large, suited to my rank and inclination, and because my family was well provided for there, in house facilities, schools, living, and agreeable society.

Whilst, on the other hand, Washington was for many (to me) good reasons highly objectionable. Especially because it is the political capital of the country and focus of intrigue, gossip, and slander. Your personal preferences were, as expressed, to make a new department East adequate to my rank, with headquarters at

Washington, and to assign me to its command — to remove my family here, and to avail myself of its schools, etc.; to remove Mr. Stanton from his office as Secretary of War, and have me to discharge the duties.

To effect this removal two modes were indicated: to simply cause him to quit the War Office building and notify the Treasury Department and the Army Staff Departments no longer to respect him as Secretary of War; or to remove him, and submit my name to the Senate for confirmation. Permit me to discuss these points a little, and I will premise by saying that I have spoken to no one on the subject, and have not even seen Mr. Ewing, Mr. Stanberry, or General Grant since I was with you.

It has been the rule and custom of our army since the organization of the Government that the second officer of the army should be at the second (in importance) command, and remote from general headquarters. To bring me to Washington would put three heads to an army,— yourself, General Grant, and myself,— and we would be more than human if we were not to differ. In my judgment it would ruin the army, and would be fatal to one or two of us.

Generals Scott and Taylor proved themselves soldiers and patriots in the field, but Washington was fatal to both. This city and the influences that centred here defeated every army that had its head here from 1861 to 1865, and would have overwhelmed General Grant at Spottsylvania and Petersburg had he not been fortified by a strong reputation already hard earned, and because no one then living coveted the place. Whereas in the West we made progress from the start, because there was no political capital near enough to poison our minds and kindle into light that craving itching for fame which has killed more good men than bullets. I have been with General Grant in the midst of death and slaughter — when the howls of people reached him after Shiloh; when messengers were speeding to and fro between his army and Washington, bearing slanders to induce his removal before he took Vicksburg; in Chattanooga, when the soldiers were stealing the corn of the starving mules to satisfy their own hunger; at Nashville, when he was ordered to the "forlorn hope" to command the army of the Potomac, so often defeated —

and yet I never saw him more troubled than since he has been in Washington, and been compelled to read himself a "sneak and deceiver," based on reports of four of the Cabinet, and apparently with your knowledge. If this political atmosphere can disturb the equanimity of one so guarded and so prudent as he is, what will be the result with one so careless, so outspoken as I am? Therefore, with my consent, Washington never.

As to the Secretary of War, his office is twofold. As Cabinet officer he should not be there without your hearty, cheerful consent, and I believe that is the judgment and opinion of every fair-minded man. As the holder of a civil office, having the supervision of monies appropriated by Congress, and of contracts for army supplies, I do think Congress; or the Senate by delegation from Congress, has a lawful right to be consulted. At all events, I would not risk a suit or contest on that phase of the question. The Law of Congress of March 2, 1867, prescribing the manner in which orders and instructions relating to "Military Movements" shall reach the army gives you, as Constitutional Commander-in-Chief, the very power you want to exercise, and enables you to prevent the Secretary from making any such orders and instructions, and consequently he cannot control the army, but is limited and restricted to a duty that an auditor of the Treasury could perform. You certainly can afford to await the result. The executive power is not weakened, but, rather, strengthened. Surely he is not such an obstruction as would warrant violence or even a show of force which could produce the very reaction and clamor that he hopes for, to save him from the absurdity of holding an empty office "for the safety of the country."

With great respect,

Yours truly,

W. T. SHERMAN.

HEADQUARTERS MILITARY DIVISION OF THE MISSOURI,

ST. *Louis, Mo., Feb*. 14, 1868.

To THE PRESIDENT:

Dear Sir: It is hard for me to conceive you would purposely do me an unkindness, unless under the pressure of a sense of public duty, or because you do not believe me sincere.

I was in hopes, since my letter to you of the 31st of January, that you had concluded to pass over that purpose of yours, expressed more than once in conversation, to organize a new command for me in the East, with headquarters in Washington; but a telegram from General Grant of yesterday says that "the order was issued ordering you" (me) "to Atlantic division"; and the newspapers of this morning contain the same information, with the addition that I have been nominated as "Brevet General." I have telegraphed to my own brother in the Senate to oppose my confirmation, on the ground that the two higher grades in the army ought not to be complicated with brevets, and I trust you will conceive my motives aright. If I could see my way clear to maintain my family, I should not hesitate a moment to resign my present commission and seek some business wherein I would be free from those unhappy complications that seem to be closing about me, spite of my earnest efforts to avoid them; but necessity ties my hands, and I must submit with the best grace I can, till I make other arrangements.

In Washington are already the headquarters of a department, and of the army itself, and it is hard for me to see wherein I can render military service there. Any staff-officer with the rank of Major could surely fill any gap left between those two military offices; and by being placed in Washington I shall be universally construed as a rival to the General-in-Chief, a position damaging to me in the highest degree. Our relations have always been most confidential and friendly, and if, unhappily, any cloud of difficulty should arise between us, my sense of personal dignity and duty would leave me no alternative but resignation. For this I am not yet prepared, but I shall proceed to arrange for it as rapidly as possible, that when the time does come (as it surely will if this plan is carried into effect), I may act promptly.

Inasmuch as the order is now issued, I cannot expect a full revocation of it, but I beg the privilege of taking post at New York, or any point you may name within the new military division other than Washington.

This privilege is generally granted to all military commanders, and I see no good reasons why I, too, may not ask for it; and this simple concession, involving no public interest, will much soften the blow which, right or wrong, I construe as one of the hardest I have sustained in a life somewhat checkered with adversity.

With great respect, yours truly,

(Signed) W. T. Sherman, Lieutenant-General.

HEADQUARTERS MILITARY DIVISION OF THE MISSOURI, St. LOUIS, Feb. 14, 1868.

Dear Brother:

I am again in the midst of trouble, occasioned by a telegram from Grant saying that the order is out for me to come to the command of the military division of the Atlantic Headquarters at Washington. The President repeatedly asked me to accept of some such position, but I thought I had fought it off successfully, though he again and again reverted to it.

Now, it seems, he has ordered it, and it is full of trouble for me. I wrote him one or two letters in Washington which I thought positive enough, but have now written another, and if it fails in its object I might as well cast about for new employment. The result would be certain conflict resulting in Grant's violent deposition, mine, or the President's.

There is not room on board of one ship for more than one captain.

If Grant intends to run for President I should be willing to come on, because my duties would then be so clearly defined that I think I could steer clear of the breakers,—but now it would be impossible. The President would make use of me to beget violence, a condition of things that ought not to exist now.

He has no right to use us for such purposes, though he is Commander-in-Chief. I did suppose his passage with Grant would end there, but now it seems he will fight him as he has been doing Congress. I don't object if he does so himself and don't rope me in....

If the President forces me into a false position out of seeming favor, I must defend myself. It is mortifying, but none the less inevitable. Affectionately,

W. T. SHERMAN.

[TELEGRAM.]

WASHINGTON, Feb. 14, 1868, F*rom St. Louis, F*eb. 14, 1868.

To GENERAL U. S. GRANT,

Commander U S. Army:

Your despatch informing me that the order for the Atlantic Division was issued, and that I was assigned to its command, is received.

I was in hopes I had escaped the danger, and now, were I prepared, should resign on the spot, as it requires no foresight to predict such must be the inevitable result in the end.

I will make one more desperate effort by mail, which please await.

(Signed) W. T. Sherman,

Lieutenant-General.

[TELEGRAM.]

Dated, ST. Louis, Feb. 14, 1868.

RECEIVED AT HOUSE OF REPRESENTATIVES, Feb. 14th.

To HON. JOHN SHERMAN:

Oppose confirmation of myself as Brevet General on ground that it is unprecedented, and that it is better not to extend the system of Brevets above Major-General. If I can't avoid coming to Washington, I may have to resign.

W. T. Sherman, Lieutenant-General.

HEADQUARTERS MILITARY DIVISION OF THE MISSOURI, ST. LOUIS, MO., Feb. 17, 1868.

Dear Brother:

I have asked the President to let me make my headquarters in New York instead of Washington, making my application on the ground that my simply being in Washington will be universally construed as rivalry to General Grant, a position which would be damaging to me in the extreme.

If I must come to Washington, it will be with a degree of reluctance never before experienced. I would leave my family here on the supposition that the change was temporary. I do not question the President's right to make the new division, and I think Congress would make a mistake to qualify his right. It would suffice for them to nonconfirm the Brevet of General. I will notify you by telegraph when the matter is concluded.

Affectionately,

W. T. SHERMAN.

[TELEGRAM.]

RECEIVED, WASHINGTON, Feb. 20, 1868.

FROM ST. LOUIS, MO., Feb. 20, 1868.

To GENERAL U. S. GRANT:

The President telegraphs that I may remain in my present command. I write him a letter of thanks through you to-day. Congress should not have for publication my letters to the President, unless the President himself chooses to give them.

(Signed) W. T. Sherman,

Lieutenant-General.

HEADQUARTERS ARMY OP THE UNITED STATES, WASHINGTON, Feb. 21, 1868.

Dear Sir: By General Grant's direction I enclose a copy of a despatch from General Sherman, seeming to indicate his preference that the correspondence in question should not now be made public.

Respectfully yours,

C. B. Comstock., B.B.S.

HON. JOHN SHERMAN,

United States Senate.

A few days after this, General Sherman went to Washington in response to the President's order, and while there had several interviews with the President relating to the change of his command. He objected very strongly, as has been seen, to any such change, because he felt that he could not hold a command in Washington without interfering with Grant's interests, and because he had a rooted objection to living in Washington in the midst of the turmoil of politics. These objections were embodied in three letters which General Sherman wrote and showed to Grant before he sent them to the President. One of them found its way into the public press, and created a disturbance which called forth the following letters.

HEADQUARTERS ARMY OF THE UNITED STATES,
WASHINGTON, D.C., Feb. 22, 1808.

HON. J. SHERMAN,

United States Senate.

Dear Sir: The "National Intelligencer of this morning contains a private note which General Sherman sent to the President whilst he was in Washington, dictated by the purest kindness and a disposition to preserve harmony, and not intended for publication. It seems to me the publication of that letter is calculated to place the General in a wrong light before the public, taken in connection with what correspondents have said before, evidently getting their inspiration from the White House.

As General Sherman afterwards wrote a semi-official note to the President, furnishing me a copy, and still later a purely official one sent through me, which placed him in his true position, and which have not been published, though called for by the "House," I take the liberty of sending you these letters to give you the opportunity of consulting General Sherman as to what action to take upon them. In all matters where I am not personally interested, I would not hesitate to advise General Sherman how I would act in his place. But in this instance, after the correspondence I have had with Mr. Johnson, I may not see General Sherman's interest in the same light that others see it, or that I would see it in if no such correspondence had occurred. I am clear in this, however: the correspondence here enclosed to you should not be made public except by the President, or with the full sanction of General Sherman. Probably the letter of the 31st of January, marked "confidential," should not be given out at all.

Yours truly,

U. S. GRANT.

The following letter was addressed to the "National Intelligencer," a Washington newspaper.

UNITED STATES SENATE CHAMBER, WASHINGTON, Feb. 22, 1868.

Gentlemen: The publication in your paper yesterday of General Sherman's note to the President, and its simultaneous transmission by telegraph unaccompanied by subsequent letters withheld by the President because they were "private," is so unfair as to justify severe censure upon the person who furnished you this letter, whoever he may be. Upon its face it is an informal private note dictated by the purest motives,—a desire to preserve harmony,—and not intended for publication. How any gentleman receiving such a note could first allow vague but false suggestions of its contents to be given out, and then print it, and withhold other letters because they were "private," with a view to create the impression that General Sherman in referring to ulterior measures suggested the violent expulsion of a high officer from his office, passes my comprehension. Still I know that General Sherman is so sensitive upon questions of official propriety in publishing papers, that he would rather suffer from this false inference than to correct it by publishing another private note; and as I knew that this letter was not the only one written by General Sherman to the President about Mr. Stanton, I applied to the President for his consent to publish subsequent letters. This consent was freely given by the President, and I therefore send copies to you and ask their publication.

These copies are furnished me from official sources; for while I know General Sherman's opinions, yet he did not show me either of the letters to the President, during his stay here, nervously anxious to promote harmony, to avoid strife, and certainly never suggested or countenanced resistance to law — or violence in any form. He no doubt left Washington with his old repugnance to politics, politicians, and newspapers very much increased by his visit here.

UNITED STATES SENATE CHAMBER, Feb. 23, 1868.

Dear Brother: I received your letters and telegrams, and did not answer because events were moving so rapidly that I could say nothing but might be upset before you got the letter.

Now you can congratulate yourself upon being clear of the worst complications we have ever had. Impeachment seems to be a foregone conclusion so far as the House of Representatives is concerned, based upon the alleged *forcible* expulsion of Stanton. No one disputes the right of the President to raise a question of law upon his right to remove Stanton, but the forcible removal of a man in office, claiming to be in lawfully, is like the forcible ejectment of a tenant when his right of possession is in dispute. It is a trespass, an assault, a riot, or a crime, according to the result of the force. It is strange the President can contemplate such a thing, when Stanton is already stripped of power, and the courts are open to the President to try his right of removal. The President is acting very badly with respect to you. He creates the impression that you acted disingenuously with him. He has published your short private note before you went to Annapolis, and yet refuses to publish your formal one subsequently sent him, because it was "private." The truth is, he is a slave to his passions and resentments. No man can confide in him, and you ought to feel happy at your extrication from all near connection with him.... Grant is anxious to have your letters published, since the note referred to was published. I will see Grant and the President this evening, and if the latter freely consents, I will do it informally; but if he doubts or hesitates, I will not without your expressed directions. In these times of loose confidence, it is

246

better to submit for a time to a wrong construction, than to betray confidential communications. Grant will, unquestionably, be nominated. Chase acquiesces, and I see no reason to doubt his election....

Affectionately,

JOHN SHERMAN.

HEADQUARTERS MILITARY DIVISION OF THE MISSOURI,

St. *Louis, Mo.,* Feb. 25, 1868.

Dear Brother:

I am in possession of all the news up to date,— the passage of the impeachment, resolution, etc., — but I yet don't know if the nomination of T. Ewing, Senior, was a real thing or meant to compromise a difficulty.

The publication of my short note of January 18th, is nothing to me. I have the original draft which I sent through Grant's hands, with his endorsement back to me. At the time this note must have been given to the reporter, the President had an elaborate letter from me, in which I discussed the whole case, and advised against the very course he has pursued, but I don't want that letter or any other to be drawn out to complicate a case already bad enough.

You may always safely represent me by saying that I will not make up a final opinion till called on to act, and I want nothing to do with these controversies until the time comes for the actual fight, which I hope to God may be avoided. If the Democratic party intend to fight on this impeachment, which I believe they do not, yon may count 200,000 men against you in the South. The negroes are no match for them. On this question, the whites there will be more united than on the old issue of Union and Secession. I do not think the President should be suspended during trial, and if possible, the Republican party should not vote on all side questions as a unit. They should act as judges, and not as partisans. The vote in the House, being a strictly party vote, looks bad, for it augurs a prejudiced jury. Those who adhere closest to the law in this crisis are the best patriots. Whilst the floating politicians here share the excitement at

Washington, the people generally manifest little interest in the game going on at Washington....

Affectionately yours,

W. T. SHERMAN.

UNITED STATES SENATE CHAMBER, WASHINGTON, March. 1, 1868.

Dear Brother: Your letter of the 25th is received. I need not say to you that the new events transpiring here are narrowly watched by me. So far as I am concerned, I mean to give Johnson a fair and impartial trial, and to decide nothing until required to do so, and after full argument. I regard him as a foolish and stubborn man, doing even right things in a wrong way, and in a position where the evil that he does is immensely increased by his manner of doing it. He clearly designed to have first Grant, and then you, involved in Lorenzo Thomas position, and in this he is actuated by his recent revolt against Stanton. How easy it would have been, if he had followed your advice, to have made Stanton anxious to resign, or what is worse, to have made his position ridiculous. By his infernal folly we are drifting into turbulent waters. The only way is to keep cool and act conscientiously. I congratulate you on your lucky extrication. I do not anticipate civil war, for our proceeding is unquestionably lawful, and if the judgment is against the President, his term is just as clearly *out* as if the 4th of March, 1869, was come. The result, if he is convicted, would cast the undivided responsibility of reconstruction upon the Republican party, and would unquestionably secure the full admission of all the States by July next, and avoid the dangerous questions that may otherwise arise out of the Southern vote in the Presidential election. It is now clear that Grant will be a candidate, and his election seems quite as clear. The action of North Carolina removed the last doubt of his nomination.

Affectionately yours,

JOHN SHERMAN.

HEADQUARTERS MILITARY DIVISION OF THE MISSOURI,

Dear Brother: I don't know what Grant means by his silence in the midst of the very great indications of his receiving the nomination in May. Doubtless he intends to hold aloof from the expression of any opinion, till the actual nomination is made, when, if he accepts with a strong Radical platform, I shall be surprised. My notion is that he thinks that the Democrats ought not to succeed to power, and that he would be willing to stand a sacrifice rather than see that result.... I notice that you Republicans have divided on some of the side questions on impeachment, and am glad you concede to the President the largest limits in his defence that are offered. I don't see what the Republicans can gain by shoving matters to an extent that looks like a foregone conclusion.

No matter what men may think of Mr. Johnson, his office is one that ought to have a pretty wide latitude of opinion. Nevertheless the trial is one that will be closely and sternly criticised by all the civilized world....

Your brother,

W. T. SHERMAN.

At this time John Sherman writes from Washington:

You notice the impeachment proceedings have commenced. As a matter of course, I have nothing to say about them. It is strange that they have so little effect on prices and business. The struggle has been so long that the effect has been discounted....

The President was very anxious to send you to Louisiana, and only gave it up by reason of your Indian command. He might think that your visit to Europe now was not consistent with the reason given for your remaining at St. Louis. Still, on this point you could readily ask his opinion, and if that agrees with Grant's, you need feel no delicacy in going. No more favorable opportunity or time to visit Europe will likely occur....

And General Sherman responds: —

I hardly know what to think of the impeachment. Was in hopes Mr. Johnson would be allowed to live out his term, and doubt if any good will result by a change for the few months still remaining of his term. A new Cabinet, and the changes foreshadowed by Wade's friends, though natural enough, would have insufficient time to do any good. I have a private letter from Grant as late as March 18, but he says not a word of his political intentions. So far as I know, he would yet be glad of a change that would enable him to remain as now....

CHAPTER IX

In July, 1867, the President approved an act providing for the establishment of a commission empowered to visit the different Indian tribes then at odds with the Government, to listen to their grievances and to make treaties of peace with them. General Sherman was appointed on this commission, and spent the spring of 1868 visiting these different tribes. His letter of June 11th is written from New Mexico, and that of the 17th from Denver, while on this duty.

St. Louis, April 26, 1868.

Dear Brother: I notice the Indians are getting restless.

This is natural, for the department has been unable to fulfil any of the promises we held out to them of ploughs, seed, cattle, etc., to begin their new life of peace.

I feel reluctant to go further in these naked promises, as I fear our Government is becoming so complicated, that it is very venturesome to make promises in advance. I have the written guarantee of the Secretary of the Interior and of the committees on Indian affairs, and will try and impress on the Indians that our work is preliminary and not final or conclusive....

Affectionately,

W. T. SHERMAN.

Fort Union, New Mexico, June 11, 1868, Thursday.

Dear Brother: I have now been in New Mexico three weeks along with Col. Tappan, peace commissioner, for the purpose of seeing the Navajos, and making some permanent disposition of them. By a debate in the Senate I see you have a pretty good idea of their former history. These Indians seem to have acquired from the old Spaniards a pretty good knowledge of farming, rearing sheep, cattle, and goats, and of making their own clothing by weaving blankets and cloth. They were formerly a numerous tribe, occupying the vast region between New Mexico and the Colorado of the West, and had among them a class of warriors who made an easy living by stealing of the New Mexicans and occasionally killing....

We found 7200 Indians there, seemingly abject and disheartened. They have been there four years. The first year they were maintained by the army at a cost of about $700,000, and made a small crop. The second year the cost was about $500,000, and the crop was small. Last year the crop was an utter failure, though all the officers say they labored hard and faithfully. This year they would not work because they said it was useless. The cost has been diminished to about 12 cents per head a day, which for 7000 Indians makes over $300,000, and this is as low as possible, being only a pound of corn, and a pound of beef with a little salt per day.

Now this was the state of facts, and we could see no time in the future when this could be amended. The scarcity of wood, the foul character of water, which is salty and full of alkali, and their utter despair, made it certain that we would have to move them or they would scatter and be a perfect nuisance. So of course we concluded to move them. After debating all the country at our option, we have chosen a small part of their old country, which is as far out of the way of the whites and of our future probable wants as possible, and have agreed to move them there forthwith, and have made a treaty which will save the heavy cost of their maintenance and give as much probability of their resuming their habits of industry as the case admits of....

Of course I have noticed Grant's acceptance. I take it for granted he will be elected, and I must come to Washington. I shall not, however, commit myself to this promotion till he is not only elected but until he vacates and I am appointed and confirmed....

Yours affectionately,

W. T. SHERMAN.

DENVER, June 17, 1868.

Dear Brother:

Yesterday it rained very hard, whereby the telegraph was interrupted so that our despatches are mutilated. Yet they contain enough to show that impeachment was not made final by the vote of Saturday. I notice that some feeling is exhibited against Henderson. I believe, of course, that he has been actuated by the best and most honorable motives. He certainly carefully heard every word of testimony, and all the arguments, and if these led him to the conclusion that the case was not [made] out, he was bound to vote accordingly. If party discipline is to ride down a man's sense of honor and right,

Republican government cannot and should not last many years.

In our Indian matters I think we are making as much progress as could be expected. The great bulk of the Sioux have agreed to move to the Missouri where they will be too far away from the railroad to be provoked to do it damage, and where the appropriations for their benefit can be more economically and faithfully applied. Some small bands will always be warlike and mischievous, but the game of war will be simplified by their separation. The same as to the Cheyennes, etc., below the Arkansas. The commission for present peace had to concede a right to hunt buffaloes as long as they last, and this may lead to collisions, but it will not be long before all the buffaloes are extinct near and between the railroads, after which the Indians will have no reason to approach either railroad....

Affectionately,

W. T. SHERMAN.

In July he writes again from St. Louis: —

Of course Grant will be elected. I have just travelled with him for two weeks, and the curiosity to see him exhausted his and my patience. He is now *cached* down at his ranch eleven miles below the city....

In September John Sherman writes from Philadelphia: —

Grant will surely be elected. If not, we shall have the devil to pay, and shall have to fight all our old political issues over again. All indications are now in favor of the overwhelming defeat of Seymour on account of the rebel and Copperhead stand of the New York convention...

And later he writes from Washington: —

I resume at once the canvass, and am working very hard. The election of Grant seems our only salvation from serious trouble.

HEADQUARTERS MILITARY DIVISION OF THE MISSOURI,
Sept. 23, 1868.

Dear Brother:

The Indian War on the plains need simply amount to this. We have now selected and provided reservations for all, off the great roads. All who cling to their old hunting grounds are hostile and will remain so till killed off. We will have a sort of predatory war for years, every now and then be shocked by the indiscriminate murder of travellers and settlers, but the country is so large, and the advantage of the Indians so great, that we cannot make a single war and end it. From the nature of things we must take chances and clean out Indians as we encounter them.

Our troops are now scattered and have daily chases and skirmishes, sometimes getting the best and sometimes the worst, but the Indians have this great advantage, — they can steal fresh horses when they need them and drop the jaded ones. We must operate each man to his own horse, and cannot renew except by purchase in a distant and cheap market.

I will keep things thus, and when winter starves their ponies they will want a truce and shan't have it, unless the civil influence compels me again as it did last winter.

If Grant is elected, that old Indian system will be broken up, and then with the annuities which are ample expended in connection with and in subordination to military movements, will soon bring the whole matter within easy control. Then there are $134,000 appropriated for the Cheyennes and Arapahoes, all of whom are at war, and yet the Indian Bureau contend they are forced by law to invest it in shoes, stockings, blankets, and dry goods for these very Indians. They don't want any of these things, but if it could be put in corn, salt, and cattle, we could detach half the hostiles and get them down on the Canadian, two hundred miles south of the Kansas road.

Grant is still at Galena, and I doubt if he will get to Washington till the November election is over. I have written to him to come down here to the Bair which begins October 5, but the Democrats are so strong and demonstrative here that I think he is a little turned against St. Louis....

Yours affectionately,

W. T. SHERMAN.

John Sherman spent the summer of 1868 working hard in the canvass for the State election in Ohio. He writes on October 14, from Mansfield: —

The October election is now over, but I do not yet know precise results. I write, supposing that the [Republicans have carried Ohio and Pennsylvania and perhaps Indiana. Grant is much stronger than our State or Congress ticket, and will get thousands of floating and

Democratic votes. I regard his election as a foregone conclusion. This canvass has been very severe upon me and I shall now take a rest. If you would like to join me, we can go to the Lake and have some fine sport hunting and fishing. This relaxation will do us both good.

On October 30, General Sherman writes from St. Louis, assuming that Grant will be elected: —

The election is so near at hand that further speculations are unnecessary. I have written to Grant that I can readily adjust my interests to his plans; but if he has none fixed, I prefer he should go on and exercise his office of Commander in Chief till the last moment, stepping from one office to the other on the 4th of March next, and calling me there at the last moment. I have told him I don't want to be in Washington till I can assume the command and exercise the positive duties of Commander in Chief....

Yours affectionately,

W. T. SHERMAN.

Meantime the election had taken place, and resulted in the election of General Grant by a very large majority in the Electoral College.

St. LOUIS, MO., NOV. 23, 1868.

Dear Brother: valuable in the Senate, as the Governor of Ohio and the Legislature would fill your vacancy with a Democrat.

Don't approach Grant in person if you want anything. Put it in plain writing so emphatic that he will know you are in earnest and not yielding to personal importunity.

Yours affectionately,

W. T. SHERMAN.

Washington, D.C., Dec. **6,** 1868.

Dear Brother:

I never expected to be appointed Secretary of the Treasury, as you suggest he might, for if he thought of it I could not accept by reason of the political complication of the Ohio Legislature. I should be gratified with the offer and opportunity to decline, but I suppose in this matter he will not choose to deal in compliments....

Affectionately,

JOHN SHERMAN.

HEADQUARTERS MILITARY DIVISION OF THE MISSOURI, St. LOUIS, Mo., Dec, 20, 1868.

Dear Brother:

Grant and I at Chicago had one or two stolen interviews in which he said he would leave me, as I wished, at St. Louis till the last minute, viz., March 4, and he assured me that he would oppose, if it came to him, any change as to the law in the matter of the office of General, or the diminution of salary. The only trouble is in my successor. Halleck is out of the question. Meade comes next on the list, but is not a favorite. Sheridan comes next in order and is Grant's preference, *I think*. Thomas could not be passed over if by the accidents of war Sheridan had not *already* got *over Mm.*

Thomas is universally esteemed, but was not made a regular Major General till his battle of Nashville. Whereas Sheridan, at least 13 years younger in service, was made a Major General for his

Winchester battle the summer previous. So I think Sheridan will be chosen by Grant as Lt. Genl. Say not a word of this, as Grant will not wish to act till the last minute of time.

We had the most enthusiastic meeting at Chicago possible, and on the whole it was the best meeting we ever had or ever will have again. All persons, Grant included, volunteered the most fulsome eulogies of my short address of welcome, which is badly reported in the telegraphic despatches, but it was carefully written out and will be correctly printed when the whole proceedings are booked.

Yours,

W. T. SHERMAN.

UNITED STATES SENATE CHAMBER, WASHINGTON, Dec. 24, 1868.

Dear Brother:... Your reception speech was universally approved. I saw Grant after his return here, and he was quite exultant over the whole affair. He takes all things tranquilly....

I am in real embarrassment about questions that I must now act upon. My conviction is that specie payments must be resumed, and I have my own theories as to the mode of resumption, but the process is a very hard one, and will endanger the popularity of any man or administration that is compelled to adopt it. Our party has no policy, and any proposition will combine all other plans in opposition to it....

Affectionately,

JOHN SHERMAN.

HEADQUARTERS MILITARY DIVISION OF THE MISSOURI, ST. LOUIS, Dec. 28, 1868.

Dear Brother:

Of course I don't profess to understand either your bill or Mr. Morton's. I should like to see a consolidated 5 per cent bond gradually substituted to replace the present bonds, to the extent of 2000 millions, requiring 100 millions annually for interest, and a greenback for the balance of debt, say fire hundred millions, and all other paper money withdrawn and prohibited. I think Grant won't commit himself to more than the general idea that the debt is sacred, and leave Congress to devise the ways and means. He will of course try all means of practical economy. I agree with him perfectly that no more money subsidies on land grants should be made now or until the debt is in good shape....

Affectionately,

W. T. SHERMAN.

HEADQUARTERS MILITARY DIVISION OF THE MISSOURI, St. LOUIS, Mo., Jan. 6, 1869.

Dear Brother: ever a country was too much governed; ours is. Congress ought to set the example of short sessions.

Yours affectionately;

W. T. SHERMAN.

The following letter was written from St. Louis at the end of February just after General Sherman's return from a Southern trip, which proved very interesting to him.

My visit South was in every sense agreeable. My old friends in Alexandria did all they could to make us welcome, and I was not allowed to pay a cent on steamboat, at the hotel, or anywhere. I visited several plantations and saw negroes at work for wages, and seemingly as free and as conscious of their freedom as the blacks of Ohio. Boyd was perfectly grateful for the books you sent him, which were in the library and marked with your name. I found my own portrait, in full uniform, in the main hall, and in the library many books on our side of the war. Boyd asked me for army and navy registers, post surveys, and railroad surveys, and other national books that I have and will send him. Of course they have their old prejudices, and labor to prevent their cause from sinking into one of pure malignity, — but as to the future, he promised me to teach his pupils to love and honor the whole country. He preserves all my old letters, and we looked over many, in every one of which I took the highest national grounds and predicted the ruin of their country.

The marble tablet which was built over the main door on which was cut the inscription By the liberality of the general government. The Union — esto perpetua," was taken out and was found broken in pieces. I saw the deposition to that effect in Boyd's possession, but lie could not say if Valias did it of himself, or on the order of the board of supervisors.

You remember attention was called to that inscription by my original letter of resignation, and it is probable the rebels made Valias take it out; anyhow Boyd has ordered an iron casting of same size and same inscription, and promised me to place it over the door in lieu of the marble, too much broken up to be replaced.

In hTew Orleans I was cautioned against going to Alexandria, which was burned down at the time of the Banks expedition, but I never received more marked attention by all classes, and not a word or look reached me but what was most respectful and gratifying. In like manner I had the most pressing invitations to stop at Jackson and Canton, Miss., both of which places were destroyed by me. I do think some political power might be given to the young men who served in the rebel army for they are a better class than the adventurers who have gone South purely for office.

Affectionately,

W. T. SHERMAN.

In May, 1869, General Sherman took command of the army, succeeding General Grant, and moved to Washington. As Senator Sherman also lived there, no letters appear during the summer of this year.

HEADQUARTERS ARMY OF THE UNITED STATES.
WASHINGTON, D.C., Sept. 12, 1869.

Dear Brother:

Statutes do not clearly define the spheres of each, and a natural conflict or suspicion arises. United in one person settles all disputes. In the present attitude of things, it would be a good thing to dispense with a Secretary of War, and unite Army and Navy in one representative in the Cabinet, and let the Internal Revenue go into the Cabinet....

Yours,

W. T. SHERMAN.

MANSFIELD, OHIO, Oct. 10, 1869.

Dear Brother:... The panic in New York, though disastrous to a few, will do good. It will prove the absolute necessity of getting upon a specie basis. This process is a hard one and will affect the popularity of Grant's administration, but it must be gone through with....

Affectionately,

JOHN SHERMAN.

In the summer of 1870, General Sherman went West to the Pacific on a pleasure trip, getting back to Washington about the middle of October. It is this trip to which Senator Sherman refers in the following letter.

MANSFIELD, OHIO, Oct. 21, 1870.

Dear Brother: I have kept the general run of you during your trip, and therefore know what a fine reception you had on the coast.

It is a fatiguing trip, and no wonder that Lizzie is worn out by it. I have spent the summer very quietly and pleasantly, most of the time at home. I did my share of the work in the canvas at Ohio and Indiana, but it was a languid one. I am getting tired of the ceaseless struggle of political life, and above all dread the contest next summer, when, if I am a candidate, I shall have to encounter the combined opposition of every Democrat and of every Federal office-holder in Ohio....

Affectionately,

JOHN SHERMAN.

HEADQUARTERS ARMY OF THE UNITED STATES, WASHINGTON, D.C., March 21, 1871.

Dear Brother: A few days ago at the request of a mutual friend, I sent to General J. E. Johnston at Savannah, the eight volumes of the report of the committee on the conduct of the war.

In writing him I called his attention to the recent feeling here on the subject of the Ku Klux, and that I did not believe he or the Confederate officers were either the instigators, or passive aiders of these disgraceful acts....

Affectionately, etc.,

W. T. SHERMAN.

General Sherman, while Commander of the Army, made frequent tours of inspection through the West.

FORT RICHARDSON, TEXAS, May 18, 1871.

Dear Brother: I have been skirting the frontier of Texas, from San Antonio to this place.

Now, for the first time, we meet mails coming from the direction of St. Louis, and have New York "Herald" of May 1, 2, and 3. I see the "Herald" is out in full blast for me as President. You may say for me and publish it too, that in no event and under no circumstances will I ever be a candidate for President or any other political office; and I mean every word of it....

Affectionately, etc.,

W. T. SHERMAN.

HEADQUARTERS ARMY OP THE UNITED States,
WASHINGTON, D.C., July 8, 1871.

Dear Brother:

I saw General Grant when he was here some days ago, and we talked about... and my published declination of a nomination by either party. I told him plainly that the South would go against him *en masse*, though he counts on South Carolina, Louisiana, and Arkansas; but I repeated my conviction, that all that was vital at the South was against him, and that negroes were generally quiescent and could not be relied on as voters when local questions become mixed up with political matters. I think, however, he will be renominated and re-elected, unless by personally doing small things, to alienate his party adherence of the North....

My office has been by law stript of all the influence and prestige it possessed under Grant, and even in matters of discipline and army control I am neglected, overlooked, or snubbed. I have called General Grant's attention to the fact several times, but got no satisfactory redress.

The old regulations of 1853, made by Jeff Davis in hostility to General Scott, are now strictly construed and enforced; and in these regulations the War Department is everything, and the name of General, Lieutenant-General, or Commander-in-Chief even, does not appear in the book. Consequently, orders go to parts of the army supposed to be under my command, of which I know nothing till I read them in the newspapers; and when I call the attention of the Secretary to it, he simply refers to some paragraph of the Army Regulations. Some five years ago there was a law to revise these Regulations, and to make them conform to the new order of things, and to utilize the experiences of the war. A Board was appointed here in Washington, composed of Sherman, Sheridan, and Anger, that did so revise them, and they were submitted to Congress with the approval of General Grant; but no action was taken. But now a new Board is ordered to prepare another set, and this Board is composed of a set of officers hardly qualified to revise the judgment of the former Board. I propose patiently to await the action of this Board, though now that war is remote, there is little chance of Congress giving the army a thought at all; and if these new regulations were framed, as I suppose, to cripple the power of the General, and to foster the heads of staff departments, I will simply notify the President that I cannot undertake to command an army with all its staff independent of the Commander-in-Chief, and ask him to allow me quietly to remove to St. Louis, to do such special matters as may be committed to me by the President, and leave the Army to be governed and commanded as now, by the Secretary of War, in person. This cannot occur for twelve months....

I have said nothing of this to anybody, and will not do anything hasty or rash; but I do think that because some newspapers berate Grant about his military surroundings, he feels disposed to go to the other extreme....Affectionately,

W. T. SHERMAN.

MANSFIELD, OHIO, July 16, 1871.

Dear Brother:

He will be nominated and I hope elected. So shall I; and it is better for the country that, in our relative positions, we are independent of each other. I hope you and he will preserve your ancient cordiality; for though he seems willing to strip your office of its power, yet I have no doubt he feels as warm an attachment for you as, from his temperament, he can to any one. You have been forbearing with him, but lose nothing by it. I have seen nothing in the course of the Republican party unfriendly to you. I know you have hosts of friends in our party who would resent any marked injustice to you....

Affectionately yours,

JOHN SHERMAN.

HEADQUARTERS ARMY OF THE UNITED STATES,
WASHINGTON, D. C., Oct. 14, 1871.

Dear Brother: The Ohio election is now over, and you have a clear working majority in the Legislature. So I infer you are safe for another six years in the Senate. I hope so, and was told by Mr. Delano, in the cars coming East, a few days since, that you were sure of reelection.

I understood from one of his revenue officers along, that Delano was not even a candidate for the Senate.

Some time ago Admiral Alden invited me to go out to the Mediterranean with him in the *Wabash* Frigate, to sail in November. I have pretty much made up my mind to go, and President and Secretary have promptly consented....

I made the condition myself, that, though I shall arrange to be gone five months, I would hold myself prepared to come back within thirty days of notice by telegram....

Yours affectionately,

W. T. SHERMAN.

MANSFIELD, OHIO, Oct. 17, 1871.

Dear Brother: Your note of the 14th is received. I am glad you are going to Europe, and under such favorable auspices.

You are sure of a hearty reception there, and you will be greatly entertained and instructed by wonders that must be seen as well as read of.... It is generally conceded that I shall be elected, though it is not sure. No doubt a majority of Republicans favor me, but combinations are often made, and may be in this election....

Affectionately,

JOHN SHERMAN.

U. S. FRIGATE WABASH, CADIZ, Dec. 21, 1871.

Dear Brother:

I have had a good chance to visit Madeira, Cadiz, Xeres, and Seville, and now we proceed to Gibraltar, where I shall leave the ship and go to Malaga, Granada, Cordova, Toledo, Madrid, Saragossa, and Barcelona. Thence we shall cross the Pyrenees into France at Pepignan, Marseilles, and Nice, to rejoin the ship. I can then learn if Admiral Alden can in the ordinary course of his duty go to Naples, Syracuse, Malta, and Alexandria, in which case I can see the Valley of the Po, the Mont Cenis tunnel, etc., to Rome and Naples in time to join the ship at, say, Naples....

Truly, etc.,

W. T. SHERMAN.

Nice, Jan. 19, 1872.

Dear Brother: The telegraph announces your re-election, and as quite a number of Americans and even foreigners have congratulated me on your re-election I can but join in the general acclaim. This carries your political career two years after Gen. Grant's second term.

Yours truly,

W. T. SHERMAN.

COMMITTEE OF Finance,

U. S. **Senate, Washington,** Jan. 26, 1872.

Dear Brother:... Congress is going on with its usual round of debate and delay. I am quite busy with taxes and tariff, and spend most of the time in committee. My re-election has got to be an old story. As the session approached, the opposition to me in my own party died away, and I received the unanimous vote. Still there were five or six Republicans who were disposed to enter into the new party movement, among them Howard and certain Cincinnati members. They disavowed any hostility to me, but were inclined to support Cox as an Anti-Grant or new departure candidate. Perhaps if the whole body of the Democrats had gone into this movement it might have resulted in my defeat; but this was found impracticable, and so I was elected by seven majority over all. I think General Grant has found out that my strength in Ohio was equal to his own. I was in Columbus for one week, but was not put to either unusual trouble or expense, and now hold the office as independent in promise as any member of the Senate.... You are to have a grand trip. Your movements are observed and commented upon here kindly. By all means take it easy and don't hurry....

Your affectionate brother,

JOHN SHERMAN.

Rome, Feb. 21, 1872.

Dear Brother: I received yours of 26th of January here at Rome, and have been so busy that really I have had no time to write my home letters. We have been here ten days, and now start for Naples, where we shall stay a week, and then for Malta, Alexandria, Constantinople, and the East. We are everywhere received with every honor and attention; indeed too much for our own comfort and advantage. No nation or people seem to be held in such estimation as the Americans....

The Italians are a kind, good people, and are winning their place among the scientific men of the world. Some of their modern railroads evince a talent in that branch worthy the old days of the Coliseum.

The unification of Italy seems to grow in strength, and the Pope, though obstinate, is in no manner interfered with in his office, and I think in time he will realize that he is stronger by being entirely disconnected with the administration of a petty state or kingdom. This is the opinion also of many Catholics. It is possible that some want the Pope to be considered somewhat of a martyr, but those who control the government here understand well enough the problem.

The King is at Naples, but his son Prince Humbert has been extremely polite to us and has tendered all proper attentions.

I do not see but the people are as free here as in Prance or other neighboring countries, there being substantially a free press, and thus far we have not even been called on for our passports, a perfect contrast to the annoyances of former times. Italy is full of Americans and we meet everywhere our country people, who seem to take the lead as sculptors, painters, travellers, etc....W. T. Sherman.

CONSTANTINOPLE, April 16, 1872.

Dear Brother: I have been here eight days, and have seen everything that interests travellers, and was to have started to-day for Odessa and the Crimea by the regular Russian steamer *Vladimir;* but last night when dining with the English Charge the Sultan's Grand Master of Ceremonies called, and expressed the Sultan's wish that I would postpone my departure, as he expressed his desire to see me, and was so situated that he could not until to-morrow. Of course I was compelled to defer my departure and now I am undecided.... Soon after our arrival the Sultan received us with marked favor, and afterwards entertained us at breakfast; but he gave to Ered Grant, as Prince Royal, the post of honor. We infer that the reason he has asked me to postpone my departure is to show me personally that he meant nothing wrong, which of course I knew he did not, for it was a subject of joke. The Russian Ambassador and English have entertained us, and they knew perfectly our relative ranks....

Yours truly,

W. T. SHERMAN.

PARIS, PRANCE, July 16, 1872.

Dear Brother:... Of course I have watched the progress of political events as they appear from this standpoint, and feel amazed to see the turn things have taken. Grant, who never was a Republican, is your candidate; and Greeley, who never was a Democrat but quite the reverse, is the Democratic candidate. I infer that Grant will be re-elected, though several shrewd judges insist that Greeley will be our next President.... There are a great many Americans located here in business or prolonged stay, that constitute a society in themselves. They try to monopolize my spare time, yet I have managed to see M. Thiers, and the officers of Versailles,— having dined with the President,—and I am this moment back from a tour of the southern line of forts, Valerien, D'Issy, Vanves, and Montrouge, guided by a staff-officer especially appointed; and I have appointed another day of next week to complete the circuit. *Bn route* to Paris I saw Strasbourg, Wissembourg, Saarbruck, Metz, and Sedan, so that I shall be able to understand the angry controversies that are sure to arise in the progress of the trials that I see it is resolved to put Bazaine and others through.... Choosing between the two candidates on national grounds, I surely prefer Grant; as to platforms and parties, of course I regard these as mere traps to catch flies, but with General Grant as President, there will likely be more stability and quietude, which the country needs....

Truly yours,

W. T. SHERMAN.

MANSFIELD, OHIO, Aug. 4, 1872.

Dear Brother:... Just now all interest is centred upon the Presidential election. As you say, the Republicans are running a

Democrat, and the Democrats a Republican. And there is not an essential difference in the platform of principle. The chief interest I feel in the canvass is the preservation of the Republican party, which I think essential to secure the fair enforcement of the results of the war. General Grant has so managed matters as to gain the very bitter and active hostility of many of the leading Republicans, and the personal indifference of most of the residue. He will, however, be fairly supported by the great mass of the Republicans, and I still hope and believe will be elected. The defections among Republicans will be made up by Democrats, who will not vote for Greeley.

The whole canvass is so extraordinary, that no result can be anticipated. You will notice that Sumner, Thurman, Banks, and others are for Greeley, who is probably the most unfit man for President, except Train, that has ever been mentioned. I intend to support Grant fairly and fully, as best for the country and Republican party.

Affectionately yours,

JOHN SHERMAN.

Mansfield, Ohio, Oct. 10, 1872. *Dear Brother:* Your letter came in my absence. The election is over, and clearly indicates the re-election of Grant. I do not see any occasion of a further contest, but I presume it will be continued until November....

Affectionately yours,

JOHN SHERMAN.

From 1872 to 1874, the two brothers lived near each other in Washington. In the fall of 1874, General Sherman obtained permission to transfer his headquarters to St. Louis, and removed there with his family. He did this in order to remove himself from further official contact with General Belknap, then Secretary of War, who was issuing many military orders and making many military appointments without General Sherman's knowledge or approval. Two years later, after General Belknap's resignation as Secretary of War had been accepted, the office of General of the Army was reinvested with the powers which had formerly belonged to it.

Thereafter General Sherman willingly removed back to Washington and reestablished his headquarters there.

HEADQUARTERS ARMY or THE UNITED STATES,
WASHINGTON, D.C., Aug. 28, 1874.

Dear Brother:... Don't ever give any person the least encouragement to think I can be used for political ends. I have seen it poison so many otherwise good characters, that I am really more obstinate than ever. I think Grant will be made miserable to the end of his life by his eight years' experience. Let those who are trained to it keep the office, and keep the Army and Navy as free from politics as possible, for emergencies that may arise at any time.

Think of the reputations wrecked in politics since 1865.

Yours affectionately,

W. T. SHERMAN.

And a few days later he continued: —

No matter what the temptation, I will never allow my name to be used by any party; but I don't think it would be prudent to allow the old Democrats to get possession of the Government; and hope the Republicans will choose some new man, as like Mr. Lincoln as you can find. Or else let us unite on Blaine, or even Washburne....

HEADQUARTERS ARMY OP THE UNITED STATES, St. Louis,
Mo., Oct. 23, 1874.

Dear Brother:

I am in easy communication with, and in perfect harmony with, the real working army....

But if let alone, I will do what devolves on me by law and custom, and endeavor to injure no one; but of those fellows in Washington who have served through several great wars, and boast that they have never heard a shot, and never had to do the dirty work of campaigning, I will speak out and Congress will have to notice it.

The Republican newspaper in Washington, their organ, intimates that inasmuch as I have removed from Washington, I am not in harmony with the Administration and should resign. By my office I am above party, and am not bound in honor or fact to toady to anybody. Therefore I shall never resign, and shall never court any other office, so they may reserve their advice to men who seek it....

I have always expressed a desire that some good man, a statesman of experience if he can be found, be selected for President. General Grant has had enough to recognize the obligation of the country to the army, and the time has come to return to the civil list. In no event and under no circumstances will I yield to this, my final determination....

Yours affectionately,

W. T. SHERMAN.

HEADQUARTERS ARMY OP THE UNITED STATES, St. LOUIS, MO., Dec. 10, 1874.

Dear Brother: I have just received from the President's secretary a note, saying he may want me to attend a dinner and reception he proposes to give the King of the Sandwich Islands, and I have answered that on a two days' notice I can be there....

Affectionately,

W. T. SHERMAN.

The "Louisiana matters," referred to in the letters of January 7 and February 3, were the reconstruction difficulties which so many of the Southern States were experiencing. General Sherman objected to the detailing of army officers to assist the State authorities in keeping the peace.

HEADQUARTERS ARMY or THE UNITED STATES, St. Louis, Mo., Jan. 7, 1875.

Dear Brother: I see my name was used in the debate yesterday on Louisiana matters.

Neither the President or Secretary of War ever consulted me about Louisiana matters. Sheridan received his orders direct from the Secretary of War and Adjutant-General Townsend, and started on telegraphic notice, writing me ,a short note stating the fact, and that the Secretary of War would explain to me.

The latter sent me a copy of the orders and instructions by mail, which I received after General Sheridan had gone, and I simply acknowledged their receipt.

I have all along tried to save our officers and soldiers from the dirty work imposed on them by the city authorities of the South; and may, thereby, have incurred the suspicion of the President that I did not cordially sustain his force. My hands and conscience are free of any of the breaches of fundamental principles in that quarter. And I have always thought it wrong to bolster up weak State governments by our troops. We should keep the peace always; but not act as bailiff constables and catch thieves. That should be beneath a soldier's vocation. If you want information of the conditions up the Red River, call for a report recently made by Lieutenant-Colonel Morrow, personally known to you....

As ever, your brother,

W. T. SHERMAN.

HEADQUARTERS ARMY OF THE UNITED STATES, ST. LOUIS, MO., Jan. 23, 1875.

Dear Brother:

You will be surprised and maybe alarmed, that I have at last agreed to publish in book form my Memoirs of a period from 1846-65, in two volumes, prepared at great cost of labor and care.

I have carefully eliminated everything calculated to raise controversy, except where sustained by documents embraced in the work itself, and then only with minor parties. I submitted the manuscript to last summer, and he was emphatic that it ought to be published in the interest of history. Bancroft did the same, though he never saw the manuscript, and I thought I had best show it to but few, as after all the responsibility rests on me....

Affectionately,

W. T. S HERMAN.

HEADQUARTERS ARMY OF THE UNITED STATES, ST. LOUIS, Mo., Let). 3, 1875.

Dear Brother: I read carefully your speech, and your reasoning is very close; much more so than Thurman's and others, and I was glad you could make so good a defence. I know that our soldiers hate that kind of duty terribly, and not one of those officers but would prefer to go to the plains against the Indians, rather than encounter a street mob, or serve a civil process.

But in our government it is too hard for our troops to stand up in the face of what is apparent: that the present government of Louisiana is not the choice of the people, though in strict technical law it is the State government. I recognize the great necessity of standing by the *lawful* On the Louisiana matters.

State government, but the soldiers do not. The quicker you allow the people to select their own governors the better, and if necessary pile on the effort to secure a fair election, and prevent intimidation of voters.

I was always embarrassed by the plain, palpable fact, that the Union whites are cowardly, and allow the rebel element that loves to fight, to cow them. Until the Union whites, and negroes too, *fight* for their own rights they will be trodden down. Outside help sooner or later must cease, for our army is ridiculously small, in case of actual collision. It is only the memory of our war power, that operates on the rebel element now. They have the votes, the will, and will in the end prevail. Delay only gives them sympathy elsewhere....

Affectionately,

W. T. SHERMAN.

HEADQUARTERS ARMY OF THE UNITED STATES, ST. LOUIS, MO., March 18, 1875.

Dear Brother:

To-morrow Generals Sheridan and Pope will meet here to discuss the Indian troubles. We could settle them in an hour, but Congress wants the patronage of the Indian bureau, and the bureau wants the appropriations without any of the trouble of the Indians themselves. I don't suppose in the history of the world there is such a palpable waste of money as that bestowed on the Kiowas, and no wonder our government is sinking deeper and deeper into debt. We have spent in the past seven months, at least half a million dollars in bringing down these Indians, and this is the fourth time since I have personal knowledge of the fact....

Yours affectionately,

W. T. SHERMAN.

CHAPTER X

General Sherman's Memoirs were first published in 1875, and called forth a storm of criticism, to which the following letter refers.

HEADQUARTERS ARMY OF THE UNITED STATES, ST. LOUIS, Mo., May 25, 1875.

Dear Brother:... no matter how unwise were my conditions with Johnston they were *secret,* and his [Stanton's] divulgence was a betrayal of me; and Stanton knew it. At all events, he himself made so much clamor that history is not perfect unless the matter be wholly explained, and I think I have done it fairly.

... I believe, had I submitted to Stanton's and Halleck's insults of 1865, I should have been swept aside like any other piece of war rubbish at the reorganization of the army....

Yours affectionately,

HEADQUARTERS ARMY OF THE UNITED STATES, **St.** LOUIS, **Mo.,** NOV. 17, 1875.

Dear Brother:... Belknap Has acted badly by me ever since lie reached Washington....

General Grant promised me often to arrange and divide our functions, but he never did, but left the Secretary to do all those things of which he himself, as General, had complained to Stanton. I don't think I ever used the expression often imputed to me of saying that the Secretary of War is only a clerk to the President. It is the opinion of many lawyers that the Secretary of War himself has no right to issue a military order to officers and soldiers — that his office is civil etc., etc. The President is constitutional commander-in-chief, and when the Secretary issues his order he ought to recite the fact; whereas orders are issued by the Adjutant-General by order of the Secretary of War. This is done daily, and I cannot command unless orders come through me, which they do not, but go straight to the party concerned. This is the real question at issue between us. Congress ought to clearly define the relation between the Secretary of War and a General of the army. It is not the case now, but the

274

Secretary of War exercises all the functions of the Commander-General under a decision of the Attorney-General....

Yours, etc.,

W. T. SHERMAN.

HEADQUARTERS ARMY OF THE UNITED STATES, ST. LOUIS,
Mo., Dec. 29, 1875.

Dear Brother:... As to the army, I agree that it is entirely too costly. Twenty-five thousand soldiers with a due proportion of officers ought to be maintained at less than present estimates, which I see are stated at forty and also at fifty-five millions. This must embrace appropriations for forts, harbors, etc., whose disbursements fall under the engineer and other bureaus of the War Department. The heaviest cost to the army is in these expensive bureaus of which we have ten, all of which have a head in Washington and run, as it were, a separate machine. I have no hesitation in saying that if the Secretary of War has the lawful power to command the army through the Adjutant-General, then my office is a sinecure and should be abolished. Instead of being useful, it is simply ornamental and an obstacle to unity of command and harmony of action. No two men can fulfil the same office; and the law should clearly define the functions of each, or mine should be abolished....

Yours affectionately,

W. T. SHERMAN.

HEADQUARTERS ARMY OP THE UNITED STATES, ST. LOUIS, MO., Feb. 1, 1876.

Dear Brother:... Your letter endorsing Hayes is first-rate, and meets general approval. I agree with you that no one should be the President unless he was with us heart and soul in the Civil War; and Hayes fills the bill perfectly.

I should be delighted to have him nominated and elected.

The Democrats, in turning between the Democrats of the North and South, will probably commit a mistake that will reunite the Republicans.

I see the "Herald," in an elaborate and good article on saving money in the War Department estimates, criticizes the sending of officers abroad at public expense, instancing my case. Not one cent of my expenses was paid by the Government. I availed myself of the frigate *Wabash* to reach Gibraltar, whither she was bound in her course to the Mediterranean. I paid my mess-bill, which amounted to $130 (more than the price of passage over in a Cunarder).

If you happen to see one of those reporters, you could say as much. I will not, because on searching they will find that not a cent was paid for my expenses abroad....

Yours affectionately,

W. T. SHERMAN.

HEADQUARTERS ARMY OF THE UNITED STATES, St. LOUIS, Mo., March 10, 1876.

Dear Brother: I have purposely refrained from writing to you my opinions and feelings on the terrible fate that so suddenly has befallen General Belknap, because I want to say truthfully that I have never asked you to advocate my cause or to be compromised by my mistakes. I am proud of your position in the Senate, and would not have you to risk it by even the faintest partiality to your brother. But people will ask you what was the real reason why I left Washington; did I have knowledge of frauds and peculations? and was I not bound to reveal them? You may answer positively that I had no knowledge except what Congress and the President had. It was not my office to probe after vague rumors and whispers that had no official basis. The President and Belknap both gradually withdrew from me all the powers which Grant had exercised in the same office, and Congress capped the climax by repealing that law which required all orders to the army to go *through* the General, and the only other one, a joint resolution that empowered the General to appoint "traders."

The consequence was that orders to individuals of the army went over my head to them, and reports went back without coming through me, as required in every military service on earth....

I have now from Moulton two letters, and from Dayton one. In all which is stated that the new Secretary, Judge Taft, has spoken kindly of me, and expressed a desire to meet me in Washington. I will not go to Washington unless ordered, and it would be an outrage if Congress, under a temporary excitement, should compel my removal back. I came out at my own expense, and never charged a cent for transportation, which I could have done. I can better command the army from here than from there. The causes that made a Belknap remain and will remain....

If you see Judge Taft, say to him that my opinion is that I can fulfil any general policy he may prescribe, and enforce any orders he may give better from St. Louis than Washington.

Affectionately, etc.,

W. T. SHERMAN.

There are two ways to govern the army, — one *through* its generals, and the other through the staff. If orders and instructions are made to individuals composing the army *direct* by the Adjutant-General, and not *through* the commanding General, the latter is not only useless but an incumbrance, and had better be away. But if Secretary Taft is willing to trust me to execute and carry into effect his orders and instructions, all he has to do is to order, and he will find me ready.

Affectionately,

W. T. SHERMAN.

During the next three years (end of 1877 to 1881) the brothers were so much together that their correspondence contains nothing of continuous interest. General Sherman removed to Washington, and John Sherman lived there as Secretary of the Treasury. In the summer of 1881, John Sherman was in Mansfield, and the General sent him frequent bulletins from Washington as to President Garfield's condition after he was shot. John Sherman returned to Washington before the President's death.

TELEGRAMS.

THE WESTERN UNION TELEGRAPH Co.,

Dated, **WASHINGTON,** D.C., July 2, 1881.

Received at **MANSFIELD, OHIO,**

3 P.M.

To Honorable John Sherman:

President Garfield was shot in the back toward the right side, the ball ranging downwards — not yet found. Pulse good and appearances favorable.

Has been brought to the White House. The assassin is from Chicago, an ex-consul at Marseilles, described as a lawyer, politician, and theologian. He is in custody. All sorts of rumors afloat, but the above is all that is known to me. I went in person to the depot immediately, and found all his Cabinet present.

W. T. SHERMAN,

General.

WESTERN UNION TELEGRAPH Co.,

Dated, **WASHINGTON,** D.C., July 2, 1881.

Received at **MANSFIELD, OHIO,** 8.45 **A M.**

To Honorable John Sherman:

Dispatch received. Just come from White House. Saw and talked with General Garfield. Mind and memory clear, and he is personally hopeful. The doctors shake their heads. Situation most serious, but I cannot help hoping that the ball has not traversed the cavity of the stomach, as the wound indicates. Mrs. Garfield and all the family are with him.

W. T. SHERMAN.

WESTERN UNION TELEGRAPH CO., WASHINGTON, D.C., July 3, 1881.

Received at **MANSFIELD, OHIO,** 4.15 **P M.**

To Honorable John Sherman:

Dispatch received, I am this minute back from the White House. Doctor Bliss surgeon, in attendance on President Garfield, authorized me to report that all the symptoms continued most favorable, and that he believed in ultimate recovery.

W. T. SHERMAN.

WESTERN UNION TELEGRAPH Co.,

Dated, **WASHINGTON,** D.C., July 4, 1881.

Received at **MANSFIELD, OHIO,** 1.40.

To Honorable John Sherman:

I am just back from the White House. The President is reported to have passed a night of pain, which gave rise to unfavorable reports; but the attending physicians, Bliss, Barnes, Woodward, and Reyburn, have made public the bulletins. Each warrants us to hope for recovery. Everything here is as quiet as the Sabbath.

W. T. SHERMAN, General.

Here the letters begin again.

**HEADQUARTERS ARMY OE THE UNITED STATES,
WASHINGTON,** D.C., July 13, 1881.

Dear Brother: Nobody now sees the President except the doctors, and we are compelled to base our opinions on the bulletins which are sent by telegraph all around the country.

These warrant us to believe that Garfield will recover, but after a long, painful process, leaving him crippled or emaciated. It is too bad that the law is so unequal to the punishment of the man who intended to murder him....

Yours,

W. T. SHERMAN.

HEADQUARTERS ARMY or THE UNITED STATES, Aug. 25, 1881.

Dear Brother: The President's condition is now absolutely critical, and surely many days cannot now pass without some turn. He is so weak now that he cannot endure a relapse....

Yours affectionately,

W. T. SHERMAN.

HEADQUARTERS ARMY OF THE UNITED STATES, WASHINGTON, Aug. 29, 1881.

Dear Brother:... The President is sensibly better to-day, and all the friends and family feel encouraged. If to-morrow he be on the upward mend I shall go to *New* York, *New* London, Worcester, and Boston, to be gone ten days, but if you have occasion to write, the letter will be forwarded. But you may be sure that I shall be here in case of necessity. The Cabinet desire that the prisoner, Guiteau, be regularly tried by the courts. We can defend the jail against the world, unless there be treachery. But when the time comes to take him from the jail to the court-house we cannot use soldiers, for the law prohibits their use as a *posse comitatus.* I apprehend no violence here even if the President dies, but sooner or later Guiteau will die. The feeling is too universal for him ever to escape.

Affectionately,

W. T. SHERMAN.

The following letter is published, not for the purpose of calling attention to the incident of which it speaks, but because of the interesting facts regarding the allowances, etc., to army officers.

WASHINGTON, D.C., Feb. 28, 1882.

HON. JOHN SHERMAN,

United States Senate.

When a senator or member of Congress discovers in some newspaper a statement which he considers offensive to himself, he rises to a question of privilege, and makes his statement of facts. How when an outsider finds himself misrepresented in the Congressional Record, I suppose he may rise and make his statement of facts.

In the Congressional Record, Saturday, February 25th, the Hon. James B. Beck is reported as having said that General Sheridan had come to Washington at an expense to the United States of a thousand dollars, to assist in having his father-in-law, General Rucker, made a brigadier-general and quartermaster-general for the purpose of being retired with increased pay. I know that General Sheridan was ordered to come to Washington by Secretary of War Lincoln, for an entirely different matter, at an expense of not to exceed $200, viz. eight cents a mile, coming and going by the shortest possible mail route, according to a law made by the Congress of which Mr. Beck was a member.

Mr. Beck is further reported to have said that General

Sherman was in the habit of travelling, with his large staff, in palace cars at the expense of the United States, nominally to inspect posts, but really for pleasure. Now this is so totally untrue, and so diametrically opposed to my usage, that I am simply amazed. Not a cent can be drawn from the Treasury of the United States without the warrant of law. I never hired a palace car in my life, surely not at the expense of the United States, for no quarter-master would pay the voucher, and if such voucher exist, it can be had on demand of any senator.

General Sherman, like every army officer, is entitled by law, and receives eight cents a mile when travelling on duty. My duty and inclination carry me to the remotest parts of our country, where travel usually costs from ten to twenty-five cents a mile.

I think the law ought to provide me a palace car, and I think Mr. Beck agrees with me, and supposes such to be the fact. I have not a particle of doubt he sup posed such to be the fact, else he would not have asserted it on the floor of the Senate; but I beg you will on some opportune occasion tell him it is not true, but on the contrary, that the Government expects me to make tours of the Indian frontier chiefly at my own cost. The general or lieutenant-general draws the same travelling allowance as a second lieutenant. No more and no less.

The general of a department has the right to inspect every post of his command, so the General of a division is expected to be familiar with the condition of every post within his sphere of command; and, of course, the commanding general has a similar right. Without this right an intelligent commander would be impossible.

By this system I am kept informed of everything pertaining to the military establishment in peace as well as war, and the constant inquiries by Committees of Congress can thus alone be answered, and I will not alter or change my plans to suit Senator Beck.

I believe it is construed as discourteous to refer to a senator in debate by name,— thus you are addressed as the Honorable Senator from Ohio,— but I infer the rules of the Senate are not so punctilious about the names of outsiders. Thus Senator Beck spoke of Generals Sheridan and Sherman by name, and not by office.

We are not ashamed of our names, and have no objection to their free use on the floor of the Senate. We fear nothing, not even a positive misstatement, but it surely adds nothing to the dignity or manliness of a senator to attempt to misrepresent an absent officer of the common Government, sworn to obey its laws, and to submit to such measures as it, in its wisdom, may prescribe....

W. T. SHERMAN, General.

Before the Act of Compulsory Retirement of Army Officers at the age of sixty-four years (passed 1882,) all retirements were made at the will of the President. General Ord's retirement by President Hayes greatly distressed General Sherman, as it came at a time when General Ord could ill afford to be retired, and when he had every right to expect that General McDowell, his senior in age as well as rank, would be retired first. This case was the immediate cause of the staunch support which General Sherman gave to this bill; so after its passage, when it was suggested that an exception be made in his own case, he refused to allow it. He was retired February 8, 1884, but had already removed to St. Louis with his family several months previous to this date in order to allow General Sheridan to take command of the army at the opening of Congress.

WESTERN UNION TELEGRAPH Co.,

Dated, Los **ANGELES, CAL.,** April 15, 1882.

To HON. JOHN SHERMAN,

United States Senate, Washington, D.C.

Letter of eighth received. I do not expect to reach Washington, D.C., till about May 12th, and do not ask Congress to make any exception in my case. If officers generally are disqualified for efficient service at sixty-two years, the law should so declare it and no chance be allowed for a repetition of the terrible discrimination made in General Ord's case. Compensation to retired officers should vary according to length and quality of service, and a vote of thanks by Congress to general officers should have some value. There are only five such now surviving, and, like the Supreme Court, they should retain their salaries without other allowances. You may announce these as my opinions.

W. T. SHERMAN,

General.

HEADQUARTERS ARMY OP THE UNITED STATES, WASHINGTON, D.C., June 7, 1883.

Dear Brother: I expect all alteration to be complete by the time we reach there, early in October, and after a short pause I will come on to Washington, write up all by reports, and then ask the President to order me to St. Louis to await my retirement February 8, 1884, and by or before December 1st of this year to install General Sheridan in command of the army, *vice* Sherman retired.

It is better that the change should occur with the new Congress. The country is now generally prosperous, and the army is in reasonably good condition, considering the fact that peace and politics are always more damaging than war....

Later he writes from St. Louis: —

I have fixed November 1st as the day for transferring the command of the army to Sheridan. This will enable me to conclude my report, and in like manner enable Sheridan to submit to Congress any special matters he may deem proper.

On the whole, the time is most opportune, and I think I can leave my post with the general respect of my fellows....Affectionately,

W. **T. SHERMAN.**

In the spring of 1884, after General Sherman's retirement, his name was prominently mentioned as a possible candidate for the Presidency in the coming campaign. As he had done on several previous occasions, he refused to allow his name to be used.

UNITED STATES SENATE, WASHINGTON, D.C., Jan. 29, 1884.

Dear Brother:... You are probably right in your treatment of the Presidential nomination. Most of the talk in your favor is no doubt honest and sincere, but some of it, I am sure, is to crowd off other candidates, or for selfish motives. A nomination is far from being equivalent to an election. The chances are for the Democrats, but for their proverbial blundering. An election would be a misfortune to you, while the canvass would be painful to all the family. Still, having fairly and fully stated your opposition to being a candidate, and having given fair notice of your purpose to decline, it is better not to say anything more about it. The papers will think you protest too much.

It now looks as if Logan may get the nomination.

Affectionately yours,

JOHN SHERMAN.

ST. LOUIS, Feb. 24, 1884.

Dear Brother: I think I have owed you a letter some time. I have nothing new. Days, weeks, and months glide by, and my mail brings the most conglomerate stuff possible, — letters asking for autographs, photographs, donations, tokens, such as saddles, swords, muskets, buttons, etc., etc., which I used in the war, — many letters predicting that I will be the next President, and that the writer foresaw it and was the first to conceive the thought.... I notice with satisfaction that my name is being gradually dropped, and that my sincerity is recognized. What your party wants is a good, fair executive, and of these you have plenty, — Edmunds, Harrison, Gresham, Logan, etc., etc.... I wish to remain absolutely neutral. Gresham has a fine war record, and is as honest, outspoken, judicious a man as I know among my old soldiers. I also think highly of Calkins of Indiana and Ballantine of Nebraska.

Affectionately yours,

W. T. SHERMAN.

UNITED STATES SENATE, WASHINGTON, D.C., March 7, 1884.

Dear Brother:... I have made up my mind to be silent and neutral, and I think that it is your best course. You did not want the nomination. I would gladly take it as an honorable closing of thirty years of political life, but I will neither ask for it, scheme for it, nor have I the faintest hope of getting it, and at the end of my present term I intend to retire from my political life and take it easy.

One thing you ought to have, and I think Congress would readily grant it if acceptable to you, and that is the detail of a staff-officer to help you with your military correspondence, to travel with, you, and aid you in the social duties that will always cling to you while you live....

Affectionately yours,

JOHN SHERMAN.

UNITED STATES SENATE, WASHINGTON, D.C., May 4, 1884.

Dear Brother:... While in Ohio I heard a great deal of politics, and chiefly about the nomination for the Presidency. It is certain that if Blaine is not nominated in the early ballots a movement will be made for your nomination, and if entered upon will go like wild fire. Some one should be authorized to make a definite and positive refusal if you have concluded to decline the nomination if tendered. My own opinion is still that while you ought not to seek, or even beforehand consent, to accept a nomination, yet if it comes unsought and with cordial unanimity you ought to acquiesce. I believe it would be best for the country, honorable to you and your children, and far less irksome than you have thought. It would be the safe result of what is like to be a severe contest.... If desired by me I could have the solid vote of Ohio, but I see no prospect or possibility of my nomination, and not much of my election if nominated, but yours is easy. Blaine could readily turn his strength to you if he cannot get a majority, and I think means to do so. All well here.

Affectionately yours,

JOHN SHERMAN.

St. LOUTS, May 7, 1884.

Dear Brother:... The more I reflect, the more convinced I am that I was wise and prudent in taking the exact course I have, and that it would be the height of folly to allow any false ambition to allow the use of my name for any political office.

John B. Henderson is my neighbor here, is a delegate at large to the Chicago Convention, and will, if need be, announce my unalterable purpose.... Why should I, at sixty-five years of age, with a reasonable provision for life, not a dollar of debt, and with the universal respect of my neighbors and countrymen, embark in the questionable game of politics? The country is in a state of absolute peace, and it would be a farce to declare that any man should sacrifice himself to a mere party necessity. Surely you do not rate Hayes or Arthur as great men, yet each gave the country a good administration,...

If you count yourself out, I will be absolutely neutral, and honestly believe we are approaching that epoch in our history when King Log is about as good as King Stork. Queen Victoria has proven about the best executive a nation has ever had, and we shall be lucky in securing a man of moderate ability and reasonable presence.

Yours affectionately,

W. T. SHERMAN-.

ST. Louis, June 7, 1884.

Dear Brother: Now that the Convention at Chicago has nominated Blaine and Logan, I feel such a sense of relief that I would approve of anything. My instructions to Henderson, verbal, telegraphic, and written, were all short, emphatic, and clear, and, so far as I am concerned, all may be published; viz. first, to do what was possible to prevent even the mention of my name; and, second, that though there should occur a break after the first ballots, and my name should be presented as a compromise, to decline; and, lastly, if in spite of such declination I should be nominated, I would decline with an emphasis which might be construed as disrespectful to the Convention itself, which, of course, I do not want to do.

I would not for a million of dollars subject myself and family to the ordeal of a political canvass and afterwards to a four years' service in the White House. You and Blaine and others have been trained in a different school,— quite different,—and have a perfect right to aim for the highest round of your ladder.... Here at this point I must confide to you, in absolute confidence, that I was in possession of a letter from Blaine, all in his own hand, marked "Strictly, absolutely confidential," which I now possess, with a copy of my answer, with others from various people, all to the same effect,— that in case of a break and deadlock between Blaine and Arthur it was inevitable that my name would be used, and that I had no more right to decline than if I had received an order as lieutenant of the army. When you come here sometime I will show you these letters, but I must not part with them. I had expected that my letters in answer, in case of a break — which all seemed to expect — would compel the Convention to turn to you, Edmunds, Hawley, or Gresham, and it may be that my positive manner carried conviction of my sincerity and stubbornness, and helped to bring about the nomination of Blaine and Logan. Anyhow, I escaped, and that to me was salvation....

Affectionately yours,

W. T. SHERMAN-.

ST. *Louis,* June 15, 1884.

Dear Brother: I am just back from a trip to Carthage, Joplin, etc., in Southwest Missouri. Thence to Kansas City in a week, and find an unusual pile of letters for answer, yours of June 11th among the number. This calls for an answer, for I fear even you suppose I was coquetting with the Chicago Convention. Of course this is not true, and if you could be here to see the letters and telegrams received by me marked "Strictly confidential," from parties even you cannot conjecture, you would have to admit that my course was fair, honest, and straightforward....

Henderson, and Henderson alone, had a scratch of pen or even telegram which could be tortured into authority to personate me. I talked with him before I went to Washington, and explained fully that in no event and under no circumstances would I assent to the use of my name as a Presidential candidate. He contended that no American citizen could disobey the "call of his country," but I insisted that the Chicago Convention was not this country....

Yours affectionately,

W. T. SHERMAN.

The next three letters refer to a controversy between General Sherman and Mr. Jefferson Davis, which was published in the newspapers at the time.

ST. *Louis, Mo.*, Dec. 4, 1884.

Dear Brother:... We have several posts of the Grand Army here, one of which, Frank Blair Post No 1, invited me to assist in the dedication of their new hall. I could not well decline, and attended. The hall was well filled, but it is against the customs and rules for reporters to be present. I saw none, but there must have been two at least who reported what little I had to say differently. Still my speech was most imperfect and condensed, emphasizing what I said of Jeff Davis, and induced somewhat by the regular speaker of the evening, who preceded me.

I congratulated them upon having secured so good a hall in so good a neighborhood; said that I was glad to see the interest manifested; that it was well for old soldiers thus to meet to interchange the memories of the war, and to impress its lessons on the rising generation; that I noticed a tendency to gloss over the old names and facts; that it was not a "war among the States," a war of "secession," but a "conspiracy" up to the firing on Sumter, and a "Rebellion" afterwards; that, whilst in Louisiana long before Mr. Lincoln was inaugurated, I saw evidences of the "conspiracy," among them the letter written in January by Slidell and Benjamin, then United States Senators under the oath, written on paper dated "United States Senate," etc., addressed to T. o. Moore, Governor of Louisiana, to seize the United States Arsenal at Baton Rouge; that afterwards, during the progress of the war, I had seen letters of Mr. Davis — a chest full at Jackson, Miss., sent to Washington — proving such "conspiracy," and subsequently I had seen a letter of Mr. Davis showing that he was not sincere in his doctrine of secession, for when some of the States of the Confederacy, in 1865, talked of "separate State action," another name for "secession," he, as President of the Confederacy, would resist it, even if he had to turn Lee's army against it. I did see such a letter, or its copy, in a captured letter-book at Raleigh, just about as the war was closing.

Mr. Davis, in a card addressed to the "Republican" of this city, published by it and generally copied, pronounced this false, calls on me to produce the identical letter, or to stand convicted of being a slanderer. Of course I cannot for an instant allow Mr. Davis to call on me for any specific document, or to enter up judgment on the statement of a newspaper. Still, I believe the truth of my statement can be established. I will not answer Mr. Davis direct, nor will I publish anything over my signature, but I will collect evidence to make good my statement. The particular letter shown me at Raleigh may be in the public archives at Washington, as I am sure that the box or chest was sent from Jackson, Miss.; but I apprehend that the papers gathered at Fayetteville, Raleigh, and Chapel Hill University were of those taken in hand by my two adjutants, Generals Sawyer and Rochester, brought to St. Louis, assorted and arranged as part of the records of the "Division of the Missouri," and sent to Chicago at the time General Sheridan relieved me. These records were consumed in the great fire of Chicago, 1871, but of the existence of such a letter I have not a particle of doubt. Of course I cannot recall the words, but the general purport was such as to recall to my mind the old fable of the Farmer and the Ox: "It makes all the difference in the world whether your bull gores my ox or mine yours."

I have made some inquiries of Col. E. N. Scott, in charge of the Rebellion Records, Union and Confederate, and if the correspondence between Mr. Davis and the State Governors is among these records, Mr. Davis will have his letter. I am not the custodian of the records of the war, which fill many buildings in Washington. As to Davis' opinions at that date, January and February, 1865, I can, I think, obtain secondary proof, being promised an original letter from Thad. Stevens to Herschel Y. Johnson, captured and still retained by a sergeant in the Union Army.

As to the "conspiracy," the proof is overwhelming. As to Davis' opinions in the winter of 1864-65, I am equally satisfied, but may not be able to prove by his own handwriting....

Affectionately yours,

W. T. SHERMAN.

ST. *Louis,* Dec. 7, 1884.

HON. JOHN SHERMAN,

Washington, D. C.

Dear Brother: In my letter a few days since, I referred to a letter of Hon. Thad. Stevens. I meant, of course, Hon. A. H. Stephens of Georgia. I now enclose a copy of that letter under cover of a note to Col. E. N. Scott, in charge of the General Eecords. I want you to read that letter carefully and then send it to Scott to be preserved among the archives. Such letters contain more real truth than official papers. It was from such papers that I gained the most valuable information of the actual condition of facts. Hundreds of similar letters reached me, and I fear we were not careful enough in their preservation.

They make up the unwritten history or traditions of the war, one of the principal objects of the Grand Army of the Republic. Affectionately yours,

UNITED STATES SENATE, WASHINGTON, D.C., Dec. 10, 1884.

Dear Brother:... I can see how naturally you spoke of Jeff Davis as you did, and you did not say a word more than he deserved. Still he scarcely deserves to be brought into notice. He was not only a conspirator, but a traitor. His reply was a specimen of impotent rage. It is scarcely worth your notice, nor should you dignify it by a direct rejoinder. A clear, strong statement of the historical facts that justified the use of the word "conspirator," which you know very well how to write, is all the notice required. Do not attempt to fortify it by an affidavit, as some paper says you intend to do, but your statement of the letters seen by you and the historical facts known by you are enough. I have had occasion, since your letter was received, to speak to several senators about the matter, and they all agree with me that you ought to avoid placing the controversy on letters which cannot now be produced. The Records have been pretty well sifted by friendly rebels, and under the new administration it is likely their further publication will be edited by men who will gladly shield Davis even at the expense of a Union soldier. The letter of Stephens to Johnson is an extraordinary one. Its publication will be a bombshell in the Confederate camp. I will deliver the copy to Colonel Scott tomorrow. One or two paragraphs from it go far to sustain your stated opinion of Jeff Davis....

Very affectionately yours,

JOHN SHERMAN.

In January, 1885, John Sherman was elected to the United States Senate for the fifth time, and writes to his brother about it.

... My re-election to the Senate for the fifth time is unprecedented in the history of Ohio, and for this I am indebted to the difficulty of selecting from among younger men of equal claims and calibre.... I also feel that it is the highest point of my political life, for if I live to the end of my term I shall be seventy years old. I have had enough of the contentions of political life and wish now to take a tranquil and moderate course, which, indeed, is the best for the country, now that we have no great, exciting questions to decide. The view expressed in my speech (a well-printed copy of which I will try to send you) is my sincere view of the situation. The dangers before us ,are election frauds and labor difficulties. These will be local at the beginning, but may involve the whole country.

And General Sherman answers: —

I have received your letter of the 16th, and somehow felt unusually gratified that you had been elected senator for the fifth time in the State of Ohio. This is a great honor, and I feel my full share of satisfaction. I believe the Senate of the United States to be the equal in intellectual capacity of any deliberative body on earth....

In the following October, General Sherman writes from St. Louis of the elections in Ohio.

The newspapers here now state that the Ohio election has gone fairly and conclusively to the Republicans, and pronounce you as the cause. So, apart from the immediate results and the influence it may have on other elections, it will introduce the "Bloody Shirt" as a part of the Republican doctrine. Of course the name "Bloody Shirt" is pure bosh, like the old political cries of "Black Republicans," "Niggers," etc., etc., so familiar to us in 1860-61. I understand your position to be that by Section 2, Article 14, Amendments of the Constitution, by which Representatives in Congress are apportioned, the South gained in numbers, and yet practically have defeated the main purpose of the Amendment. Now, as Congress had the power to enforce that Section by the Fifth Section, I am asked why it was not done when the Republicans had the Government. So far as I can learn the negroes at the South are protected and encouraged in gaining property and education; also in voting when their vote does not affect the result. But the feeling is universal against their "ruling white men." How force or law can be brought to bear is the most difficult problem I can conceive of, and I think you are perfectly right in making the issue; a good result will follow from its fair, open discussion. My notion is that the negro himself will have to fight for his right of suffrage, but the laws of the United States for electing Members of the House should be made as strong as possible, to encourage the negroes in voting for their candidates, and, if need be, fighting for their right when they have an undoubted majority....

Affectionately yours,

W. T. SHERMAN.

ST. *Louis,* Nov. 8, 1885.

Dear Brother:... I have been importuned from every quarter to write or say something about the "Depew" revelations, but have steadily refused anything for publication. But a few days ago Blaine wrote me confidentially, as he wanted information in the preparation of his second volume. I have answered him, sending copies of letters and papers from my private files,

which I believe established these points. The attempt to send General Grant along with Lew Campbell to Mexico in October, 1866, had no connection with Congress's final quarrel with President Johnson, which did not happen till after January 14, 1865, and then only because Grant allowed Stanton to regain his office as Secretary of War, after forcing him to contend for it in the courts. Indeed, Grant served in Johnson's Cabinet during Stanton's suspension, viz., from August, 1867, to January, 1868, and was, to my personal knowledge, on friendly terms with Johnson. The real cause for their quarrel was that article in the "National Intelligencer," January 14, 1868, when four members of the Cabinet accused Grant of prevaricating and deceiving the President. I was present when Grant made his explanation of the whole case to Johnson, and I understood the latter to express himself as satisfied. But the newspapers kept it up, and made the breach final and angry.

I do not believe that Johnson ever contemplated the use of force against Congress, and am equally sure that Grant, at the time, had no fear or apprehension of such a thing....

Affectionately yours,

W. T. SHERMAN.

ST. *Louis,* Feb. 23, 1886.

Dear Brother: I owe you a personal explanation as to why I did not come to Washington during my last visit East. After positively refusing to attend the banquet to the Loyal Legion at Cincinnati (President Hayes the Commander), I was persuaded at the last minute that I ought to go. After I had packed my valise, I heard of General Hancock's death, made one or two despatches to General Whipple as Adjutant-General, my former Aide, asking Mm to communicate with me at the Burnet House. On arrival, I was met by President Hayes and General Cox and others, who explained that [by] the death of General Hancock, the president of the Order of the Loyal Legion, they had been forced to modify their programme, and that I must respond to the memory of General Hancock. I was kept busy all that day by a stream of visitors, and when the company had assembled for the banquet, full four hundred in the room, without notes or memoranda, I spoke for about ten minutes. My words were taken down and sent off without a chance of revision, but I afterwards learned that Mrs. Hancock was especially pleased. At the Burnet House I got all the notices of the funeral, which compelled me to travel to New York. *En route* was delayed a couple of hours by the flood in Delaware. It was two o'clock at night before I could lie down, and I had to be up at six to go down to the Battery, where the funeral was to commence. We were kept busy till night, when Miles and I went to Elly's for dinner, and it was midnight when we got to the Fifth Avenue Hotel...

Affectionately yours,

W. T. SHERMAN.

ST. LOUIS, April 3, 1880.

Dear Brother:... I shall go to California to be in San Francisco August 3d-5th for the Encampment of the G. A. B., when, of course, I shall be forced to say something. It occurs to me that I should say something about the annexation of California to the Union. I know that Webster advised a friend of his as early as 1843-44 to go to California, because it surely would on

the first pretext be captured and held by the United States.

I have all the executive documents for 1847, also the special Mexican War correspondence, but I fail to find Corwin's speech where he used the expression that were he a Mexican he would welcome the enemy (the Americans) "with bloody hands to hospitable graves." Can you get this speech for me, or an extract? I know that General Taylor believed that Texas did not reach the Rio Grande but was bordered by the River Nueces, and that the proclamation of war was based on an error that "American blood had been shed on American soil," and now comes Grant, who expresses more than a doubt if the first blood shed — Palo Alto — was not on "Mexican soil." Notwithstanding this, I believe the annexation of California was essential to the world's progress at that date. The Mexicans had held it for a hundred years without material improvement, whereas under our domination it at once began that wonderful development which we now experience....

Affectionately yours,

W. T. SHERMAN.

SENATE CHAMBER, WASHINGTON, D.C., April 6, 1886.

Dear Brother: Yours of the 3d is received. The speech of Mr. Corwin, to which you refer, was made in the United States Senate on the 11th of February, 1847, on the Mexican War. It is a very long speech, and is to be found on pages 211-218. Enclosed is the extract you refer to: —

"If I were a Mexican I would tell you, 'Have you no room in our own country to bury your dead men? ' If you come into mine we will greet you with bloody hands, and welcome you to hospitable graves.".. . .

The speech of Corwin's is worth reading through, as it gives fully his idea of the injustice of the war with Mexico, which I think was shared by the great body of intelligent people in the North, but was opposed by the cry "Our country, right or wrong!" which perhaps after war commences is the best public policy....

Affectionately yours,

JOHN SHERMAN.

Dear Brother: Your letter was duly received, and the quotation from Corwin's speech will be all I want. I remember the fact that when General Taylor's army marched from Corpus Christi, Texas, to Matamoras, it was generally noted that what few people were encountered south of the Nueces were all Mexicans. Their (Mexican) maps made Texas cease at that line, and our only title to that part of the country was Texas' claim to the Rio Grande as the boundary, so that the army officers, notably General Taylor, always ridiculed the action of the President and Congress — "whereas American blood has been shed on American soil," etc., etc.

Nevertheless war did exist and did continue till we had acquired California, New Mexico, etc. Our payment to Mexico of $15,000,000 at the end of the war was an act of generosity, and made our title one of purchase rather than conquest. Mexico never could have developed California as we did, and without California we could not have filled up the intervening space....

Affectionately,

W. T. SHERMAN.

In June, 1886, General Sherman removed from St. Louis to New York, where he lived for two years at the Fifth Avenue Hotel, and afterwards bought a house on Seventy-first Street. Referring to his removal to the East, John Sherman writes in June, 1886: —

. . . . It is well, too, that the drift of events brings you eastward. You must be aware that the wonder has been that, having the whole country to choose as a home, you should settle upon St. Louis. I could understand it, but many others do not. Almost daily I am asked when the General is coming back to Washington, and always with the earnest hope that it will be soon and to stay....

From this time on the brothers saw each other constantly, and their letters, referring chiefly to family and social affairs, are infrequent and disconnected. On February 1, 1887, General Sherman sends his brother a letter of advice regarding a Southern trip, which John Sherman took in the spring of that year.

... I came near closing without answering the part of your letter most important. I certainly do feel competent to advise about that contemplated trip. Go south *via* Richmond to Atlanta, Savannah, Jacksonville, Florida, by the St. John's to Enterprise and Sanford, visiting St. Augustine *en route*. At Sanford go by rail to Tampa, and if the railroad is finished, to Charlotte Harbor on the Gulf side, whence a steamer goes to Havana. Much of the interior of Cuba can be reached by rail,— Santa Rosa and Matanzas. The last-named is to me the finest place in Cuba. March and April are good months there. May and June are too hot. You will meet acquaintances everywhere. There are a great many beautiful places along the St. John's River, with good boats, hotels, and accommodations of all sorts, and the same in Cuba. I am sure that the railroad is finished to Charlotte Harbor, but you can learn the best way to reach Cuba from the Post-Office Department. On the Gulf side of Florida, you have the cluster of islands, leaving only the ninety miles of open sea from Key West to Havana, made in a single daylight.

Havana is a very interesting city, though for a week's stay I would prefer Matanzas and the interior bay.

Affectionately,

W. T. SHERMAN.

The end of the next letter, referring to the return of captured rebel flags, is published in order to explain in some measure General Sherman's silence on this matter, which was so widely and freely commented upon at the time.

New YORK, FIFTH AVENUE, June 26, 1887.

Dear Brother: I have just returned from Saratoga and Lake George, and am now arranging for Providence, E.I., where on the Fourth of July there is to be inaugurated an equestrian statue of General Burnside. I was always one of Burnside's personal friends, but after the battle of Chattanooga or Missionary Ridge, and after I had forced my Amy of the Tennessee to march by land 450 miles in October, November, 1863, from Memphis to Chattanooga, General Grant, finding the Fourth Corps — General Gordon Granger — moving too slow, called on me to go to his relief at Knoxville, which I did effectually and conclusively. Burnside in Knoxville reporting to Mr. Lincoln direct, treated his siege as a question of supplies, viz., that his supplies would be exhausted about December 3d, when want would compel him to surrender. I was therefore forced to march my already weary Army of the Tennessee near 136 miles in four days, or be held responsible for the terrible consequences of his surrender. I forced my men at twenty-six miles a day, and when I got to Knoxville I found inside a fine pen of cattle, and was invited to dine with Burnside at a dinner with a roast turkey, tablecloth, knives, forks, and spoons, which I had not seen for years. My Memoirs described the literal truth, but Burnside's friends thought it hard on him, and now I shall go to the dedication of his monument to apologize for telling the truth. Others may orate, I will not. I will simply assert a personal friendship. Burnside was not a combative man. He was kind, good, and patriotic, as you saw him in the Senate, but he did not come up to the occasion. In war we must use all forces, and now when we look back we recognize the qualities of each. Burnside was a good man, but he was not a war soldier.

The New York papers make out that you and I differ. Of course, we all differ. I stand by the authorities.... Mr. Cleveland is President, so recognized by Congress, Supreme Court, and the world. Now, by the Fifth Article of War, made the law before you were born, every officer of the Army of the United States who speaks disrespectfully of the President of the United States becomes a felon the same as one who has committed murder, felony, forgery, treason, or any crime, and could be punished at the discretion of a court-martial. I am still an officer of the army, and cannot violate this law. Of course I know Drum, the Adjutant-General. He has no sympathy with the army which fought. He was a non-combatant. He never captured a flag, and values it only at its commercial value. He did not think of the blood and torture of battle j nor can Endicott, the Secretary of War, or Mr. Cleveland.... Still, in

Republics majorities govern, and since only one in sixteen go to war, non-combatants always govern. The soldier who fights must take a back seat and apologize for his vehemence in action. Grant had to apologize, Sheridan to shelter himself behind his most proper orders to devastate the Valley of the Shenandoah, and Sherman to be abused and assailed for the accidental burning of Columbia in the day of Republican rule.... In 1861-65 we fought for union and right. The soldiers restored to Congress full power, and returned to their civil vocations. Congress surrendered the country to the non-combatants, and now it is questionable whether Lincoln or Jeff Davis was the Union man. Jeff now says he never meant war. He thought that they would be allowed to do as they pleased without war. Lincoln was the assailant, Davis only on the "defensive-offensive."

MANSFIELD, OHIO, Sept. 3, 1887.

Dear Brother: Your letter of the 27th came as I was starting for the Ohio Fair. From thence I went to Lancaster, and found all well.... My trip to the Pacific over the Canadian Railroad was a great success. We travelled 7000 miles without fatigue, accident, or detention. We stopped over at the chief points of interest, such as Toronto, Montreal, Sudbury, Port Arthur, Winnipeg, Calgary, Banff, Donald, Glacier House, Vancouver, Victoria, Seattle, and Tacoma, and yet made the round trip within the four weeks allowed. We did not go to Alaska, because of the fogs and for want of time. The trip was very instructive, giving me an inside view of many questions that may be important in the future. The country did not impress me as a desirable acquisition, though it would not be a bad one. The people are hardy and industrious. If they had free commercial intercourse with the United States, their farms, forests, and mines would become more valuable, but at the expense of the manufactures. If the population of Mexico and Canada were homogeneous with ours, the union of the three countries would make the whole the most powerful nation in the world. I am not so sure but this would be a good thing to do....

Affectionately yours,

JOHN SHERMAN.

New YORK, Sept. 6, 1887.

Dear Brother: I am sorry you lost the trip to Alaska, but it will give you an excuse for making it at some future time. I have never been there, and feel little curiosity about it. My judgment at present is that we want no more territory. If we could take in the territory of Ontario it would make a good State, but the vast hyperborean region of the North would embarrass us with inchoate States and Territories without a corresponding revenue. I am dead opposed to any more of Mexico. All the northern part is desert, like the worst parts of Texas, New Mexico, and Arizona, further south the population is mixed Spanish and Indian, who never can be harmonized with our race. Eight millions of such people would endanger our institutions. We have already enough disturbing influences.

Affectionately yours,

W. T. SHERMAN.

General Sherman writes in October, 1887, referring to his retirement: —

Dear Brother:... I am perfectly content to have retired when I did, as the present *regime* makes Sheridan command of the army a farce. The army is drifting back into the same old condition, when Jeff Davis was Secretary of War, when secretaries and other clerks gave military orders to General Scott and those under him. In case of a new war, army commanders will be hampered just as we were in 1861....

NEW YORK,

Fifth Avenue Hotel, April 1, 1888.

Dear Brother:... This morning at breakfast I received a note from Gen. B. F. Butler, asking me to say when he could see me. I supposed it was about a son of his nephew George and Rose Eytinge, about whom I had written him two months ago. After breakfast I went to the office and found that he was in Boom 1, on the ground floor, so I went there. He was alone, and asked me to be seated. I commenced to speak of his grand-nephew, when he said that was not the reason of his call. He then took up the conversation, and said that the country was in real danger, revealed by the death of the Chief Justice, that there was a purpose clearly revealed for the old rebels to capture the Supreme Court, as shown by the appointment of Lamar and the equal certainty of Waite being succeeded by a Copperhead or out and out rebel; that in the next four years Miller and Bradley would create vacancies to be filled in like manner, thus giving the majority in that court to a party which fought to destroy the Government, thereby giving those we beat in battle the sacred fruits of victory. That is a real danger....

Affectionately yours,

W. T. SHERMAN.

1319 K ST., *Washington,* D.C., Nov. 9, 1889.

Dear Brother:... The coming session of Congress is to be an important one, not in a political sense but in a business sense. The tariff, commercial relations with American States, and differences with Canada are likely to occupy a good deal of time, and in all of these I shall have to take a part. What is worse, we will have the distribution of many offices. Harrison holds on to this dangerous power, and is likely to distribute it during his entire term. If so, he will not have another. Cleveland did the same and lost. A President should, within the first few months of his term, fill all the most important appointments, and then he may hope to recover from the effect before his term closes. But I suppose you are not interested in these things, and I begin to regard myself as a spectator rather than an actor. It is not at all likely that I shall ever seek or accept an office again....

Affectionately yours,

JOHN SHERMAN.

NEW YORK, NOV. 12, 1889.

Dear Brother: I was very glad to receive your full letter of November 9th, to hear that you are safely back at your Washington home, and take the recent election so philosophically. I wanted Poraker to succeed, because he was one of my young soldiers. He cannot be suppressed, and will turn up again. I think you are also wise in your conclusion to retire gracefully at the end of your present term. To be a President for four years is not much of an honor, but to have been senator continuously from 1861 to 1892 — less the four years as Secretary of the Treasury — *is* an honor. Webster and Clay are better known to the world than Polk and Pierce. As to myself, I continue pretty much as always in universal demand for soldiers' meetings, college commencements, and such like things — always with a promise that I will not be called on to speak, which is always broken — worse still, generally exaggerated by reporters....

Affectionately,

W. T. SHERMAN.

SENATE CHAMBER, WASHINGTON, D.C., July 21, 1890.

Dear Brother:... You are living the life proper for your position and services, — everywhere welcome, all you say and do applauded, and secure in a competence and independent in all things. I will deliver your message to Edmunds, but you will not probably find him at Burlington, August 20th. We are to have important questions before us, but I mean to act not as a laborer but as an umpire. I am for peace at home and abroad, and if I cannot do much that is actively good I will try and prevent harm, and if possible will tranquilly glide down the rest of the road of life, enjoying all I can and helping those who deserve help.

Affectionately yours,

JOHN SHERMAN.

New York, July 22, 1890.

Dear Brother: I was gratified by the general tone and spirit of your letter of yesterday, just received. You surely in the past have achieved as much success in civil affairs as my most partial friends claim for me in military affairs. It is now demonstrated that with universal suffrage and the organization of political parties no man of supreme ability can be President, and that our President with only four years is only a chip on the surface. Not a single person lias been President in our time without having been, in his own judgment, the most abused, if not the most miserable, man in the whole community. Your experience has simply been with nominating conventions. It would have been tenfold worse had you succeeded in obtaining the nomination and election.

I had a letter from General Alger yesterday, asking me to ride in the procession at Boston, August 12th, in full uniform, to which I answered No with an emphasis. I will attend as a delegate from Missouri, as a private, and will not form in any procession, horseback or otherwise. It is cruel to march old veterans five miles, like a circus, under a mid-day sun for the gratification of a Boston audience....

Affectionately yours,

W. **T. SHERMAN.**

New York, Tuesday, Feb. 3, 1891.

Dear Brother: I am drifting along in the old rut in good strength, attending to about four dinners a week at public or private houses, and generally wind up for gossip at the Union League Club. Last night, discussing the effect of Mr. Windom's death and funeral, several prominent gentlemen remarked that Windom's fine speech just preceding his death was in line with yours on the silver question in the Senate, and also with a carefully prepared interview with you by George Alfred Townsend, which I had not seen. I have ordered of my book-man the New York Sun" of Sunday, February 1st, which contains the interview.

You sent me a copy of your bill in pamphlet form, which, was begged from me, and as others naturally apply for copies I wish you would have your secretary send me a dozen, that I may distribute them.

All well here and send love.

Your affectionate brother,

W. **T. SHERMAN.**

THE END.

BIG BYTE BOOKS is your source for great lost history!